MW01256269

America's

Deadliest Battle

MODERN WAR STUDIES

Theodore A. Wilson
General Editor

Raymond Callahan
J. Garry Clifford
Jacob W. Kipp
Jay Luvaas
Allan R. Millett
Carol Reardon
Dennis Showalter
David R. Stone
Series Editors

AMERICA'S DEADLIEST BATTLE

Meuse-Argonne, 1918

Robert H. Ferrell

University Press of Kansas

© 2007 by the University Press of Kansas
All rights reserved

Published by the University Press of
Kansas (Lawrence, Kansas 66045), which
was organized by the Kansas Board of
Regents and is operated and funded by
Emporia State University, Fort Hays
State University, Kansas State University,
Pittsburg State University, the University
of Kansas, and Wichita State University

Library of Congress Cataloging-in-
Publication Data

Ferrell, Robert H.
America's deadliest battle : Meuse-
Argonne, 1918 / Robert H. Ferrell.
p. cm. — (Modern war studies)
Includes bibliographical references and
index.
ISBN-13: 978-0-7006-1499-8 (cloth : alk.
paper)
1. Argonne, Battle of the, France, 1918.
2. United States. Army—History—World
War, 1914–1918. 3. World War, 1914–1918—
Campaigns—Meuse River Valley. I. Title.
D545.A63F477 2007
940.4'36—dc22
2006029077

British Library Cataloguing-in-Publication
Data is available.

Printed in the United States of America

10 9 8 7 6 5 4 3 2 1

The paper used in this publication
meets the minimum requirements of
the American National Standard for
Permanence of Paper for Printed Library
Materials Z39.48-1992.

In reading history . . . we must remember that the orders of the practical, two-fisted soldiers, interpreted long afterwards by an anemic professor of history, form a picture very different from the actual facts.

Major General George Van Horn Moseley,
"One Soldier's Journey"

CONTENTS

*A photograph section
appears following
page 93.*

All the maps, with the exception of maps 11 and 13, are from *American Armies and Battlefields in Europe* (Washington, D.C.: Government Printing Office, 1938), the army's official guide published under the supervision of General Pershing; it was reprinted by the army's Center of Military History in 1995. Several maps contain signs for stops and arrows for routes, referring readers to portions of the guide's text.

PREFACE AND ACKNOWLEDGMENTS

As the twenty-first century progresses, the last veterans of World War I are passing from the scene. In 2006, perhaps twenty remained of the nearly 4 million Americans in the army and the half a million in the navy in 1917–1918. Their numbers were considerable until the 1970s and 1980s, but today, these veterans are all centenarians, and in a year or two they will be gone.

World War I has been largely forgotten. People today know little about it; they have no idea what issues caused the European war in 1914 or how it turned into a world war with the United States' entrance in 1917. They have little understanding of the nation's experience in the war, and the individual engagements have entered the dark corridors of history.

In the fashion of present-day historical writing, I suspect I will be criticized for writing about a single battle, even if it was the largest one of the war—the Meuse-Argonne, which lasted for forty-seven days, from September 26 to November 11, 1918. It will seem too small a subject, lacking the expansiveness that historical writing is expected to embody. My fellow historians consider military history old-fashioned. But surely World War I was the root of the horrendous events—in terms of lives lost—of the twentieth century and, by extension, the twenty-first. World War II, the cold war, and terrorism can be traced to the war of 1914–1918, leading to events that in earlier times (notably, the nineteenth century) would have been unimaginable.

In World War I, the appearance of a huge American army in France was decisive, and in that army's history, the most important battle was the Meuse-Argonne. Although that battle was a success, the cost in human casualties was high, which is my reason for writing about it. There were 26,277 men killed and 95,786 wounded, making it the deadliest battle in all of American history. It also was the largest, with 1.2 million men at the front. Still, the battle has received little attention for many years. The only book on the subject, *Our Greatest Battle,* by military historian Frederick Palmer, was published in 1919.[1]

I am greatly indebted to historians of America's participation in World War I. Some years ago, Edward M. Coffman published a remarkably accurate and well-written account of what he described as, in the phrase of the Wilson era, "the war to end all wars." Donald Smythe's two-volume biography of General John J. Pershing stands as a beacon in the literature of American military history. Similarly valuable are Allen R. Millett's biography of General Robert L. Bullard and Forrest C. Pogue's biography of General George C. Marshall. General James L. Collins Jr. presided over the U.S. Army's Center of Military History for years and edited General Marshall's manuscript on the American Expeditionary Forces. Through books and lectures, Russell F. Weigley almost single-handedly created interest in military history among the officers and men who made it; a whole generation of U.S. Army historians owes a great deal to Weigley. David F. Trask has also contributed significantly to the scholarship, both military and civil, about World War I. In addition, James J. Cooke has written division and topical histories, John S. D. Eisenhower has a notable general account, and Alfred F. Hurley is the biographer of General William Mitchell. And all students who seek to write about the United States in 1917–1918 must thank a new generation of scholars typified by Carol Byerly, Mark E. Grotelueschen, Kenneth E. Hamburger, Jennifer D. Keene, Timothy D. Nenninger, and James W. Rainey.

My thanks to Jeffrey M. Flowers of the Manuscript Division of the Library of Congress; Timothy Nenninger and Mitchell A. Yockelson of the Modern Military Branch of the National Archives; and Richard J. Sommers, David A. Keough, and Richard Baker of the U.S. Army Military History Institute, which is part of the Army War College in Carlisle Barracks, Carlisle, Pennsylvania.

Maps of the Lost Battalion were drawn by John M. Hollingsworth. Betty J. Bradbury was the skilled word processor.

My appreciation to the staff of the University Press of Kansas, notably Linda Lotz, who copyedited the manuscript; Susan Schott and Larisa Martin; and especially director Fred M. Woodward, who has turned Kansas into a powerhouse among university presses. He has been a friend for twenty years and, on occasion, an acutely wise counselor. In the case of this book, he provided its title and, more than that, made it better by pointing out literary errors and logical mistakes along the way.

My thanks, as always, to Carolyn and Lorin, and now Amanda.

CHAPTER ONE

Preparation

Two immense tasks confronted the United States on April 6, 1917, when the nation entered the world war: industrial mobilization and preparation of the army to fight in France. Both ultimately affected the battle of the Meuse-Argonne.

The first, industrial mobilization, was nearly a failure because President Woodrow Wilson simply could not manage it. In the years before 1917, this highly regarded chief executive had displayed a mastery of domestic politics that had brought memorable, progressive legislation, including the Federal Reserve Act (long overdue) and the act creating the Federal Trade Commission. Wilson's presidency was marked by moral leadership of a high order; no tincture of scandal—either personal or political—accompanied it. But for all his admirable qualities, Wilson was not the manager of mobilization that the country needed in 1917–1918. He could not put his mind to the great projects he had begun.

Wilson was a man of peace to the core of his being. After his election in 1912, he wrote to a friend that it would be an irony of fate if he ended up leading the nation into war. After a German submarine sank the liner *Lusitania* in May 1915, Wilson made a speech in Philadelphia in which he said there was such a thing as a man being too proud to fight—after the deaths of 1,198 men, women, and children, including 128 Americans. Former president Theodore Roosevelt, Wilson's opponent in 1912, said publicly that if he had been president the ship never would have been sunk; he told military writer Frederick Palmer that he would have sent Germany an ultimatum and seized any German ships in American harbors. To explain his lack of action, Wilson told Palmer that people east of the Alleghenies would have supported war after the *Lusitania,* but those west of the Alleghenies would not have.[1] About the same time, he stated that war would not accomplish anything permanent. In the autumn of 1915 the president read in the *Baltimore Sun* that a group of army officers at the War College in Washington were planning for war, and he instructed the acting secretary of war, Henry S. Breckinridge, to find out whether this were true and, if so, to order all the officers out of the city. Wilson never ventured far from his antiwar position. He was never at ease as a war leader, regardless of what he said out of expediency. When he went to the peace conference in Europe, his generals and European leaders implored him to tour the battlefields, but he put it off for as long as he could and then devoted only a few days to the distasteful task. He did not find time to visit the Meuse-Argonne.

Another quality that accompanied the president's views on war was his tendency to resort to oratory rather than action at a time when the ends were less important than the means. The president believed that words were vital; in the beginning was the word. This principle had taken him far in politics. Oratory had come in with Daniel Webster, Henry Clay, and John C. Calhoun and did not go out until after the world war and the introduction of amplification (loudspeakers), radio, and eventually television. Wilson's leading biographer and the editor of sixty-nine volumes of his papers wrote that oratory was the president's principal attribute as a public figure.[2] Wilson believed that he could resolve problems by taking his listeners to the high places from which they could see the valleys and villages below.

Given the nation's need to mobilize industry to produce ships and weapons to allow the army to get to France and fight on the western front, there was no time to waste in turning industry to this purpose. But despite the president's announcement of this need, he did little or nothing to achieve it. He did not sense that leading such a great enterprise would require him to get into the details of the work; he had to know what was going on, and he needed to confer with experts and appoint them to supervise war production.

Warning signs were visible not long after the declaration of war, but the president paid little attention, with the inevitable result. The first failure appeared in shipbuilding.[3] The situation had been addressed the year before the war when, to oppose Roosevelt's urging of mobilization, the president had sponsored a program known as preparedness, one aspect of which was to increase the merchant marine. Wilson appointed a shipping board that was coheaded by the builder of the Panama Canal, Major General George W. Goethals. The general was a talented administrator, but he butted heads with his civil counterpart, William G. Denman, and little happened until the president dismissed them both and appointed two civilians. The more dominant was Charles M. Schwab, the head of Bethlehem Steel and a former assistant to Andrew Carnegie. Schwab followed the same course that Goethals might have taken, had he possessed support. But during this administrative confusion, precious time was lost in what proved to be a complicated effort.

The shipbuilding program was given the highest priority, for in 1917 there were hardly enough ships to carry more than a fraction of a large army to Europe. The total transatlantic tonnage was only 1 million, the same as in 1810. For a short time in the first part of the nineteenth century, tonnage had gone up, but by 1860 American ships carried only 65 percent of American commerce. During the Civil War, as a result of Confederate raiders such as the *Alabama,* tonnage fell to a quarter of the overseas trade, and in subsequent years it fell to less than 10 percent. With the invention of iron and then steel ships, the United States lost its advantage in the construction of wooden ships because of Europe's cheaper metals and much cheaper wages (European ships cost 25 to 50 percent less than American). Then in February 1917 came the crisis: the German government engaged in unrestricted submarine warfare to prevent all commerce with the British Isles, which meant the sinking of all ships approaching British ports. In that month, submarines sank 536,000 tons of Allied shipping, followed by 603,000 tons in March and nearly 1 million in April. As the rate of sinkings to launchings approached two to one, if not three to one, among shipyards all over the world, the supply of shipping decreased dramatically.

After April 1917 the capacity of American shipyards increased sixfold under the government program; 1,284 ways were in operation, double the number in the rest of the world. The shipbuilding workforce rose from 45,000 to 380,000. The largest yard was at Hog Island, a muddy acreage near Philadelphia, where pile drivers produced what amounted to a shipbuilding city. It was larger than the seven largest shipyards in

England. Hog Island turned into an enormous enterprise, assigned the task of producing, launching, and finishing two hundred ships. It had a projected production of fifty ships on the ways, with room for fifty at the piers. Each ship required 250,000 parts, and Hog Island had 250,000 piles of parts brought in by fifty miles of rail sidings. Cranes lifted the parts into hulls, and workers used the team method, moving from way to way. One did ribs, another bulkheads, and another decks, turning out 4,600-ton cargo carriers and 5,000-ton combination cargo and troop carriers. The speed of the cargo vessels was eleven to twelve knots; combination ships could travel fifteen to sixteen knots.

The prospect was exhilarating. At Hog Island, a ship could be built in eighty-seven days, requiring thirty-five more to finish. At this single yard, with all the ways working, a ship could be launched every other day. The national shipbuilding project was getting into high gear by early summer 1918, and on a single day, July 4, yards across the country launched 300,000 tons of ships.

But the program got started too late, and few yards launched ships in time to assist the war effort. Hog Island launched its first, the *Quistconck* (Indian for "Hog Island"), on August 5, 1918, and delivered it on December 3. The program faltered, and tonnage went up only because of the commandeering of German ships that had taken refuge in American harbors at the outset of the war, as well as those of neutrals that had stayed in port because of the threat from submarines. A few ships came from the Great Lakes, bisected and taken through the Welland Canal. An attempt to build composite ships, with steel frames and wooden plates, failed because of the ships' structural weakness. They proved suitable only for coastal runs, where they freed a few ships capable of transatlantic passage. The total new tonnage was 664,000 in 1917 and 1.3 million in 1918—a miserable performance. The entire shipbuilding program produced only 107 steel, 67 wooden, and 4 composite ships.

The lack of ships in 1917–1918 adversely affected the American contribution to the war, and when the Allies realized this (belatedly), they did something about it. Early in 1918, fearful of a great German offensive, the British government removed ships from Mediterranean runs and other employment and sent them to the United States to bring over American divisions. Half of all troops in the American Expeditionary Forces (AEF) were brought over by the U.S. Navy; the rest were transported by Allied ships. For the navy, this meant packing the men into holds and assigning bunks on twelve-hour shifts—doubling the capacity of transports.

Getting the men to France was just part of the problem. Creating an infrastructure to receive them proved daunting. Ports in France were insufficient and needed to be enlarged and new ones constructed, if possible. The rail network from the ports up to the Lorraine sector, where the Americans were supposed to deploy, was as primitive as the port structure. French resources were few; the years of war had starved industry of steel and other necessities. The Americans lacked the ships to bring over the necessary materials, and the problem continued until the end of the war.

The effects of the shipping crisis were felt in all directions. The AEF needed trucks—or if not trucks, then horses and mules—to carry the men and their baggage. American industry could have turned out trucks in huge quantities, but there was no space aboard ships to carry them. Thus, truck transport ceased in January 1918. Animals could not be sent from the United States because of the same space problems, and animal transport likewise ceased the same month. Army procurement officers sought to purchase horses and mules in Europe, but they were in short supply and expensive, costing up to $400. The animals that were available were often of poor quality, having been rejected by the French army. Few American divisions were able to obtain enough animals to fill their tables of organization. Moreover, caring for the animals they did have was time-consuming. They had to be fed, meaning that oats and forage had to be found in large quantities. They also had to be curried. And when they went to the front, their high silhouettes made them vulnerable to artillery and machine gun fire, and those that were killed had to be buried. Owing to this lack of trucks and animals, many divisions went to the front with insufficient transport, and many men, mostly infantrymen, had to walk the fifty miles (eighty kilometers) between St. Mihiel and the Meuse-Argonne carrying eighty-pound packs, leaving them in less than optimal physical condition when they entered battle.

Like the shipbuilding program, airplane production was also ineffective.[4] Failure occurred in the details. Secretary of War Newton D. Baker was the initial enthusiast for a production program, and he let it be known that $600 million would allow the building of the greatest air fleet ever devised. The president's adviser, Colonel Edward M. House, told the nation's chief executive that all he had to do was give the word. Wilson gave the word, Congress appropriated $640 million, and the details intervened. One problem was acquiring the lumber to build frames—five thousand feet were needed to get five hundred feet without a cross or spiral grain. Flax from Ireland to cover the frames was unavailable, and cotton needed different dopes that were hard to come by. Motors were also a problem, and only after many changes did the government decide on the excellent twelve-cylinder Liberty motor, resulting in the production of 13,547 engines, of which 4,435 went overseas. Few planes ever went overseas. Baker originally promised twenty thousand, but the figure decreased to seventeen thousand, fifteen thousand, two thousand, and finally, thirty-seven. On February 21, 1918, the War Department announced that the first American-built planes were en route to the front; in reality, a plane had gone from the factory to an aviation field (in America) for a radiator test. The commander of the AEF, General John J. Pershing, received 1,213 American-made British DeHavilland 4s, known as flying coffins because the fuel tanks exploded on landing. Most AEF planes were foreign built. Of the 6,364 used by the army in France, evenly divided between service and training types, 4,874 were French, 258 British, and 19 Italian.

Airplanes in quantity were unavailable from the Allies until the summer of 1918 (shortly before the Meuse-Argonne), and never in sufficient numbers. Air service pilots had only a short period of instruction before having to oppose the skilled German pilots. There was also little time for training with the divisions in artillery spotting, which is so essential to the forward movement of troops.

Production of artillery was another mobilization failure.[5] Army officers urged the production of a three-inch gun known as the French 75, wrongly believing that this fine artillery piece was superior to the army's similar gun, the Model 1902. Mass production of the 75 proved impossible. The gun had been made by artisans and demanded rigid tolerances. Too late, officers went back to the Model 1902, but Pershing had to use 1,828 French 75s. Similarly, no American-made six-inch (155-mm) howitzers or guns (a howitzer has a lower muzzle velocity than a gun and delivers curved fire) reached France before the armistice.[6] The War Department obtained plans for 155-mm howitzers from Schneider in France, and by October 1917 it had changed the specifications from metric measurements to the American system. It awarded separate contracts for tubes, carriages, and recoil mechanisms. The American Brake Shoe and Foundry Company of Pennsylvania received a contract for three thousand tubes, and seven months later, twelve a day were coming down the line. Maxwell Motor Company and Ford Motor Company both produced carriages, Ford turning out 4,373. The difficulty was the recoil mechanism, or recuperator, which needed forgings weighing 3,875 pounds. Companies shied away from the task. A contract eventually went to Dodge Brothers, and at the time of the armistice, Dodge was turning out sixteen a day. In contrast, for 155-mm guns, the Midvale Steel Company was already making tubes and carriages for the British army, and all the War Department had to do was place an order. The department bought French blueprints for the recuperators, and they proved to be more difficult to manufacture than the mechanisms for howitzers; Dodge Brothers had made only one by the time the war ended.

It is impossible to know what the failure to produce three-inch guns and especially 155-mm howitzers and guns meant for the Meuse-Argonne. Nevertheless, it seems certain that if American-made artillery had been available, the army would have used all of it, which would have drastically reduced casualties. In the summer of 1917 the War Department sent a mission under Colonel Chauncey Baker to consult with AEF officers and establish tables of organization for the divisions' supporting units. A member of the Baker board was Colonel Charles P. Summerall, an artillerist, who became a corps commander in the Meuse-Argonne. He argued vociferously and undiplomatically for more artillery but was voted down. The board and the AEF officers allotted each division one artillery brigade, no more.

In the Meuse-Argonne, Summerall's position proved correct. If more 75s and 155s had been available, the AEF's attacks might have gone very differently. In the first weeks of battle, the divisions needed more artillery. The 75s provided barrage fire ahead of advancing troops, and those walls of fire saved lives. But the 75s were short-range guns, and it was difficult to get them forward. They could not get up the poor roads, and taking them through open terrain was awkward; even though the 75 was nominally a light gun, it weighed four tons with its carriage and required six horses. The army could have used many more 155-mm howitzers and guns with their longer ranges. When Summerall's two divisions became the point units in the attack of November 1, 1918, the First Army was under a new and imaginative artillery commander, and with the corps commander's delighted assent, he gave the 2nd Division three artillery brigades and the 89th two. The guns took out everything in front of them, and the infantry lines swept forward without opposition.[7]

The country's production of tanks was as inconsequential as its production of ships, planes, and artillery, although for a different reason. There was not so much a failure in production as a lack of direction from either the army's leaders in Washington or the commander of the AEF, Pershing, about what should be done. Employment of tanks in dramatic if not always effective numbers had come late in the war. The British used them at Cambrai in November 1917 with devastating effect; they did not anticipate their success, and there were no follow-up troops. In just a few days a German counterattack took back the territory that had been gained. On August 8, 1918, the British tank force struck again at Amiens, this time with the infantry following up.

At the outset of U.S. entry into the war, the War Department considered the production of tanks, and the AEF organized a provisional tank brigade. The problem with tanks, however, was that they were not battleworthy; the attrition rate was 25 percent daily. Their speed was so slow (five miles an hour) and their armor so thin that any artillery piece could hole them. The Germans brought up long-barreled rifles (with three times the bore of regular rifles) mounted on tripods, and these primitive antitank guns were effective. Tanks also broke down from mechanical failure, motor malfunctions, and loss of treads. For such reasons, the 6.5-ton Renault tanks used by the Americans—360 at St. Mihiel on September 12–16, 1918, and 140 in the Meuse-Argonne—proved ineffective. The heavy French St. Chaumond Schneider tanks were mechanically impossible, and the Americans did not receive enough thirty-ton British tanks to become competent in their use.

Tank production in the United States was too little too late. The Ford Motor Company was slated to produce fifteen thousand three-ton light tanks, but by the end of the war it had produced only fifteen. By autumn 1918 American production of Renault tanks started to move, the first coming off the line in October and two arriving in France on November 20. An Anglo-American project for fifteen hundred thirty-ton tanks got under way, with the Americans providing Liberty engines and the rest of the driving mechanism and the British providing the armor plates; these tanks were scheduled to become available in 1919.

It is intriguing to consider what might have happened if the Wilson administration had gone to the automotive industry and asked for a tank design that combined speed and armor. The industry was highly developed, the best in the world, and such a request would not have been beyond its capability. When the AEF organized its tank brigade, there was enough experience even in that small unit to make excellent technical suggestions to the manufacturer of the French light tank.[8] After a tour of the plant, the Americans recommended a self-starter; a double-cased, felt-lined fuel tank to prevent leaking if hit by enemy fire; a mount for either a machine gun or a 37-mm gun; and a bulkhead to protect the crew from engine fire. Detroit engineers could have outdone Renault in terms of speed and armor, but instead, the industry (with the exception of Ford's three-ton experiment) accepted European tank designs and lacked sufficient encouragement to produce them.

American industry also failed to provide the AEF with munitions: powder, shells, and cartridges. It was unable to produce anything beyond the quantities it had supplied to the Allies in the period of neutrality, 1914–1917. Upon entry into the war, the army's procurement officers were uncertain how many divisions would go to France, so they placed no extra orders with the powder industry.[9] When it became likely that a huge army would be sent, they contracted with the nation's principal powder maker, E. I. Du Pont de Nemours. It was the largest government contract in American history: $90 million for the construction of new plants, and $155 million for orders. Six days later Secretary Baker refused the contract, calling it excessive; Du Pont had asked for an additional 15 percent commission on the plants' construction, believing them to be useless in peacetime. Baker told Pierre S. Du Pont that President Wilson had decided to construct government plants and win the war without Du Pont. It was at this time that General Pershing cabled the War Department about his need for ammunition, which the French had promised but failed to deliver. The department could do nothing and cabled in reply that "the French Government must furnish it, for there is no other way of getting it. At the present time there is not in this country any actual output of ammunition of the types mentioned. None has been expected."[10] Confusion reigned for four months until the secretary realized that contractors for government plants would have to consult Du Pont, because that company was the only American firm with the know-how to produce smokeless powder, TNT, and picric acid. In negotiations, Du Pont proved willing to construct a plant for an acceptable sum: $1. The arrangement was for two plants—one constructed by Du Pont in Nashville, named Old Hickory, and the other built by the government in Charleston, West Virginia, named Nitro. Du Pont's plant required less money and was already in production when the war ended, although not up to capacity. The government plant went into production on the day of the armistice. Contention over public versus private ownership had delayed the munitions program until it was too late. Meanwhile, British and French production increased sufficiently to supply the AEF, although the troops had some shortages in the Meuse-Argonne caused by a lack of transportation from railheads to the front.

American industry supplied the AEF in only two types of arms—machine guns and rifles. Ever since the Gatling brothers had invented the machine gun in 1861, the War Department had been slow to understand its importance. Seeking to sell it, the brothers had followed the troops of the Union army, using their employees to man the gun and show it off. The army adopted the gun in 1866, but it then shifted its interest to artillery shells that threw shards in all directions, shrapnel that promised to do the work of machine guns. In desperation, another American inventor, Hiram Maxim, sold his gun to the Germans.

In 1912 the War Department's table of organization for infantry regiments allotted four machine guns to a regiment. In the era of neutrality the department's lack of attention continued, and in 1917 its inventory totaled fifteen hundred guns of four types. A machine gun board adopted the heavy Browning machine gun and the Browning automatic rifle; these were first-rate weapons that were easily produced, and they proved so satisfactory over the following years that the army used them again in World War II and the Korean War. Light Brownings began to come off the assembly lines in February 1918 and heavy Brownings in April, enough to make a difference in the last weeks of the war. Until then, the Americans used the heavy British Vickers and French Hotchkiss guns. For automatic rifles they used the French Chauchats, which jammed regularly because of dust or overheating. These guns fired half as many bullets as the excellent British Lewis guns. As for rifles, in 1917 there were the Springfield 1903s, but only 600,000 of them—not enough. The Springfields came from a single government arsenal that managed to turn out 300,000 more by the end of the war. Many AEF divisions used a modified version of the British Enfield that was heavier than the Springfield and had an inferior sight. Produced in American factories and known as the Lee-Enfield, it took Springfield ammunition.

The second national task—preparing the army to fight in France once war was declared—encountered the same difficulties that dogged industrial mobilization. Again, the trouble was a lack of leadership, this time within the War Department in Washington. If Woodrow Wilson was no war leader, neither was Newton D. Baker. After a year of inaction, General Peyton C. March became chief of staff of the army and brought order out of chaos.

At the outset, Baker seemed to be the individual who could manage the War Department. In 1916 then secretary of war Lindley M. Garrison had proposed a reorganization of the army that included more federal control over the National Guard, an institution of pride within the individual states. President Wilson believed that this was more control than the country would support. Garrison made an issue of his program and resigned. His successor, Baker, had the full support of the president. The two men had met when Wilson was a professor at Princeton and taught courses at nearby Johns Hopkins in Baltimore and Baker was a student in one of Wilson's courses. They even ate at the same boardinghouse. Baker also had administrative experience. He had become a lawyer and assisted Cleveland's reform mayor, Tom Johnson. Baker followed Johnson as mayor and fought for a three-cent ice cream cone, a three-cent streetcar fare, and dance halls where young men and women could meet each other in wholesome surroundings. It was during his administration that Cleveland's city council financed the local symphony orchestra for an annual sum of $10,000, an unheard of profligacy. Wilson offered him the job of secretary of the interior in 1913, which Baker declined, but he accepted the War Department post three years later.

Upon taking office, Baker made an unfortunate decision that guaranteed his ineffectiveness for the rest of his tenure. He decided that, as a civilian, he would not interfere with military affairs. This was an egregious error; the department needed all the help it could get. Baker's decision not to intervene was based on a confrontation between President Jefferson Davis and General Robert E. Lee during the Civil War. Once, when Davis offered military advice to Lee, the general unbuckled his sword and offered it to Davis, who in embarrassment declined to accept it. Baker's decision also may have been influenced by his physical stature. He was a small, slight man, not much over five feet tall, and the generals tended to tower over him; when he sat behind his huge desk, he usually kept one leg folded under him, giving the appearance of greater height. He may have been overly impressed by the air of command he encountered in the old State, War, and Navy Building, a great pile of masonry next to the White House that had been built during the era of President Ulysses S. Grant. For whatever reason, historical or otherwise, Baker removed himself from decisions of military importance. During the war he spent most of his time defending the army; the rest of the time he concentrated on the well-being, legally and morally, of the men in the training camps (dealing with harassment by officers such as Major General Leonard Wood, who mistreated conscientious objectors, and the temptations of men serving far away from their families and friends).

Baker tolerated—indeed, admired—three incompetent chiefs of staff until he finally chose a fourth, which may have been his principal achievement as secretary of war. The first three should never have been appointed. Major General Hugh L. Scott was a relic of the Indian wars. He began his service as a replacement for an officer killed with General George A. Custer at Little Big Horn in 1876. Heavily mustached, with a square face and flashing eyes (the air of command), he was slow-witted and out-of-date when it came to military affairs. Upon taking office, Wilson had appointed him brigadier general for personal reasons: the president had known Scott's brother on the Princeton faculty, and they had been on the same side in a controversy over reforms of the social fraternities and control of the graduate school. There was precedent for doing so; in 1906 President Roosevelt had passed over hundreds of ranking officers to appoint Captain Pershing a brigadier general, but Scott was hardly in Pershing's class.

Rank did nothing to improve Scott's abilities, and when he became chief of staff he spent his days writing memoranda in a large hand on small pads of paper. He was largely unaware of events in Europe. He even inquired of an assistant, Colonel Robert E. Lee Michie, "Michie, everybody's talking about the battle of the Marne. What happened at the battle of the Marne anyway?" In the department he apparently spent a good deal of time sleeping. In 1918, after his retirement as chief of staff, Baker and General March visited Scott's command, a training camp, and were appalled by a forty-five-minute disquisition on the meaning of the feathers in an Indian headdress. March relieved and retired Scott upon his return to Washington.

Scott's successor, General Tasker H. Bliss, was no better, but for a different reason. He was alert but was essentially a theorist, with little experience leading troops. In 1912 he had commanded combined maneuvers of the Regular Army and the National Guard in Connecticut, where he had insisted to the umpire, Robert L. Bullard (later a lieutenant general and commander of the Second Army of the AEF), that the troops halt on the rut of one wagon wheel not another, a distance of three and a half feet.[11] After the war Bliss performed diplomatic tasks for the president; he was one of the delegates to the peace conference, where he drew up memoranda.

The third chief of staff was only an acting chief. Major General John Biddle, an engineer, filled in for Scott and Bliss when they were out of the country. He did not consider himself suited for the office of chief of staff, a sure sign of inability. In 1918 Biddle commanded American troops in England, where he received visiting British and American dignitaries.[12]

Last among the chiefs of staff, but far more important than his three predecessors put together, was March. A tall man with a large nose and a wispy goatee, he had an imperious air that was no facade; he was efficient to the point of ruthlessness. He had been Pershing's chief of artillery, and the commander in chief of the AEF had recommended March to Baker, thinking that he could control him (actually, Biddle had been Pershing's first choice). But March put his hand to everything and pushed in the direction of efficiency. Almost overnight he changed the War Department. When he walked into the State, War, and Navy Building on his first evening in Washington, he found only one officer at work and bags of unopened mail stacked outside one of the offices. Furious with this nine-to-five mentality, he let his anger be known, and the next night the offices were bright with lights.

Typical was the way March handled relations with Baker. Although the secretary had chosen not to do much, March ensured that he did less. The two had adjoining offices, and early in March's tenure, Baker used a buzzer to summon March to his office. The buzzer had been there a long time, and Baker had used it with March's predecessors. March came in, the two took care of the business at hand, and the chief of staff left. He summoned an assistant and told him to pull the buzzer's wires out of the wall. Under March, more tasks went to Goethals, whom he put in charge of all army supply, and what March and Goethals did not do was handled by assistants such as Captain Robert E. Wood (promoted to brigadier general and, after the war, in charge of Sears, Roebuck). March saw to it that draftees—a draft was instituted in May 1917—filled the training camps and sent them to ports of embarkation on the East Coast, where they were packed into ships' holds and headed to France. He provided the divisions that his European opposite, Pershing, needed. Had March not been in charge at the War Department in the spring of 1918, the troops never would have gotten there.[13]

General March failed in only one respect in his work as chief of staff, and that was the matter of training. It was one thing to get the men into camps and then across to France, but quite another to make them proficient in the work of soldiering and prepared for what they would encounter on the western front. The men were trained so quickly, and in many cases wrongly, that no amount of efficiency in Washington and no will to achieve could turn the divisions into effective fighting units. They had to learn by experience, on the front itself, when they came up against the German army's efficiency and paid the price of instruction by the enemy—the heavy casualties in the Meuse-Argonne.[14]

The initial problem in the United States was a delay in the construction of training camps. It was decided to build huge cantonments consisting of tent camps in the South and barracks camps in the North. Construction of the camps took six months, so the cantonments were not ready until September 1917, and construction continued into the winter. This was much too slow, and the War Department should have used its powers of persuasion with local contractors. When March published his memoirs years later, he excoriated his predecessors for their slowness. In fairness, however, upon U.S. entry into the war it was unclear whether Britain and France needed credits and munitions or troops. Not until the end of the year did it become evident that they desired troops. Still, Secretary Baker had announced an emergency program of training camp construction and should have carried it out as such, if only as a precaution against what proved to be a miscalculation in the Allies' requirements.

Once the men arrived at camp, there was a lack of weapons with which to instruct them. They reached the cantonments only to discover that their heavy weapons would be available once they got to France. Artillery brigades could not train without their French guns. A Stokes mortar platoon in the 82nd (the AEF used the British-made Stokes) saw no such weapons until its arrival in France. Machine guns were mostly unavailable. A soldier assigned to the 160th Machine Gun Company of the 90th Division was in training for two months before the division sailed in June 1918, and he did not see a machine gun until a few weeks before going to the front. Even rifles were not always available, and men trained with Krag-Jorgensens left over from the Philippines; the army had 200,000 of them. Stories circulated that men without rifles trained with broomsticks. This was almost true; the 82nd used four-inch boards to cut out approximations of rifles.[15]

Because of equipment shortages, officers assigned the men to tasks that were supposedly related to training, such as physical exercise. Men from cities may have benefited, but farm boys did not need it. Officers resorted to close-order drill, which had little use on a battlefield. In the eighteenth century, when armies came from the dregs of humanity, it held troops together when they marched through forests (red coats also helped), and it looked good to outside observers. Its rudiments could be learned in fifteen minutes, and the men spent hours and hours on it. Harvard professor William L. Langer, a recruit in 1917, complained in a history of his regiment that the men did "squads east and west" long after the experience had the slightest value.[16] Training time was also spent "policing" the grounds outside the tents or barracks. In sandy ground the men raked everything so that the rakes' teeth erased all footprints; the last man finished by trailing a rake behind him.

Actual training time was devoted to learning trench warfare, the kind of war that had prevailed on the western front since the first weeks of 1914. The Allies and the War Department believed that what had gone on in northern France for three years would continue. The Allies sent instructors to the camps to help train the Americans in digging and sandbagging trenches, including secondary and tertiary trenches, with dugouts to protect troops under fire. Recruits also practiced the use of the bayonet, the supposed weapon of choice of a soldier emerging from a trench. As members of the AEF learned, however, bayonet practice was a waste of time. Bayonets were the most overrated weapons of the war, and AEF surgeons saw almost no bayonet wounds because attacking troops could not get close enough to the enemy to use them, especially if the defenders possessed machine guns. Bayonets had only two uses: to hang gear on and to dig foxholes when shovels were not available.

Departing divisions had to be brought up to strength, and the War Department had no replacement depots, so it took men from divisions in training. Cantonment commanders thus found their training schedules in turmoil. Over a period of months the 80th Division was affected by the transfer of 87,000 men, three times its strength. In November 1917 the 78th's training started, and January levies reduced it by two-thirds; in April it was half strength. In June it sailed, filled with recruits. General Pershing was always critical of the War Department, in particular its fracturing of training schedules, and in this case he had a point. "Although the War Department eventually established a replacement system, as urgently recommended by me, it was done too late to be of material benefit even to the last divisions that came over in the fall of 1918."[17]

Just as the training of individuals was often inefficient, so was unit training in companies, battalions, regiments, brigades, and divisions. This led to a huge problem in the Meuse-Argonne, where units had to stay together despite rugged terrain and German fire. Units were large: companies consisted of 250 men, battalions 1,000, regiments 4,000, brigades 8,000, and divisions 28,000. Size made control difficult. Training schedules did not call for much unit training, and division maneuvers were rare. In the 35th Division, which went to pieces after four days in the Meuse-Argonne, the only such training took place just before the division sailed. Carrying packs—which would not have been the case at the front, where packs were left behind—the men marched down a road for eight miles. They refused to take the experience seriously, laughing, joking, and straggling, with troops on the flanks loping along.[18] Even though the cantonments stretched for miles, providing plenty of room to train units, War Department inspectors did not stress such training, and once the divisions got to France, it became impossible. The men were immediately on the move from the ports to the interior; upon their arrival in Lorraine, they were billeted in villages, farmhouses, and barns. In Alsace, while training in the mountainous Vosges, the 35th was strung out for twenty-five miles.

Disgusted by the War Department's handling of training, Pershing decided, with his usual steely resolution, to add three months to the department's training. That is, he would add three months if time permitted, which it often did not, because he had to put divisions into the line. For the AEF program, Pershing elaborated his own personal theories of tactics, but they were no more realistic, in terms of what was going on in the front line, than the training in the cantonments. He stressed above all else the importance of the rifle, the weapon he had known in the Regular Army in the West among the Indians, during the Spanish-American War, afterward in the Philippines, and in the expeditionary force against Pancho Villa in Mexico. He considered the rifle all-important, and officers from the training section of general headquarters (G-5) so informed their divisions. "In spite of the addition of numerous ancillary weapons to infantry units, the rifle is by far the most formidable weapon of the infantry soldier. . . . Effective rifle fire is essential to victory and is the element which most frequently determines the issue of the battle."[19] The AEF's commander in chief did not have much to say about the worst tactical problem in the Meuse-Argonne—enfilading artillery fire from heights in the Argonne or east of the Meuse, or fire from frontal batteries. As for machine guns, he advised his commanders to attend to them, even if the guns fired too rapidly to permit frontal attacks, their positions were too difficult to identify except at night, and the gunners were often in cement pillboxes impervious to rifle fire. Nor did he understand the importance of gas, which rifle fire could not eliminate because the canisters were too far above the line or contained in shells. As the organizer of the AEF, which was eventually a force of 2 million men, Pershing deserved praise; no one could have done better or even as well. As a guide to training, however, he was no better than the War Department.

CHAPTER TWO

The American Expeditionary Forces

In the beginning was President Wilson's failure to organize American industry for war and Secretary Baker's failure to supervise the War Department. Meanwhile, in 1917 the Allied armies exhausted themselves in ill-planned and exceedingly costly offensives on the western front. For the French, it was the Nivelle offensive, named after its commander, General Robert Nivelle; for the British, it was a series of engagements known collectively as Passchendaele, after a Belgian town. Both these offensives became the ultimate examples of folly by Allied commanders, proof that the world war had lost any sense of purpose and was only grinding down its participants year after year. This persuaded the leaders of the German army to believe that 1918 would bring victory, that a great offensive against the Allies would defeat them and bring their governments to sue for peace.

The Allies frantically appealed to the United States for assistance, which meant bringing over the cantonment divisions that had been formed in the autumn and early winter of 1917. They needed the manpower, whatever the divisions' lack of equipment or training. The Allies, mostly the French, would provide the equipment, and Allied commanders would train the men and get them into the line. In January 1918 the British government offered shipping to bring the divisions over, and the commander in chief of the American Expeditionary Forces, General John J. Pershing, gratefully accepted.

The result was the formation, by the end of the war, of a great American field army. As the divisions came over, the AEF commander began putting them into the line in a gingerly fashion because of their lack of training. He organized a large attack on the German salient at St. Mihiel that opened on September 12, 1918, and rolled up the sector almost the same day. A bare two weeks after St. Mihiel, he threw his divisions into the Meuse-Argonne.

It is possible to discern alternatives to the events that took place in 1917–1918, but history did not take them. French troops in Salonika and British troops in Egypt, Palestine, and Mesopotamia, should have been called home long before. The eastern Mediterranean was merely a sideshow. There were enough of these troops—on the British side, well over 1 million—to make a difference, and other British troops were available in the home islands. It was said at the time and afterward that because casualties at Passchendaele had been so heavy, Prime Minister David Lloyd George was hesitant to release these troops to his commander on the western front, Field Marshal Sir Douglas Haig. Relations between Lloyd George and Haig were poor, and the prime minister was capable of holding back reinforcements. On the American side, the Wilson administration could have organized, armed, and trained the AEF with dispatch if the president had mobilized industry and the secretary of war had mobilized the army. The Allies thus created their own crisis—the German offensive that opened in March 1918. The Americans' crisis came a few months later in the sector between the Meuse River and the Argonne Forest.

The decision to attack the British and French was made by the field commander and first quartermaster general of the German army, General Erich Ludendorff, at a meeting of his staff and principal commanders on November 11, 1917. Neither the titular commander in the west, Field Marshal Paul von Hindenburg, nor Kaiser Wilhelm II was present. Their absence was an indication that the fate of imperial Germany had passed into the hands of the military in the person of Ludendorff. This boded well for overall victory when Ludendorff succeeded, but it boded ill for the general and for Germany when he ultimately failed.

The timing appeared to be good for the German high command, for the French and British armies had been weakened by their ill-advised

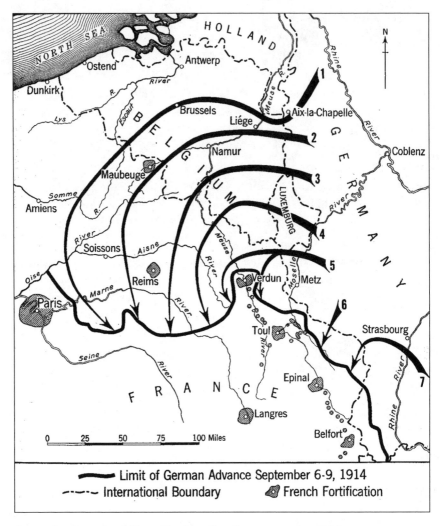

Approximate routes followed by invading German armies, 1914

attacks of the preceding months. The French had attacked on April 16, 1917, under the leadership of an overconfident General Nivelle, who had promised everything but made no preparations to obtain it. When fighting ended on May 21, there had been hardly any change in the line at a cost of 100,000 casualties, including 15,000 dead, and the destruction of the army's morale; half the divisions mutinied. A new commander, Henri Philippe Pétain, barely managed to stabilize the front using artillery rather than men. He then reorganized the troops, which took months; the general went from division to division and vowed to remedy the men's dissatisfactions, promising them generous home leaves. There were executions, but not many. The continuation of the war hung in the balance, and Pétain, who was a man of judgment, made the difference (he would lose his judgment as head of Vichy France in World War II). The French army managed two small attacks in the autumn, the limit of its capacity. Meanwhile, the British army, observing the French failure, clumsily added its offensive known as Passchendaele, commencing July 31 and ending November 10. Things went terribly wrong as driving rain waterlogged the battlefield, and artillery turned everything to mud. The advance was five miles, and the casualties were four times those in the Nivelle offensive. The British commander, Haig, was blamed for what happened. A reserved, stolid man, he seemed to have no control over the battle once it began.[1]

The failure of the Allied armies in 1917 was the principal reason for the Germans' spring 1918 offensive, although there were two others. For one, in the winter of 1917–1918 the AEF was minuscule—four divisions unprepared for service in the line—and posed no danger to Germany. The second reason was the collapse of the eastern front in Russia. A revolution in March 1917 deposed the czar and ended the empire, creating a republican government in Petersburg. Russia remained in the war, despite its increasing inability to continue fighting, until the Petersburg regime collapsed in the Bolshevik revolution in November and the new government negotiated the peace treaty of Brest-Litovsk. Russia's withdrawal from the war gave the German army the opportunity to transfer divisions from east to west, often cited as a reason why the high command attacked in the west. The command believed that it had sufficient forces at its disposal to win: 1,569,000 rifles to the Allies' 1,245,600. It withdrew thirty-three divisions, not enough to count in the spring offensive, and constituting less than 15 percent of the two hundred that attacked on March 21, 1918.[2]

Besides the propitious timing, the German field commander chose a wise place (wiser than he knew) to attack: the juncture of British and French forces along the front. His divisions attacked the British Fifth Army, the least prepared of the four British armies and the one that had sustained the greatest losses at Passchendaele. At Haig's order, the Fifth Army had taken over thirty miles of adjoining French front because the French occupied more front than the British did and were unable to

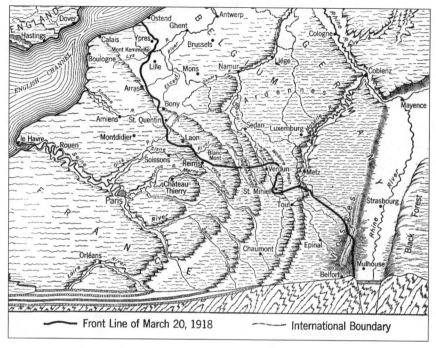

— Front Line of March 20, 1918   - - - - - International Boundary

Diagram of western front

organize a reserve. The Fifth Army commander, Sir Hubert Gough, in-
herited a mass of poor trenches and did not have enough laborers to redo
them. He engaged most of his 40,000 laborers in building roads.[3]

The German commander made every effort to ensure success by en-
gaging in thorough preparation. He divided the forces for Operation Michael into categories. First were forty mobile divisions with full battalions
of 850 men; second were thirty attack divisions. He assigned the best
equipment to these two groups. Mobile division commanders saw to it
that everyone capable of doing so went to school to study Hutier tactics,
named for General Oskar von Hutier, victor of the battle of Riga in 1917.
Hutier had defeated the Russians by using infiltration, bypassing strong
points, and overwhelming back areas before front-line enemy troops un-
derstood what was happening. He would be one of the commanders on
March 21. Third were the trench divisions, the leftovers; they furnished
equipment for the others and were expected to stand behind the mobile
and attack divisions, taking the brunt of any failure.

The high command arranged for a massive artillery preparation and rolling barrage to soften the Allied line before the mobile and attack divisions confronted it. Heavy and light guns stood wheel to wheel; there were guns to obliterate dugouts, guns for shelling the line, and mortars for machine gun positions. A large airplane and balloon force photographed Allied positions. Four thousand men worked on analyzing the photographs, so that artillery and mortars would not waste fire. The command gave attention to machine guns—light for advancing troops, and heavy against tanks, if any appeared. The heavies were to go forward in groups of two or three. Each four-man crew carried a total of five thousand rounds of ammunition, enough for four bursts of three minutes. Commanders also prepared quantities of gas. The German army had introduced gas at Ypres in 1915, and Hutier had used it before Riga. The Germans were far more adept than the Allies at releasing the dread contents of the canisters or sending gas over in shells, the latter containing high-explosive charges to confuse the troops and conceal the fact that they were receiving gas.

Despite this careful planning, not everything went right with the March 21 attack. The morning proved foggy, which was a boon to the attackers but also added an element of confusion. Signal rockets were impossible to read, and units became lost. The battlefield was in an area of soft, swampy ground, soaked by rain. The rolling barrage of the artillery, organized by Lieutenant Colonel Georg Bruchmueller, was adhering to a rigid schedule of one hundred yards every two or three minutes, and it got ahead of the infantry. German casualties the first day were 78,000, the highest for any day of the war.

Enough went right, however, to make the attack an enormous success. Allied intelligence had discovered the date of the attack but did not guess the power of the artillery preparation and barrage or the number of divisions, nor that it would fall on the Fifth Army. Nothing like it had been seen. The Germans drove a salient into the British line between Arras and Barisis fifty miles across and forty deep. The divisions captured thirteen hundred guns and quantities of munitions and stores. British casualties were 200,000, including 90,000 prisoners. Adjoining French forces suffered 70,000 casualties.[4]

A footnote to Operation Michael—but not so insignificant to the residents of Paris—was the gun that opened on the French capital on March 23. The eight-inch howitzer, named the Kaiser Wilhelm Geschuetz, could hurl a 264-pound high-explosive shell seventy-five miles. It fired until August, lobbing 307 shells that killed 250 people and wounded 640. A shell shattered the roof of a church crowded with worshippers. This instrument of terror caused an outpouring of refugees.[5]

Operation Michael ended on April 5. A second attack followed against the British to the north, which came within twenty-seven miles of the sea at Dunkirk. A third took place along the Chemin des Dames, an east-west ridge running parallel to the Aisne River for fifteen miles. The French had taken the ridge during the Nivelle offensive, at a heavy cost. It protected Compiègne, Soissons, and Reims. Despite American and British warnings, the French refused to believe an attack was coming, and the general in charge, Denis Duchêne, bunched his troops in the front line rather than in the second- and third-line trenches. The cost of losing the Chemin des Dames was high. The last German attacks were of lesser importance: the fourth was along the Matz River, a tributary of the Olse north of Soissons, and the fifth took Soissons and threatened Reims.

As the immense drama of the offensive played out, the need for American troops became evident, and the British government offered to provide shipping. However, an argument arose between Pershing and the Allies over what sort of troops should come over—entire divisions with support troops, as Pershing wanted, or only infantry and machine gun units. More important was the matter of amalgamating the American troops once they arrived, with Anglo-French proposals for placing them in Allied divisions in various ways, perhaps by regiments or battalions. The forum for argument was the Supreme War Council, created in November 1917 and sitting in Paris. Its political arm consisted of Prime Minister Lloyd George, Premier Georges Clemenceau of France, Premier Vittorio Orlando of Italy, and, later, President Wilson's personal representative, Colonel Edward M. House.[6] Its military arm was composed not of field commanders, which would have suited Pershing, but superfluous generals such as Sir William Robertson for Britain, Ferdinand Foch for France, Luigi Cadorna for Italy, and General Tasker H. Bliss for the United States. Their coming together marked the beginning of an effort to replace the offhand relations among the army commanders that had prevailed for three years. During the crisis over Operation Michael, Foch was appointed Allied commander in chief.

During the argument over amalgamation, the War Council saw Pershing at his argumentative best, which was impressive. The American

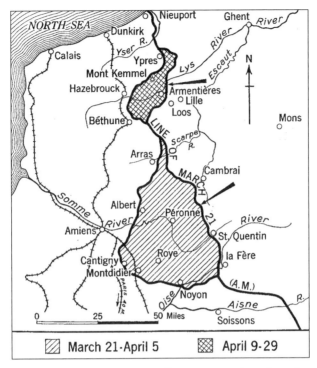

Ground gained by German offensives, March and April
1918

general believed that whatever training his troops received from the Allies would be perfunctory and that they would be cannon fodder. He considered amalgamation the end of the AEF as a force on the western front, as well as the end of any prospect that he would be more than a minor player, with little more importance than the commander of the Belgian army. He took every opportunity to make his position known. In a meeting of the council at Abbeville on May 8, he faced a test when Foch asked triumphantly, "Are you willing to risk our being driven behind the Loire?" Pershing was being asked whether, by championing an independent command, he was willing to risk the capture of Paris and perhaps the end of the war. His response was yes. The British minister of war, Lord Alfred Milner, whispered to Lloyd George behind a door, "It's no use. You can't budge him an inch." Lloyd George asked virtually the same question and got the same response. Pounding the table, the commander of the AEF said, "Gentlemen, I have thought this program over very deliberately

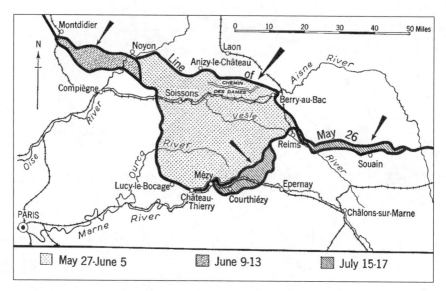

Ground gained by German offensives, May, June, and July 1918

and I will not be coerced." That night, Pershing, who could be as laconic as the British field commander Haig, wrote in his diary, "Discussion at times very lively."[7]

On two occasions Pershing gave evidence of giving in to amalgamation, but each time nothing came of his apparent cooperation. On March 28, at the height of Michael, he took the initiative by going to Pétain and then to Foch, saying that he would give all he had to the Allies. The results were minimal: the 1st Division was ordered from Lorraine to Picardy but was not used; the 2nd Division extended its sector, which was quiet; and the 26th and 42nd Divisions relieved French units, also in quiet sectors. The only American troops opposing Michael were two companies of engineers, seventy-eight of whom were casualties. On the second occasion, a request for amalgamation came from Foch on June 17, and Pershing said that he would think it over. Why he took this position is difficult to know. His leading biographer believes that Pershing was exhibiting his willingness to cooperate, although that aspect of his personality has never been celebrated. Two days after the proposal, and with the prospect (soon realized) of more enemy attacks, he wrote to General Peyton C. March in Washington: "We cannot afford to allow their morale to become too low, as there is danger of their breaking at the wrong time." He told Baker that he might go along with the Allies "to give them courage." He did nothing more.[8]

By this time, amalgamation no longer worried either Pershing or the Allies. The attacks at the Matz and at Soissons proved less threatening and petered out, and the cantonment divisions were coming over. The number of troops brought over was astonishing: 85,000 in March, 120,000 in April, and thereafter, 250,000 a month through the summer. The number also astonished the Germans. A German writer who had been an officer during the war wrote of the "great surprise" that the number of troops tripled, sextupled, octupled.[9] The 2 million troops in France by the armistice could have doubled to 4 million, or even 5 million, if the war had continued through the next year.

The coming of the American army to France made one of the most decisive changes in European affairs in the twentieth century (decades later, Pearl Harbor would begin another change in Europe's and the world's fortunes). To the Allies, it was the end of a nightmare; to the Germans, the beginning of defeat. American troops could sense the change taking place. William Langer made the crossing in the summer and wrote that to his fellow voyagers, western men from the plains and the Rockies, the ocean was new and wonderful, "the endless expanse of restlessly rolling blue water, the splendid sky." Most important, he remembered, "the sight of that tremendous convoy plowing its way ever on and on, carrying some 90,000 troops more for the Kaiser to reckon with," would have unnerved any submarine commander who happened to see it.[10]

In the spring and summer of 1918 the AEF took part in a series of engagements that could have provided combat experience for fighting in the Meuse-Argonne. Each marked increasing American participation in the line, but unfortunately, the engagements were of only modest value. The largest, St. Mihiel, was so short (September 12–16) that, with the exception of a few divisions in the Aisne-Marne offensive, little was learned. Thus, the Meuse-Argonne would be the AEF's learning experience.

Accounts of the AEF often begin with the German trench raids on the 1st Division on November 3, 1917, and March 1, 1918, and on the 26th Division on April 20. All offered small lessons. The 1st Division's initial trial, inflicted on a platoon of the 16th Infantry by 40 or 50 enemy troops, resulted in 3 Americans killed (one was shot, one had his head bashed in, and the third had his throat cut), 5 wounded, and 12 prisoners—not an impressive result for the Germans, who had 2 dead, 7 wounded, and 1 deserter. The second raid showed that an alert leadership could limit such attacks by watching for the signs of preparation, such as enemy guns ranging on small portions of the line. Before this trench raid, the men of the 18th Infantry pulled back, leaving automatic gunners in the rifle pits. The Germans sent 220 men who killed 20 Americans, wounded others, and took 12 prisoners. Enemy losses were far higher and totaled 83: 17 killed and left behind, 4 prisoners, and the others caught by American artillery fire while moving back to their lines.[11]

The third raid, on the 26th Division, was much more serious, although all these raids were insignificant compared with the German attacks against the British and French during the spring offensive. The Germans boxed in a section of the line as before, sent over 2,800 men, and held the section for twenty-four hours. Eighty-one Americans were killed, 187 were wounded, 214 were gassed, and 187 were taken prisoner or missing, for a total of 669.[12] The 26th's officers had seen the 1st Division learn from experience and ready itself for the second raid, and they might have been better prepared. It was an opportunity for Pershing to cashier the 26th's responsible officers, notably the division commander, Major General Clarence A. Edwards. Edwards had graduated last in his class at West Point and had risen in rank because he headed the War Department's Bureau of Insular Affairs. Though beloved by his men, he was a loose disciplinarian. Already under a cloud before the raid because of his refusal to accept advice from general headquarters (GHQ), Edwards was hypercritical of anything he did not have a hand in. Pershing kept him until mid-October and then sent him back to the United States for the absurd purpose of training troops. After the raid, Edwards's infantry commander, Brigadier General Peter E. Traub, was promoted and awarded the 35th Division. Traub ran his new division into a hole in the first days of the Meuse-Argonne and put it out of the line for the rest of the war.[13]

More important than these raids was an engagement at Cantigny, northwest of Montdidier, near the farthest point reached by the German attack in March. Cantigny was the first planned engagement of the American army in France. By that time, May 28, Pershing had 650,000 troops—a measure of how long it took for Americans to see real action at the front, and how exasperated the Allies had become with the AEF commander in chief's criticism and lack of cooperation. Cantigny involved a reinforced regiment of the 1st Division. Its commander, Colonel Hanson E. Ely, would become a major general commanding the 5th Division at the Meuse-Argonne. His regiment captured the village of Cantigny, a high point in the line, from which the Germans observed their enemies and directed artillery fire. Enemy casualties were perhaps 1,400, including 220 prisoners. American casualties were 1,067, including 199 dead—a high but not prohibitive cost, considering the ground captured. The difficulty at Cantigny was that the day before, the Germans had attacked along the Chemin des Dames, which forced the removal of French artillery and air support. The 1st's artillery brigade possessed the usual complement of two light regiments and one heavy one, insufficient to range back on German heavy guns. German spotting planes hovered over the lines, calling fire. As if this were not enough, fifteen thousand high-explosive shells mixed with mustard gas caught a reserve battalion, causing 800 casualties. But Ely's men held.[14]

The next actions were Belleau Wood, Vaux, and Château-Thierry, involving the 2nd and 3rd Divisions, during the Chemin des Dames attack. The commander of the marine infantry brigade—the 2nd was the only AEF division to have a marine brigade—was James G. Harbord, whom Pershing had sent in to gain experience. He allowed the marines to attack locked-in machine guns, with no artillery support.

> Five yards apart, in four ranks, twenty yards between each rank, the Marines advanced. Nothing had been seen like it, in mass innocence, in hope and at the end in unavailing heroism, since the British attack on the Somme in 1916—and it is quite possible that the lack of immediate reaction from the enemy was due to disbelief that in 1918 such naiveté could still exist. For nearly a hundred yards the Marines walked forward in silence, broken only by the thrashing of the young corn [wheat] as they waded through it, by their officers' whistles or shouted commands, and by the sounds of their own breath in throats dry with fearful excitement. Then with the sharp crack of a thousand snapping sticks, the hidden machine guns opened.[15]

The marines cleared the woods with 4,716 casualties. In contrast, the army brigade of the 2nd took Vaux in twenty minutes with 128 casualties, a set-piece fight. The lesson at Belleau Wood and Vaux was that impetuosity was unequal to calculation. At Château-Thierry a motorized machine gun battalion of the 3rd Division arrived first at the Marne, followed the next day by infantry, and did excellent work. The division commander, Major General Joseph T. Dickman, a stickler for machine guns, received corps command in the Meuse-Argonne.

Another test came in what the French called the second battle of the Marne and the Americans called the battle of Soissons, followed by the Aisne-Marne offensive. The German attack opened on July 15 in an effort to extend the Chemin des Dames salient. This time, the French pulled back all units except for suicide troops. A counteroffensive opened three days later, led by the American 1st and 2nd Divisions and a battle-tried Moroccan division. The battle was no flawless engagement. At the outset the Americans did well, but the operation showed them to be untrained, with troops plunging through the Forest of Retz at night in a confused effort to get into line behind the barrage—a rushing mass that was largely beyond the control of brigade and division commanders. The 75s did not extend the barrage far enough, and the rush to get into line left the machine gun companies, the 37-mm guns, and the mortar troops behind; when the 75s stopped, the men were on their own. They failed to stay within their assigned sectors. The Moroccan division was sandwiched by the 2nd Division on one side and the 1st Division on the other; they converged on the Moroccan sector and crowded the division out. Casualties for the Americans were high: the 1st Division had 1,393 killed outright, 373 died of their wounds, and 5,803 wounded, for a total of 7,569; the 2nd Division had 505 killed outright, 122 died of their wounds, and 2,083 wounded, for a total of 2,710.[16] After this tactically marred introduction, the French and Americans pushed the Germans back across a series of rivers—first the Marne, then the Ourcq, Vesle, and Aisne. By late August the Germans were forced to the prepared defenses of the Hindenburg Line, a point that had been the jump-off place for the March 21 attack. In five furious months the Germans had gone forward. In two months the Allies pushed them back.

Meanwhile, the British won what was perhaps the decisive battle of the war. On August 8, 1918, the British army triumphed against the German enemy, marking the end of German tactical dominance on the western front. In this attack near Amiens, which equaled Soissons in its suddenness, the British Fourth Army threw in its Australian and Canadian troops and achieved a near breakthrough using 530 heavy and light tanks.

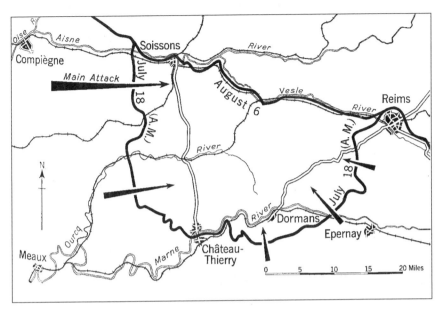

French-American counteroffensive, July 18, 1918

The defenders had never seen so many tanks, and entire units fled—a remarkable change in the Germans' behavior, which had previously been so disciplined and decisive. The tank attack marked what all historians of World War I have described as Ludendorff's "black day," employing his words. The attack came to an end on August 12, after an advance of twelve miles. Although the Germans caught some tanks with artillery fire and others suffered mechanical breakdowns, after Amiens, a German victory was no longer possible.

Ludendorff offered his resignation, but Hindenburg and the kaiser refused to accept it. It is interesting to consider what might have happened if he had been removed from command of the western front and perhaps been sent to Sweden, where he eventually ended up. The German army would have been saved the casualties it took in the remaining weeks of August as it moved back. After Amiens, Ludendorff's judgment began to fail, and he insisted on defending points that were indefensible. His commanders urged him to move the line back quickly, but he refused. The slow retreat during the Aisne-Marne offensive hurt morale. With a quick retreat, the army might have worked harder to fortify the Hindenburg Line, which was not a single line but actually several extending

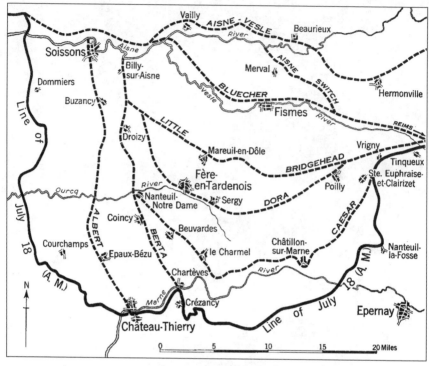

German withdrawal positions, Aisne-Marne salient

seven miles deep, consisting of trenches along strong places, pillboxes for machine guns, concrete shelters for troops, and belt after belt of staked barbed wire. With more time, the German army could have made the line impregnable against the American attack in the Meuse-Argonne and the other Allied attacks that began in September and forced Germany into an armistice.

The final engagement of the AEF before the Meuse-Argonne was St. Mihiel, involving the elimination of a salient east of Verdun. The Germans had created the salient in 1914 during the first battle of the Marne and used it in 1916 when their army attempted to take Verdun in a battle that cost the Germans and French hundreds of thousands of casualties. By 1918, St. Mihiel had lost its value. It was one of the positions that Ludendorff should have given up but did not. On July 24 Foch gave the task of eliminating it to the AEF, and the same day Pershing announced his intention to form the First Army, which he would command. The First Army came into existence on August 10. St. Mihiel would mark its first appearance in battle.

The AEF commander in chief took every precaution to win the battle that began on September 12, bringing up an overwhelming force of 230,000 American and 110,000 French troops against 23,000 defenders. He brought in all his "veteran" divisions—the 1st, 2nd, 26th, and 42nd—plus reserve divisions behind them. Massed batteries opened with a roar, and the barrage moved the sheet of flame forward, ahead of the infantry. The corps of Major General Hunter Liggett, who would command I Corps at the beginning of the Meuse-Argonne and then the First Army itself, reached the second day's goal in the middle of the first. The Germans in the salient had been warned of the attack and were preparing to pull out. In a bit of luck for the AEF, the Germans put their artillery on the roads, where the preparation fire caught it. German infantry commanders were so disgusted that they hardly opposed the attackers. The cost to the AEF was 8,182 casualties (including 1,303 killed outright and 496 who died of their wounds), rather than the anticipated 50,000. The battle was virtually over the day it began, although it was not until September 16 that the Americans could be certain that the Germans would not counterattack.[17]

Like previous American engagements, St. Mihiel displayed military lapses. Road discipline was appalling; military police were hardly in evidence, and vehicles, both horse drawn and motor, were lined up for miles in traffic jams. One of them caught Clemenceau, who was attempting to motor to Thiaucourt to welcome the liberated inhabitants. A dozen years later, in *The Grandeur and Misery of Victory,* he was still full of sarcasm: "All the representatives of the higher American military authorities openly inclined to the views of Pershing—General Bliss being the one exception. They wanted an American Army. They had it. Anyone who saw, as I saw, the hopeless congestion at Thiaucourt will bear witness that they may congratulate themselves on not having it sooner."[18] At Pétain's headquarters, Pershing's representative, Major Paul H. Clark, heard careful criticism. He was told that artillery fire had not cut the wire in front of the German trenches—men had cut it with hand tools—and was admonished that French troops would not have gone into battle until the wire had been cut.[19] In addition, tanks ran out of gasoline in the afternoon of the first day; they required three times the amount of fuel estimated,

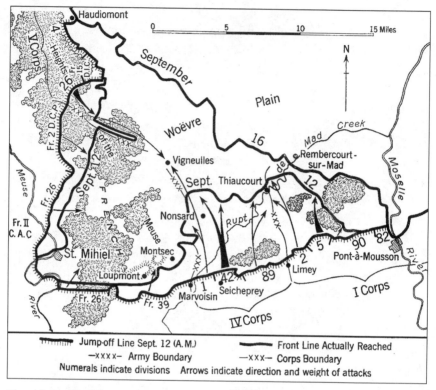

Plan of attack of First Army, September 12, 1918

and because of the traffic jams, the gas trucks could not deliver it, taking thirty-two hours to move fourteen kilometers.[20]

But St. Mihiel was a far more interesting affair than the easy victory it seemed. It involved much more than rolling up a salient with an American-commanded army and making a few errors in the process. Taking St. Mihiel just before going into the Meuse-Argonne foreclosed a strategy that had attracted Pershing and his staff since 1917. At that time, they had chosen a place in the line to the right of the French army, which had concentrated its divisions above the approaches to Paris, and to the far right of the British army, which was fighting close to the English Channel.[21] In seeking a place to put the American divisions, Pershing and his planners saw the attraction of Lorraine. The AEF could provision its divisions from ports south of the Seine, which were being underused because supplies for the British army came in at Channel ports. Divisions that were rest-ing or worn out and refitting held the line from Verdun to Switzerland; the Germans also used that part of the line as a rest area. Thus, the AEF set out a strategy to take over in Lorraine. The plan was to build up the force gradually. In 1918 the veteran divisions and any arriving divisions that were fairly well trained would take the St. Mihiel salient. In 1919 the gathered and trained AEF would attack from St. Mihiel north into the Moselle River valley and lay siege to the fortress of Metz. North of Metz lay the Briey-Longwy-Thionville triangle containing the coal and iron mines of the Saar.

It is possible that the Metz strategy would have been easier to accomplish in 1918 than taking the sector between the Argonne and the Meuse. Capturing a city known for its defenses would have won acclaim, as would taking the coal and iron of the Saar. Colonel George C. Marshall, assistant operations officer at GHQ, wrote after the war that "there is no doubt in my mind but that we could have reached the outskirts of Metz by the late afternoon of the 13th, and quite probably could have captured the city on the 14th, as the enemy was incapable of bringing up reserves in sufficient numbers and formation to offer an adequate resistance." Brigadier General Douglas MacArthur of the 42nd Division, always sure of his strategic views, reconnoitered the terrain, stood on an eminence, and observed the approaches to the city, the rail traffic in and out, and the motor traffic at night using headlights. Metz, he thought, would have been easy to take. In his memoirs, Pershing agreed.[22]

There were arguments on the other side, as well. Ten years later, General Liggett wrote that the AEF at St. Mihiel was not yet a well-oiled machine, alluding to the traffic jams, and he claimed that the terrain in front of Metz was marshy.[23] As the AEF learned in the Meuse-Argonne, September in northern France meant unrelieved rain. The waterlogged Woevre Plain would have been a major obstacle—Passchendaele all over again. The defenses of Metz also could have caused a great deal of trouble. The German group commander in the area, General Max von Gallwitz, told an American reporter in 1928 that although the army had withdrawn the bulk of war material from Metz, its defenses lay to the south and sides, where fieldworks had strengthened the forts. Overrunning such positions, he claimed, would have been "impracticable."[24]

Pershing ultimately decided in favor of the Meuse-Argonne. We do not know why exactly; it may have been a snap decision. Foch appeared at Pershing's headquarters on August 30 and argued in favor of putting

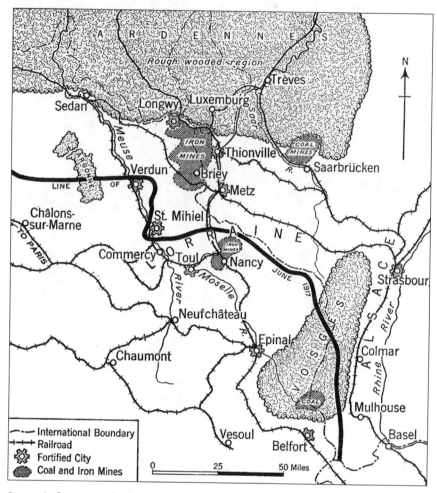

Strategic features influencing selection of Lorraine front

more troops on the Aisne. The German army, he said, was "in complete disorder and . . . we must not allow them an opportunity to reorganize." He was referring to the counterattack at Soissons and the British success at Amiens and the Aisne-Marne offensive. The British, he proposed, would continue in the direction of Cambrai and St. Quentin, the French would attack in the vicinity of Mesnil, and the Americans would bring troops from St. Mihiel into the Aisne sector. The battle in 1918, Foch stated, would be decided on the Aisne. To this Pershing replied, either argumentatively or thoughtfully, "why not that the Americans take all the sector from the Meuse to the Argonne?" The Allied commander in chief was fond of large strategic visions, some of which, his critics averred, were not completely thought out. Pershing had seen that Foch's proposal would separate American troops, and it is possible that Foch (who had become a marshal of France on August 5) anticipated this turn of the argument, although that may credit him with more guile than he deserves. For whatever reason, Foch dropped his argument for the Aisne and agreed to the Meuse-Argonne. Pershing confirmed the choice in a meeting at Foch's headquarters on September 2, and Foch issued a directive the next day that set out the final plan.[25]

It was as simple as that, and the reasoning has never been clear. What followed, however, is clear: whatever the merit of Foch's proposal and Pershing's counterproposal that led to the decision, the AEF commander in chief should have dropped the planned attack on St. Mihiel. The Germans were, after all, getting ready to give up the salient (although Pershing was not aware of it at the time), and the AEF would have saved itself the logistical difficulties of changing sectors so quickly; calculated from the end of the St. Mihiel operation on September 16, the time was only ten days.

The logistical problems of moving from St. Mihiel to the Meuse-Argonne were immense, and Pershing's decision to conduct both operations was the cause of many of them. All the paraphernalia of men at war had to be brought to the new sector. The amount of supplies brought into the Meuse-Argonne was an amazing 900,000 tons. Shells and cartridges came in at nineteen railheads and needed to be unloaded and positioned in dumps where the troops could draw them. Twenty-seven hundred pieces of heavy and light artillery had to be shifted from St. Mihiel, which could cause traffic jams if the guns slipped off the roads. Many infantrymen in the divisions had to walk the distance between the sectors—no easy task when carrying packs.

The road network between St. Mihiel and the Meuse-Argonne was mostly south-north rather than east-west, which lengthened the move. Men in artillery brigades with horse-drawn guns, together with division trains—signal, supply, and sanitary (medical)—followed along. Because of the autumnal rains, they slept in wet forests with wet feet, clothes, and blankets. Some infantrymen rode in French trucks, *camions,* driven by Annamese, whom the men mistook for Chinese. Truck transport was not much better than walking, however. The drivers were indifferently trained and drove at night without lights. The trucks, which had no springs, were excruciatingly uncomfortable, with sixteen men and packs jammed together on the floorboards for the sixteen-hour trip.

A special concern in changing fronts was caring for the horses, whose motive power barely met the AEF's requirements. Early in September, before St. Mihiel, an officer at Pétain's headquarters spoke to Major Clark about the animals, noting that American veterinarians' favorite medicine for the horses was the revolver.[26] Several thousand animals received that treatment on the way to the new sector. An artillery battalion commander who was an engineer in civil life, accustomed to analyzing motive power, noted that even at the end of the horse era, when many Americans still knew how to care for the animals, the AEF showed little judgment in handling them. Horses needed sixteen to twenty hours to eat, and there was never enough time. Forage (hay) as well as oats should have been available at or near the camps. But troops arrived to find that the only forage was five to twelve kilometers distant, so the horses were often given only oats. The famished animals bolted their food and swallowed without chewing, obtaining no nourishment; as a result, many starved during the passage.[27]

Involvement in the attack on St. Mihiel made it necessary to employ inexperienced divisions in the Meuse-Argonne. By the time First Army chief of staff Colonel (later brigadier general) Hugh A. Drum learned of the need to shift troops, it was too late to bring the four veteran divisions. This single failure—the inability to use experienced divisions—proved to be a major factor in the initial difficulties in the new sector.[28]

The operations at St. Mihiel did have the advantage of confusing the Germans over where the AEF would attack next. The AEF staff at Chaumont disguised the divisions' movement, and everything took place at night. In the daytime, Americans near the front wore French uniforms when out in the open. When artillerymen needed to lower trees to open fields of fire, they tied the tops and cut the trunks not quite through, so they could quickly chop the remainder when the time came.[29] The German army did not know what, if anything, to make of the goings-on; the signs were confusing.

All these identifications, particularly of circulation in hitherto quiet sectors, point to the possibility of an attack along the whole front from Reims to Verdun. During the daytime, only circulation far in the rear could be observed, but at night great activity reigned along our front. The noise of narrow-gauge railways, motor trucks, the unloading of heavy material, loud cries, sirens, and klaxons, could be heard throughout the whole night.[30]

The above refers to the night of September 22–23, three days before the attack. On the day before the Meuse-Argonne, German officers of the 1st Guard Division, in front of the U.S. 35th, became suspicious and captured a few French prisoners, who told them that the sector was filled with Americans. Near the Meuse they brought in an American, but that caused little concern, for Americans had already been identified in the area. Anyway, by that time it was too late to obtain reinforcements. Local commanders, if they expected an attack, could do no more than put their men on the alert and place most of them to the rear.

A colonel in the AEF medical corps, surgeon George W. Crile, founder of the Cleveland Clinic, wrote about the movement of troops into the Meuse-Argonne in his diary. In his mind's eye, on September 24 he saw a concentration of half a million men, but not one was visible; there were no road convoys beyond those of a normal day. At night, all was activity, "prowling, skulking, preparing, stalking, 500,000 armed human beings accompanied by acres of guns—paraphernalia covering the earth—a blanket of destruction ten miles deep, thirty miles long, gliding by inches, skulking by inches—hundreds of thousands of my fellow beings are dragging and lugging this vast carpet of destruction toward the enemy; thrusting its sharp and explosive edge into the enemy." He wrote about the marvelousness of this destruction, this sheet of death moving at night, and of how manhunting threw a dullness on all other sports.[31]

Dale Van Every, later a novelist and historian of the American West, remembered the days just before the attack, when the Meuse-Argonne stood in all its virginal splendor.[32] It was wonderful weather in the Argonne. Gusts of rain washed the earth, followed by days of brilliant sunshine; the hills and woods rolled up to a blue sky across which tumbled white clouds. Sunset flooded the west with red and gold, followed by nights bright with a full moon.

CHAPTER THREE

First Days

The first days of the battles of 1918 usually went well, and then trouble set in—the undue extension of salients, the outrunning of lines of supply, the increase in casualties and confusion, the Clausewitzian fog of war. No army commander wished for such experiences, and each felt certain that his planning would avoid them. Pershing was so busy during the two weeks between St. Mihiel and the Meuse-Argonne that he had no time to think about whether his battle would follow the usual pattern. He may have believed that whereas the other commanders enamored of the trenches would have the usual troubles, he would escape them because he had inculcated American tactical virtues in his men and was bound to succeed. He hoped against hope that his men would move into the sector fast, swarm over the German strong points, and get up to the Kriemhilde Stellung, the line of Grandpré, St. Georges, and Brieulles, which was where Foch expected him to go. Afterward, Pershing could look the Allied commanders in the eye—the effervescent Foch, with his schemes to deny the AEF commander in chief his just desserts; the steady and remote Pétain; and the supercilious Haig, with his uniform full of red tabs.[1]

The battle started off well, with First Army headquarters in charge, the three corps commands functioning efficiently (I Corps on the left, V Corps in the middle, and III Corps on the right), and the divisions—77th, 28th, 35th, 91st, 37th, 79th, 4th, 80th, and 33rd—sending troops into their virtual corridors moving north. Then the classic problems of attacking troops intervened. The initial sign of trouble was slowness in taking the height of Montfaucon, the Hill of the Falcon, which dominated the middle of the sector and the first of the heights constituting the whaleback. This failure was a fascinating exercise in battlefield confusion. The AEF commander had left the taking to a green division, the 79th, under the command of Major General Joseph E. Kuhn, whose performance was disconcerting. Thereafter a whole series of difficulties followed—some of them preventable, others not. In sum, they were enough to bring the opening attack—so promising, and so important to the commander in chief and to the American nation behind him—to a standstill within four or five days.

The battle opened not with a roar but with a sort of distant thunder, first from one direction, then another. It was 11:30 p.m. on September 25 when guns belonging to the French Fourth Army, to the left of the Argonne Forest, began firing in an effort to make the Germans believe that a French attack might be forming. To create further confusion, or perhaps the sense that an infantry pincer might be a sequel, guns opened to the right of the Meuse-Argonne, from St. Mihiel to the heights of the Meuse, which might also appear to be supporting an American drive toward Metz.

At 2:30 a.m. on September 26 came the guns of the Meuse-Argonne, 3,980 of them. The combination of American- and French-commanded artillery, distributed about evenly, averaged one gun every twenty-five feet. In their offensive at Soissons in July, the Germans had placed one gun every eighty feet. The guns at neither engagement were in a line, for they were echeloned, with the smallest caliber at the front—for the Americans, this meant the three-inch French 75s; for the Germans, their equivalent calibers, the 77s and 88s. Terrain, too, governed where the wheels might go; this could not be an eighteenth-century array. The guns nonetheless seemed to be everywhere. When they began firing, they sent over a quarter million rounds in three hours. The German commander, Gallwitz, remembered later that the windowpanes at his headquarters at Montmédy began to rattle.[2] A civil engineer from Ohio described it as music from a great orchestra. He heard the staccato sounds of the 75s and 155s, the three- and six-inch pieces of the artillery brigades. There were kettle drums beating, the same size guns at a greater distance, be-

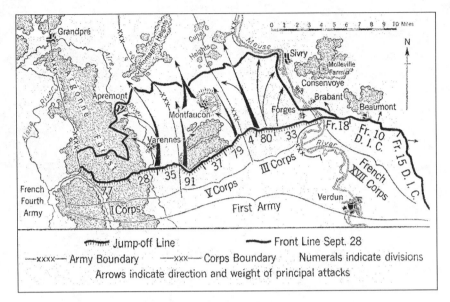

Plan of attack of First Army, September 26, 1918

longing to corps and army artillery. Behind were the thunderous explosions of the bigger guns. Behind them on railway lines stood the basses, fourteen-inch giants brought to the front later by a contingent of the U.S. Navy commanded by Admiral C. P. Plunkett. To the ear of the engineer, the bigger guns rumbled and roared. All this was accompanied by the screaming and swishing of high-velocity projectiles. And at the front itself, as darkness turned to daylight, he heard the snare drum roll of massed machine guns. It was, the engineer wrote, "the most tremendous, awe-inspiring volume of sound, not altogether unmusical, that ever jarred human ears."[3]

To veterans of the Spanish-American War of 1898, not a few of whom were in line, the fire was unbelievable. In the 37th Division, Mess Sergeant Bryan was sitting on the tongue of a rolling kitchen. He listened to the roar for ten minutes, looked around, and remarked that he had just heard more shooting in the last ten minutes than he had heard in the entire war of twenty years before.[4]

When the preparation fire ended, the barrage began at 5:30 and continued until 8:30 or 9:00, after which only corps and army artillery fired. The 75s had reached their range. Walton Clark Jr., a captain in the Second

Battalion, 108th Field Artillery Regiment, 28th Division, noticed that the blackness of the woods began to turn to gray at 4:30, and just before 5:00 there was a lull in the firing while the batteries relaid the gun sights preparatory to the barrage. He wrote that it was hard work shoving ninety-pound shells into the breeches and swabbing the guns after each shot.[5] When the barrage was over, the gunners everywhere threw themselves on the ground to rest. Meanwhile, there had been accidents. In the 122nd Field Artillery Regiment attached to the 91st Division, a man had failed to get his hand away after pulling the lanyard; the tube caught him in counterrecoil and mashed his fingers under the rollers. It took time to get them out. The crew elevated the gun almost straight up, but it was so hot they could not touch it; they took a duckboard and put it over the muzzle, and then eight or ten of them pushed the tube down. The man waited to pull out the pieces of his hand.[6]

With the opening of the barrage, the waves of infantry went forward. They did not begin from trench positions, however, for such was not the nature of the Meuse-Argonne. They walked forward across the partly caved-in enemy trenches that were now bereft of defenders, who had moved back behind the barrage to strong points. They went forward with helmets and rifles, leaving their packs in piles guarded by a soldier or two. Behind them came the mortars and 37-mm light guns—but usually not in the first waves, for the equipment was heavy and required carts— followed by the signalmen with rolls of telephone wire. The artillerymen came after, especially the light regiments with the 75s.

The infantry could see no more than thirty or forty feet because of the fog that filled the ravines; they saw only high places, pushing up like tips of mountains in a biblical flood. Some of the envelopment was actually from smoke shells thrown over by the artillery, but it was unnecessary; the fog was enough. Although the fog along the line at first appeared to be a barrier, the men later realized that it offered protection. In earlier attacks in the British and French sectors there had been morning fog, and in each case it had shielded the infantry from artillery and machine guns. On September 26 the fog lasted until midmorning, when a wan sun appeared and the terrain through which the men were passing began to come into focus—woods, fields, and ravines.

By noon the weather had become pleasant, an ideal autumn day. It was the last the men would see in the Meuse-Argonne, an area notorious for its mist and rain. In the sunshine they sought to rejoin their units after becoming separated while stumbling around in the fog. In addition, men had lost track of their units when passing through rolls of rusty barbed wire, which had to be cut with wire cutters and traversed single file. Those who went through last were often left behind.

Men went forward in extended order and avoided bunching, which had been a source of trouble at Soissons. On the first day of the Meuse-Argonne, a soldier in the 91st Division, Vernon R. Nichols, remembered his platoon being spread out according to specialty—rifle bombers first, then grenadiers, followed by riflemen. When work was to be done, a group double-timed up, forming a skirmish line with spacing as wide as fifteen yards. Thus, a high-explosive shell bursting in the middle of a group would cause no casualties.[7]

Tanks accompanied two divisions in I Corps—the 28th along the Aire and the 35th to the right—giving courage to the men behind them. The Renault tanks were not altogether effective, however. Tankers had not trained with the infantry, and on the morning of the twenty-sixth they went ahead of the infantrymen to capture Varennes and then had to go back to bring up infantry support. In addition, a few tanks assisted in the capture of Cheppy, but that was the limit of their usefulness in the Meuse-Argonne. The First Army had organized a provisional regiment of three battalions under Lieutenant Colonel George S. Patton III. The colonel considered leading the tanks, but because the two-man crews left no room for extra persons, this was impossible; also, there was no way to communicate from tank to tank, so he accompanied the force on foot. On the way to Cheppy he found a group of lost infantrymen and took them forward behind the tanks until a machine gun forced the group into shell holes. A bullet felled Patton, and he lay in a hole until stretcher bearers came up.

The attacking troops did not see many American planes. Unlike at St. Mihiel, the AEF air service was not much in evidence. In the days before the attack, the service could not conceal its planes, and squadrons flew over from St. Mihiel. After the first day in the Meuse-Argonne, the weather was uncooperative. In addition, German planes were everywhere. Seven planes belonging to an AEF air service squadron went over the line the first day, and five were lost, with eleven men dead. One of the two remaining planes returned with a dead observer shot through the mouth, and it too would have been lost if not for the heroism of the other plane's pilot, who protected it.[8]

Like the planes, the army's balloons failed to offer support for the attacking troops. Their task was to observe the enemy line and call down
targets for the artillery. But balloons filled with hydrogen needed only
bullets to set them on fire. The danger to balloons and balloonists was evident the first day of the Meuse-Argonne, as soon as the fog began to burn
off and the balloons rose. One balloon went up near Esnes, and 100,000
infantrymen watched as a German plane came out of a cloud and hit it.
One of the observers jumped with his parachute; the other hesitated,
then followed. Not content with taking down the balloon, the pilot turned
his machine gun on the second observer, an unchivalrous and unnecessary thing to do, for the burning mass of the balloon began to follow the
observer, dropping twice as fast. The flaming balloon set the parachute
on fire, and a blackened meteor fell into the woods below.[9]

The experiences of the divisions varied markedly in subsequent days
as they sought to move up as far as they could before enemy resistance
made movement impossible. In I Corps the 77th Division of New York-
ers, with replacements from the American West, attacked in the Argonne
Forest. The plan was for the French on the left and the U.S. 28th Division
on the right to place a pincer on the defenders, persuading them to give
up the Argonne. When the pincer did not happen because of French failure to attack, the task of cleaning up the forest passed to the American
division. The Argonne was formidable, "a bleak, cruel country of white
clay and rock and blasted skeletons of trees, gashed into innumerable
trenches and scarred with rusted acres of wire, rising steeply into claw-
like ridges and descending into haunted ravines, white as leprosy in the
midst of that green forest, a country that had died long ago, and in pain."[10]
The Germans knew the area, having lived in it for four years, and they
sited machine guns on what few paths existed. Artillery was unsuitable
for this terrain, and guns had to fire almost blindly. The 77th confronted
the most rugged country of any division in the Meuse-Argonne, but there
were moments of relief. Troops discovered huts and dugouts that the Germans had prepared, some of them rather amazing: drab on the outside,
with modest entrances or overhanging concrete lids, but containing wood
trim and tinted walls, mission furniture, beds with springs, and cozy fire-
places. The pavilions had electric lights, hot and cold running water, and
central areas for eating that were virtual restaurants. The Americans had
to be careful with such establishments, however, because their previous
owners had booby-trapped them.[11]

The 28th Division had the eastern edge of the Argonne and the left (and some of the right) bank of the Aire. The river was under artillery observation from the cliffs that rose into the Argonne Forest, which meant that the 28th received murderous fire. On the morning of the twenty-sixth, the opening day, it managed an advance of six kilometers. Anything beyond that led to trouble, as the next days proved. Men of the 28th discovered that their retreating enemies lived as well as those of the 77th. A member of the 112th Infantry saw pianos in some dugouts.[12] The third division in I Corps, to the right of the 28th, was the 35th, the Missouri-Kansas division. It did not have an especially difficult sector. Its problems lay elsewhere, principally in command, and are analyzed in detail in chapter 4.

The 91st Division was in V Corps, to the right of I Corps. The memoirs of Farley Granger (father of the actor of the same name) nicely caught its action on the first day. The First Battalion of the 362nd Regiment, of which Granger was an officer, passed through a series of small woods, and as the day advanced, resistance increased. After the fog lifted, there was fire from machine guns in front and to the right and artillery fire from the vicinity of Montfaucon and the Bois Emont, in the neighboring sector of the 37th Division. Granger and the men moved forward to a woods beyond Epinonville, only to be told to retire because of a proposal to shell the Germans ahead of them. They did so, but the shelling never occurred.[13]

Troops in the 91st were unaware of problems with one of the infantry brigade commanders, Brigadier General Frederick S. Foltz. The division commander, Major General William H. Johnston, ordered two infantry brigades, the 181st and 182nd, placed side by side for the initial attack. The 181st's commander put both his regiments in the line, side by side, but Foltz, commander of the 182nd, put his in a column of battalions. He thus used only one battalion out of six—hardly General Pershing's prescription for a thrusting attack toward the Kriemhilde Stellung. Johnston was advised that Foltz and his men could not get through the wire (they had no wire cutters), then that they were disorganized and desired to retire. An observing colonel from GHQ accompanying the division commander heard that the sight of half a dozen men and two animals mangled by shell fire lying beside a road had concerned Foltz.[14] Johnston relieved Foltz and put a colonel in charge.

In the sector allotted to the 37th Division, in the center of V Corps, it became clear that although the German defenders might have been few in number, they had been placed almost anywhere that allowed a machine gun nest. The 37th crossed woods and fields, and machine guns were everywhere, often in pillboxes. Snipers were in shell holes, copses, and trees. The attackers found themselves engaged in a kind of Indian warfare, "as our forefathers must have known in the forests of the New World."[15] Like the 91st, the 37th Division was not well commanded. Here again, the use of green divisions in the attack led to trouble. Major General Charles S. Farnsworth allowed his men to bunch at the front, and each evening of the advance to and beyond Ivoiry, he failed to prevent rear units from coming up behind front-line units. The Germans also gassed the three woods ahead of the division, forcing troops to cluster in narrow passageways and making the division a prime target for enemy artillery. Other troubles intervened that were not solely attributable to Farnsworth, for other divisions suffered them as well. The division's artillery could not get to the front because of the roads, which meant no artillery support. Supplies could not get up either, and the wounded could not get back. The men went forward without their packs and overcoats, and when the weather turned cold, they were chilled to the bone. By September 30 the 37th had gone as far as it could.[16] Meanwhile, V Corps suffered further embarrassment when its right division, the 79th, failed to take Montfaucon until noon of the second day, to the disappointment of General Pershing and GHQ planners.

In III Corps the attacks of the 4th, 80th, and 33rd Divisions showed more skill than those of V Corps. The 4th had a first-rate commander, Major General John L. Hines. It moved forward in excellent order, with each company guided by an engineer officer or sergeant carrying a compass with an illuminated dial, and it reached its objective by noon of the first day. The middle division, the 80th, faced terrain both easy and difficult. Two kilometers of open but hilly country allowed the men to keep in formation, but then, as if to compensate, the 80th reached woods filled with machine gun nests. Although it was an untested division, it managed its first-day assignment. That night it withdrew, and the front narrowed because of the bend of the Meuse River to the west. The 33rd Division, the best of the three, was worn out from fighting the previous month and was full of replacements. It moved north along the Meuse and halted at the marshes before Brieulles. This was the middle part of the Hindenburg Line, the Kriemhilde Stellung, which the First Army would not take until just before the general attack that began November 1—the attack that ended all opposition in the Meuse-Argonne.[17]

Sometimes a single failure is enough to cause a great enterprise to lose its momentum, stumble, and if not fall then at least come to a standstill. In the opening days of the Meuse-Argonne, this may have been the failure to take Montfaucon on the first day of the attack (the First Army took it at noon on the second day). Attacks on the western front had fallen into a distressing pattern: they started out well, but then slowed down and ended. The AEF commander in chief may have exaggerated the importance of taking Montfaucon when he claimed that the failure to do so on schedule had held up the entire First Army. But he was right in believing that his divisions had to advance as quickly as possible to overwhelm German defenses before the surprised enemy could bring up reinforcements. If the 79th had advanced with alacrity, and if the neighboring 4th, under the able leadership of Hines, had been allowed to advance in similar fashion, the history of the battle would have been quite different.

Montfaucon was an eminence easily discernible from the army's starting line six kilometers away. It commanded the terrain from Verdun to Clermont on the eastern edge of the Argonne Forest. Montfaucon was the place from which the German crown prince had surveyed the battle of Verdun in 1916, and when American troops reached it, they found the telescope the prince had used. The taking of this hill was one step in the goal of cutting the Lille-Metz railway, the four-track line supplying German divisions for half of the entire western front, from Lille to Switzerland.

The 79th Division's attack on Montfaucon started out uneventfully on the morning of September 26, but then things began to go wrong. The rolling barrage ceased as the 75s got out of range, and battalions without a curtain of fire were cut down by machine guns. It was not possible for them to move back slightly and go forward. In fact, Brigadier General Dennis E. Nolan, GHQ's chief of intelligence, visited the 79th and believed that it lost as many men going back as going forward.[18] A balloon detachment at Ivoiry in the 79th's sector working with First Army artillery reported, "Infantry can't take Montfaucon at present, need more artillery preparation."[19] The report was true enough, but what could be done to provide it?

Pershing sent word at 2:50 that afternoon, through the V Corps commander, Major General George H. Cameron, that the 79th must take Montfaucon because the delay was holding up the entire First Army. A message went from the 79th's commanding general to both of the division's infantry brigades. By this time, darkness was approaching. The 313th Infantry Regiment attacked shortly after 6:00 p.m., with two Renault tanks out in front. The machine guns opened fire, and the tankers refused to take their machines any farther; infantry nonetheless moved up, with the same result as before. In this attack the regiment lost the last of its battalion commanders. That night, division headquarters received two more orders from Pershing via V Corps, at 6:30 and 11:30, that it must take Montfaucon at once and advance three more kilometers to the vicinity of Nantillois. But by that time, the regiments were too tired to do anything.

The next morning, the twenty-seventh, with the men rested and artillery support available, the troops attacked again. The Germans resisted, but gradually the enemy moved back. By 11:55 the 311th Infantry, with assistance from a regiment of the 37th Division, was in the town.

The 79th managed to move beyond Montfaucon, up to Nantillois and beyond, but this was as far as it could go. Montfaucon was full of snipers. The men found German soldiers operating a buzzer, giving the range to guns to the north. The Germans contested every foot of the way above Montfaucon, or so it seemed. Above Nantillois the opposition stiffened so much that it was impossible to hold, and the troops fell back. A few men got as far as the Bois des Ogons, seven kilometers above Montfaucon, where they could see the town of Romagne, but they could not hold the woods and moved back. It took fifteen days of hard fighting and 6,000 casualties for the First Army to take this part of the Kriemhilde Stellung.[20]

Despite the 79th's taking of Montfaucon and reaching Nantillois and beyond, in the view of GHQ, the division had failed, principally because of timing. The AEF inspector general, Major General André Brewster, said that the division had no future other than to break up or change its number; no good soldier would want to have any connection with it.[21] Pershing took the division out of the line on September 30 and replaced it with the 3rd. A member of the 79th wrote about how encouraging it was to watch the 3rd come up, wave after wave of men, as far as the eye could see.[22]

A few years after the war, in a series of studies of AEF divisions that had performed poorly or encountered trouble, officers of the War College criticized the 79th's training, which they blamed for its failure to take Montfaucon.[23] Lack of training had made it an unreliable unit that the division commander could not rely on in battle. It had not trained enough in the United States and, upon arrival in France, had spent only 43 days in training, compared with an average of 152 days by General Pershing's "veteran" divisions.[24] GHQ and the division commander had laid out an intensive training schedule calling for five division terrain exercises beginning September 1, but the next day, the 79th began preparation for the Meuse-Argonne.

The officers pointed out another problem also related to training: the high number of replacements in the division. Just before sailing, the 79th received 58 percent of its personnel, 15,000 men. The replacements had all been inducted after May 9.

But this emphasis on training and concern about replacements failed to address the real reasons for the delay in taking Montfaucon, which were related to command and involved four well-placed generals of the AEF. One was the 79th's commander, Major General Joseph E. Kuhn, a sad example of a man who had made a reputation in the Regular Army and failed in the field. Kuhn had been first in his class at West Point. He had been an observer in the Russo-Japanese War, the first modern war of the twentieth century employing artillery and machine guns. He had served in the American embassy in Berlin in 1915–1916, an ideal assignment for what was to follow. He had been president of the War College, a small but prominent institution that was a part of the army's effort to study the tactics and strategies of other armies. The difficulty with Kuhn was that, like so many Regular Army officers, he had little experience with large bodies of troops. The presumption was that, because of his long service, he could do well in the field.

Kuhn was a poor choice as a division commander, and his two infantry brigade commanders had little if any competence. The attack brigade under Brigadier General William J. Nicholson lost contact with division headquarters almost the minute it moved out. Kuhn said afterward that Nicholson was old and of indifferent ability, but he had hesitated to relieve him before the battle because it might have disrupted the work of the brigade. The commander of the support brigade, Robert H. Noble, simultaneously lost one of his regiments—making Kuhn, in effect, a regimental commander. At midnight on September 26–27, Kuhn called Noble to division headquarters and further disorganized the division by reassigning the regiments. Nicholson had attacked with his two regiments abreast, and Kuhn ordered Noble to give the support brigade's left regiment to Nicholson and to take Nicholson's right-hand regiment. He wrote out the order, which took some time, and gave it to Noble, who then had to go forward and make the shift. Noble managed to find Nicholson's regiment, but he felt that he could not carry out Kuhn's order to attack at 4:00 a.m. until he arranged for his rear regiment to secure its area. In the advance of the preceding day, Nicholson had passed over German machine gun nests, and Noble felt that he had to get them out. He was in the process of drawing up an order to that effect when Kuhn came up at 6:00 a.m. and removed him, giving the brigade to a colonel, who finally took the men forward at 7:00 a.m., three hours late.[25]

The War College officers did not mention this command debacle, nor did they have anything to say about a failure by a brigadier general in neighboring III Corps. This failure became well known after the war and contributed to the delay in taking Montfaucon. It seemed that Brigadier General Alfred W. Bjornstad, chief of staff of III Corps, was determined to be the Lieutenant Colonel Hentsch of the First Army. (Hentsch was the hapless German general staff officer who, at the height of the battle of the Marne in 1914, had instructed an army commander to retreat and thus snatched defeat from victory.) On September 26, part of Brigadier General Benjamin A. Poore's 7th Brigade wandered over the corps and division boundary into Montfaucon. The German commander there had only a few understrength platoons, sensed that he could be cut off, and retreated. When the 7th Brigade reached its corps and division objective just after noon on the first day, its availability prompted General Hines to suggest using his 4th Division, to the right of the 79th, to move in above Montfaucon and flank the German defenders while the 79th and 37th came up from below. Bjornstad, acting in the absence of corps commander General Robert Lee Bullard, instructed Hines and, through him, Poore and Brigadier General E. E. Booth of the 8th Brigade not to enter the 79th Division's sector but to advance straight ahead.

The best explanation for his action was offered by Bjornstad himself after the war. In 1925, when he was being considered for promotion in the Regular Army to brigadier general (having been reduced to colonel), the question of his 1918 order to Hines came up during his confirmation hearings in the Senate. Bjornstad said that he had not known where the 79th's troops were and hesitated to let III Corps troops into an area where V Corps artillery might fire on them. Throughout the twenty-sixth, there also had been reports of the taking of Montfaucon, which made him think that the 4th Division's assistance to the 79th was unnecessary.[26]

Bjornstad's hearings required two published volumes of remarks by supporters and objectors, and for years after the war, believers in what the 4th Division might have accomplished argued their case. The leader of that contingent was Booth, commander of the 8th Brigade, which was in support of Poore's attack brigade. If Poore's command had not gone in above Montfaucon, Booth's 8,000 riflemen could have done it. The two brigades could have followed the taking of Montfaucon on the first day with a successful attack on the Kriemhilde Stellung before the Germans reinforced it. If that had happened, both Booth and Poore would have been promoted in the field to major general, a rank they received only after the war. Booth would not let the argument die and pursued it to the end. More than twenty years later he took the issue to Pershing, and the former commander in chief obtained a confession from Bjornstad, who had retired and may have had enough of the subject. On June 17, 1940, Pershing so informed Booth, who considered his long fight justified.[27]

Montfaucon was the first sign of trouble after the opening of the Meuse-Argonne, and it was accompanied by other difficulties that, in combination, brought the AEF's initial attack to a halt. One of them was the tiredness of the attacking troops. They had to walk or ride from St. Mihiel or elsewhere, and it was no easy trip, whatever the means. Their stay in holding areas in the wet forests produced illnesses. The author's father, a member of the 80th Division, came down with diphtheria a few days after the attack and barely survived after transport to a base hospital. In the forests the men were subject to hostile artillery fire, which made sleep difficult. The night before the attack, their own artillery made sleep impossible. During the attack the exhilaration of the moment gave them strength, but then the tiredness returned.

Another major difficulty was the scarcity of roads in the sector. The only decent road in the entire area was Route Nationale No. 46 along the Aire. The Germans had done nothing with the roads during their four-year occupation, relying on narrow-gauge railroads. American artillery shot up what remained of many of the smaller roads. Meanwhile, the AEF had not anticipated a road problem and had made no provision for the repair of existing roads or the construction of new ones. The War Department in 1917 organized two dozen engineer regiments for special tasks, which in the field were to be under army rather than division control (each division had an engineer regiment, but the duties of division engineers were not specific and the men often acted as reserve troops). Only one of the army regiments was designated for road construction, and when it arrived in France it was assigned to port construction and other duties in base areas. The engineer troops whose specialty was roads did not reach the Meuse-Argonne until the night before the battle. They found dumps containing crushed stone and other supplies, but the Services of Supply, in charge of rear areas, had taken most of their trucks.

In the opening days of the attack, the AEF compounded its ignorance of the road problem by the poor discipline on the roads that were available. As at St. Mihiel, the military police were hardly in evidence. Too much traffic tried to move up, and divisions fought over what roads they were entitled to. The 35th Division was certain that the Route Nationale belonged to it, and the 28th used it with equal assurance. The road between V Corps and III Corps meandered enough for the troops to think that it was actually two roads, leading the 37th, 79th, and 4th Divisions to crowd one another off if they could. Colonel Frederick W. Coleman of the 91st Division, which also laid claim to the road, found all four divisions converging at Avocourt. "I stayed there all day with Colonel Saville and we succeeded in getting through most of the transportation of the 91st Division, while that of the other two [three] divisions was pocketed."[28] The few military police who appeared on the scene possessed little or no rank, and a colonel like Coleman—or, at night, a simulated colonel— could produce chaos. It was easy to block a road, and troops bivouacked on them.[29] Heavy guns could swivel in the rain and mud and go sideways into a ditch. Men and trucks and horses were often in line for hours, with nothing moving. Stories of these scenes were commonplace.

> I witnessed by the faint night vision and by sound, for several kilometers along this road, one of the most complete and depressing exhibits of war that was presented on the front. The traffic was a mixture of every kind of material and personnel to be found in an army. There were French forgon wagons, chariots du parcs, lorries, camions, water carts, ration carts, ammunition carts, ambulances, automobiles of every description, entire batteries of artillery,

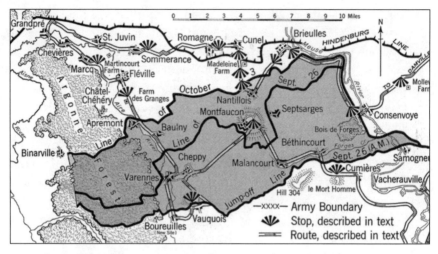

Ground gained by First Army, September 26–October 3, 1918

motorcycles and other vehicles that could not be identified in the darkness of the night. The road was narrow and only fitted for one-way traffic. Clinging to the two sloping edges of the over-burdened road were endless streams of foot soldiers going and coming, many groups of German prisoners, carrying American and German wounded on stretchers. Many heavy motor trucks and vehicles of various kinds had slid off the road into the water-filled shell holes. . . . Men were frequently clinging to the rims of deep craters into which they had slipped.[30]

Rolling kitchens could not get up to the front, nor could ammunition. An engineer wrote of a meeting between his artillery colonel and an infantry brigadier on September 29 during which General W. P. Jackson said that the men of the 37th above Nantillois were desperate for artillery support, but the engineer had no shells to provide it. Ambulances coming down met delays of twenty-four to thirty hours, leaving the wounded without food and water and lying on boards. Surgeon Harvey Cushing was horrified to receive the ambulances with their cargoes of dead.

The final factor in the halting of the attack was the appearance of German reinforcements. At the outset, the German army commander, Gallwitz, had the 76th Reserve Division west of the Argonne, the 9th and 2nd Landwehr in the forest, and the 1st and 5th Guards in the neighborhood of Apremont. He brought in five divisions on September 26–27. The defenders numbered 125,000 by September 29–30, enough to give them an edge; accepted wisdom was that an attack force needed twice as many men as its opponents—by some reckoning, three times. The German divisions were a third the size of U.S. divisions, but Gallwitz believed that by the twenty-seventh, even before he had gained an edge, his troops had stopped the advance. Ludendorff considered the twenty-seventh, "in the main," a day of success. On the twenty-eighth, "apart from certain modifications of our front which were carried out in accordance with our plans," his forces were holding. Frederick Palmer agreed with Gallwitz that "the signs of developing resistance" against the Americans developed into successful opposition on the morning of the twenty-seventh.[31]

CHAPTER FOUR

The 35th Division

Of all the divisions that took part in the opening days of the Meuse-Argonne, the 35th deserves a detailed analysis, because according to First Army leaders, its performance was the worst. This National Guard division from Missouri and Kansas collapsed after four days in the line. By September 29 it was sprawled in disorder; regiments were mixed up, with only a few companies together. Many men had gone back to where they had started on the first day of the attack, milling around in confusion. Most of these were not stragglers—that is, men who were escaping the front line; they had lost their commanders, did not know where they were, and were willing to rejoin the battle if possible. But the units were too disorganized. The division's commanding officer, Major General Peter E. Traub, asked that the division be relieved. On the night of September 30–October 1, General Pershing sent up the best relief force in the AEF, the 1st Division, and thousands upon thousands of experienced troops filled the 35th's sector. From that point on, from the area of the Aire to where V Corps' divisions held the ground east of Cheppy and Very, the commander in chief of the AEF could rest assured that everything was in order.

The question is why the 35th came apart. At the beginning of the attack in the Meuse-Argonne, the division seemed all right. It appeared to be much like the others, filled with eager young soldiers who were looking forward to their first engagement. General Pershing told General

Traub that he considered the men of the 35th the "best looking lot of men I have got in France."[1] Organized at Camp Doniphan in Oklahoma in September 1917, the division was initially commanded by Major General William M. Wright, whom the AEF commander in chief raised to corps command. In the last and altogether successful attack in the Meuse-Argonne on November 1, Pershing placed Wright in command of one of the two point divisions, and the general performed admirably. Wright's replacement in the 35th was General Traub, an experienced officer who had commanded a brigade in the 26th Division. His task after he took over in mid-July 1918 was mainly that of moving the division up toward the front, preparing it for what was to come. But then something happened.

On the morning of September 26, 1918, the men of the 35th moved out on a line of twenty-five hundred meters, brigades in column: 69th Brigade in front, with the 138th Regiment on the right and the 137th on the left, followed by the 70th Brigade at a distance of between one thousand and two thousand meters, with the 140th on the right and the 139th on the left.[2] On the right, Vauquois Hill proved not to be the obstacle the troops had feared. In earlier years, the French had purportedly lost 40,000 men trying to take it, and when French officers accompanying the 35th learned that the Americans were going to attack Vauquois, they were certain it could not be taken. In the event, the Germans stripped the hill of defenders, leaving only seventy-five men and six machine guns commanded by a nineteen-year-old lieutenant, Friedrich von Huellesheim. The lieutenant received confusing orders from his superiors: one told him to fight to the death, and the other advised him to do his best. Given the size of his force versus the strength of the Americans, and the fact that his superiors did not consider the fortification worth much, he made a token defense and surrendered.[3]

An attack on Cheppy to the north was not so easy, for in the hours between the First Army's artillery preparation and the 138th Regiment's arrival, the Germans distributed machine gunners in nests commanding the village's approaches. The situation soon became precarious. The regiment's colonel and headquarters company were pinned down in shell holes. When the colonel ventured out, a machine gunner shattered his hand, sending him back to an aid station as a casualty. What finally broke the defense was eight Renault tanks. After three hours in the shell holes,

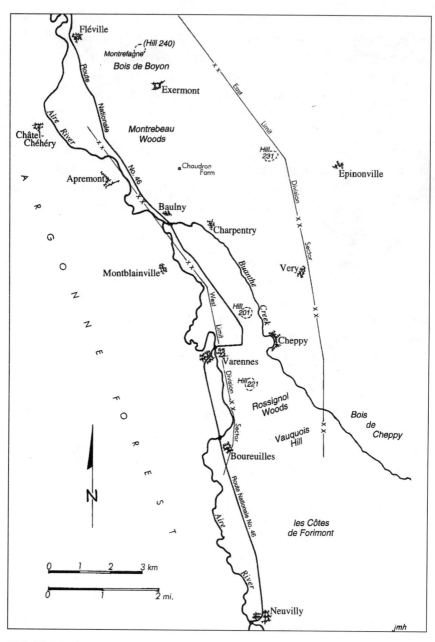

Fléville

(Hill 240)

Montrefagne

Bois de Boyon

Exermont

Châtel-Chéhéry

Montrebeau Woods

Apremont

Chaudron Farm

Hill 231

Epinonville

Baulny

Charpentry

Very

Montblainville

Hill 201

Cheppy

Varennes

Hill 221

Rossignol Woods

Bois de Cheppy

Vauquois Hill

Boureuilles

A R G O N N E   F O R E S T

Aire River

Route Nationale No. 46

Buanthe Creek

East Limit

Division

Sector

West Limit

Division

Sector

les Côtes de Forimont

N

0   1   2   3 km

0   1   2 mi.

Neuvilly

jmh

35th Division's sector

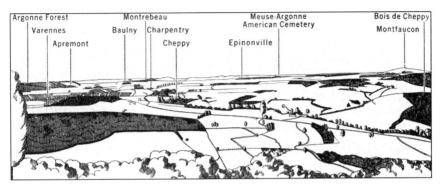

Argonne Forest		Montrebeau		Meuse-Argonne American Cemetery		Bois de Cheppy
Varennes	Baulny	Charpentry				Montfaucon
Apremont		Cheppy	Epinonville			

Panorama looking north from Vauquois Hill

the Americans saw the welcome sight of the tanks wheeling to form an attack line ten feet apart. The men formed behind them, and everything moved forward. The rest of the action on the division's right side on September 26 was less difficult; the 138th took Cheppy at 3:00, and an hour later the lead elements, followed by the 140th, were a kilometer north. By that time, night was approaching; the men found shell holes or German barracks or dugouts, ate field rations (hardtack) and cans of beef, and went to sleep.

On the left part of the division line, the 139th Regiment leapfrogged the 137th, which enemy machine guns had held up above Varennes. The 139th went on for a kilometer before meeting resistance, to a point approximately even with the division line on the right. The division advance during the first day was five kilometers.

That night, the troubles began. The 35th's artillery brigade was unable to keep up, and only a battalion of 75s—three batteries, twelve guns—was available to support the division's 5:30 a.m. attack on September 27. Road conditions were appalling, and even though artillery had priority, even over ambulances, the guns could not make it up to the front. The roads had not been used in years, and Route Nationale No. 46, which proceeded from Neuvilly through Boureulles and Varennes, contained two huge craters—one blown by the retreating French army a year before the American attack, and the other by the Germans when the Americans came in. The need to construct shooflies around the craters held up traffic during the initial day or two of the attack and forced artillery into the side roads, which were little more than paths and could not take the weight of the guns.

In addition, there was confusion over the orders for the timing of the September 27 attack. An order to attack at 5:30 a.m. came down from General Pershing, for the commander in chief desired all his divisions to move forward rapidly. Commander of I Corps, Major General Hunter Liggett, passed it on with his endorsement, and General Traub did the same thing to the brigade and regimental commanders. When it was learned that the 75s could not get up to the line, the division's chief of staff, Colonel Hamilton S. Hawkins, gave an order for a 6:45 attack. Traub countermanded Hawkins's order and went up to the line to tell brigade and regimental commanders that the attack should open at 5:30. He appeared at the dugout of the commander of the 70th Brigade, Colonel Kirby Walker, at 4:00 a.m. and told him, "It is General Pershing's order, it must be done." An argument ensued, in which Walker and his officers explained that they could not get word to the forward infantry battalions in less than forty minutes, and changing the artillery schedule for the 75-mm guns would take an hour. Regardless of what General Pershing desired, it was impossible. A compromise was worked out to begin artillery fire at 5:30 and the attack at 6:30.

Lack of artillery support caused the failure of the attack on the morning of Friday the twenty-seventh. On the right, the 140th Infantry under Lieutenant Colonel Channing E. Delaplane leapfrogged the 138th, as Hawkins's order required. Delaplane had been the division's ordnance officer until just before the battle, and he was a man of firmness; sensing the result of the night's confusion, he placed a single battalion in front and the other two behind. On the left, Lieutenant Colonel Carl L. Ristine of the 139th Infantry, also an able commander but a bit adventuresome, put two battalions in front. Both regiments attacked at 6:30 and stalled, with Delaplane managing half a kilometer and Ristine almost nothing. The artillery support was obviously poor, and German machine gunners and artillery had had the night to reinforce their positions.

When the Friday morning attack failed, Pershing sent a command down through I Corps that the 35th attack again that afternoon at 5:30. The message was plain enough: "He expects the 35th Division to move forward. He is not satisfied with the division being stopped by machine gun nests here and there. He expects the division to move forward now in accordance with orders." Meanwhile, Colonel Jens Bugge of I Corps had replaced Hawkins, whom the corps' chief of staff, Brigadier General Malin Craig, considered indecisive. Traub sent Hawkins up to the front to see if he could get things moving—this when the problem was not a lack of decision but rather too many of them.

By the time of the division's third attack at 5:30 p.m., the artillery brigade had arrived. The 129th Field Artillery Regiment had reached its destination early in the morning, in battalion strength, and all battalions of the 75s were up by afternoon. The 155-mm guns of the 130th Field Artillery Regiment were in position in Varennes. The attack was a considerable success, with the artillery making the difference. That day, the two infantry regiments that had leapfrogged were brought together in a provisional brigade and attacked as one, with the other two regiments in support. On the right, Delaplane's regiment moved forward. Ristine's entered Charpentry and went on to the village above Varennes, Baulny. One battalion evidently crossed the Aire and reached Montblainville; another went as far as Montrebeau Woods, two hundred acres of trees and undergrowth, and after losing touch it fell back to the ridge above Baulny. Most of the advance occurred in the dark, which may account for its success. A sergeant in the 140th (writing years later after his retirement as an army colonel) remembered the experience vividly and concluded that if he had been a general in 1918, he would have sent his regiments in at 3:00 a.m. on Saturday, September 28, pushed them forward one to five miles, and had them dig in and wait for daylight. "That would sure raise hell with a defensive system," he noted, for when daylight came, the Germans would be fighting "forty-eight little wars on sixteen different fronts," with outpost lines crumpled and small-arms fire driving artillerymen from their guns.[4]

The night attack advanced the line by two and a half kilometers, making a total division advance on September 26–27 of seven and a half kilometers. But the division would have been better off if it had not attacked. Disorder had already appeared in the 137th Regiment, stalled above Varennes. Its colonel had physically collapsed under the strain and lay spread-eagle in a shell hole, hardly able to open his eyes. When Ristine of the 139th arrived, his regiment leapfrogged the 137th, which mixed the two. Some men of the 137th joined Ristine's regiment, while others just milled around. Then, the night after the 5:30 p.m. attack, the 139th lost its commander. Ristine was out in front leading the troops, accompanied by a few men, and in the gathering darkness he went straight ahead while the rest of his regiment turned northwest in accord with a turning of the division sector, which also widened significantly. Ristine passed into the German line and found himself surrounded by retreating enemy troops. He hid in a shell hole for a while, donned a German over-coat and helmet, moved west toward the 28th Division, and on Sunday morning, September 29, managed to get across the Aire, find the 28th, and return to his regiment. By that time, however, without his leadership the 139th, like its sister regiment the 137th, had fallen apart.

By the morning of Saturday, September 28, the German defenders had pulled themselves together, and the enemy commander, Gallwitz, had brought in reinforcements. The new men—machine gunners, like the earlier defenders—established a multitude of nests in front of the attacking Americans. All the while, German artillery was exceedingly active. Guns were on the hill known as the Montrefagne, Hill 240 above Exermont. Batteries were firing from far up the whaleback and had ze-roed in on the positions below. To the left of the 35th, the 28th Division had not gotten up to the front, nor had the 77th Division to its left. This meant that high up in the Argonne Forest, sixteen batteries around Châtel-Chéhéry were firing across the Aire at the 35th, and the batteries were in pits that the chalky Argonne soil made invulnerable to anything but direct hits. German gunners could see the 35th's men struggling for-ward out of the woods into open places. Getting out of artillery fire was a problem that the 35th could not resolve.

The attack on Saturday morning, September 28, opened in the usual way and quickly ran into trouble. Delaplane's 140th Infantry on the right moved out at 5:30, and Ristine's regiment on the left, without Ristine, at-tacked an hour later. Because of enemy artillery, the going was difficult, casualties were heavy, and ground was gained only foot by foot. The 140th received tank support at 9:30, but the Germans brought up antitank guns; the Renaults were easy to hit, and those not damaged by enemy fire succumbed to mechanical breakdowns. Distant machine guns fired over ridge crests, grazing the tops, so the spent bullets' trajectories carried them down to troops trying to shield themselves on reverse slopes. As if this were not enough, the skies also belonged to the Germans, who sent over spotting planes. The division's right-hand attack failed. On the left, the taking of Montrebeau Woods increased the mixing of the 139th and the 137th, and by the end of the day, battalion commanders came out on the north end of Montrebeau hardly knowing what regiment they were in. The attack faltered at the top of the woods.

On the morning of Sunday, September 29, a dreary, rainy day, what was left of the 35th attacked for the last time. The attack was on both sides of the line—east of Montrebeau Woods, where the 140th and 138th were, and on the left with the fragmented 139th and 137th. On the right, the 138th was to attack at 5:30, with the 140th in support, but the 138th did not receive its orders until 6:45. At 6:25, former division chief of staff Hawkins came on the scene and ordered the 140th to take the place of the 138th, but Delaplane objected because he was making plans to go forward in support. Out of the corner of his eye he thought he saw the 138th coming up, and said so. At about that time, Hawkins himself told one of Delaplane's battalions to go forward. Delaplane's brigade commander, Walker, came up and agreed that the 140th should attack in place of the 138th.[5] Delaplane went with the men, several hundred when they started, all that was left of the regiment's 4,000. They went without artillery support, as the division's artillery brigadier had started a barrage at 5:30. They were headed north a thousand meters toward Exermont. Machine gun nests that had escaped the barrage opened fire. Artillery came from Hill 240, from the whaleback, and from the Argonne. Shells and machine gun bullets were everywhere. Sergeant (later colonel) William S. Triplet never forgot the way the platoon went forward. Rain was coming down in torrents, and the men bowed their heads, hoping that their helmets would keep the water out of their eyes. Like many others of the attack force, Triplet felt a jolt, collapsed, tried to get up, and could not. The platoon's survivors continued, now running or falling. For the rest of his life—he died in 1993—Triplet could see the men running, the far-away village, and above it the Montrefagne.[6]

A small force that accompanied the 140th to Exermont on that disastrous morning was under a battalion commander of the 139th, Major James E. Rieger, who had been in Montrebeau Woods to the left of the 140th. He had sought to take his depleted companies through the woods, hoping to pick up stragglers and strays from whatever units were there. Just before entering the woods, however, he was accosted by his former brigade commander, Colonel Louis M. Nuttman, who insisted that Rieger take the force around the woods to the east rather than going through. The major objected, Nuttman insisted, and Rieger lost men to machine guns and artillery even before moving up to Exermont, where many of the rest were lost.

Delaplane and Rieger and their survivors stayed in and above Exermont as long as they could. They waited until the Germans began gathering, hundreds of men in coal-scuttle helmets and greatcoats. At about 1:30 p.m., when word came from Walker that they should go back, they slowly did so, giving up the farthest advance the division had made.[7]

On the left-hand portion of the division line, there was even less of an attack that morning, although it got off approximately on time, a little after 5:30. It consisted of 125 men led by a headquarters major, Parker C. Kalloch, who had arrived the night before. The next morning, he found the 137th's previously indisposed colonel, Clad Hamilton, back in command—of what, Hamilton was unsure—at the top of Montrebeau. Meeting the colonel at 4:35 a.m., Kalloch learned that there was to be a division attack at 5:30, leaving less than an hour, in pitch-dark, to organize it. The colonel told the major to go back in the woods and see how many men he could round up, and Kalloch returned with 125. At 5:30 he could hear no artillery barrage and waited a few minutes before starting. Like the attack of the 140th to the right, which Kalloch's force could not assist because it had not yet happened, the move forward failed. The force got as far as a ravine southwest of Exermont; stayed there until 8:00, when its right flank was turned; and went back to the woods, the men running from shell hole to shell hole and firing against the advancing enemy.[8]

What remained of Ristine's 139th Regiment took no part in the action that morning, except for the men Kalloch had found in the woods. Kalloch had no idea where those men came from and never learned their names or units, with the exception of one of the two lieutenants who led his line on each side. Ristine's replacement from I Corps, Colonel Americus Mitchell, knew the position of only a single battalion. When the attack order came, he took forward whatever men he had, picked up more as he went through Montrebeau, and got up to the top of the woods with what he thought were 400 men. At that point, he saw men coming back and assumed that they were the Kalloch force (in fact, it was a small support force for Kalloch that had gone only a short distance). Mitchell did not have enough men to accomplish anything and remained just above Montrebeau.

What saved the 35th Division that Sunday morning was a move forward by the division's 110th Engineers.[9] The regiment's colonel had gone to division headquarters to serve as division engineer, and the two small battalions, totaling 1,200 men, were being led by the senior battalion commander, Major Edward M. Stayton, from Independence, Missouri. Stayton received the order to establish a line running northeast along the ridge above Baulny, a place without natural defenses, except that it was high ground and the men could link shell holes and command the rear of Montrebeau Woods. The line was in the air, but most of the German forces were to the west, so the gap with the V Corps division to the east was manageable. The 35th's commander sent word by runner to what remained of the infantry regiments to go back to the engineers' line, behind which they could reorganize. They thus gave up Montrebeau Woods, dearly won, and when the 1st Division replaced the 35th, its men had to retake the woods, which by that time had been reinforced with wire and machine guns and snipers in trees. But for the 35th, a defensible line was better than the line attempted on Sunday morning, and the engineers' line held. On that afternoon, there was straggling below the engineers' line and the danger of its turning into a rout. Delaplane, arriving at the new line, sent his intelligence officer, Captain Ralph E. Truman (a cousin of one of the 35th's artillery officers, Captain Harry S. Truman), into the back area to round up men and stop the stragglers, which he did at gunpoint.[10] Meanwhile, corps and army artillery, thirty-one batteries of heavy guns, put down a protective arc of fire on the approaches to the new line. Days later, after relief, a count of the division's casualties estimated the loss of perhaps 8,000 men. A final count, years afterward, showed 1,204 killed or died of wounds and 5,870 wounded, for a total of 7,074.[11]

The question is why the 35th Division went to pieces in the first four days of the Meuse-Argonne, and part of the answer involves the rigidity of its direction by higher headquarters—specifically, General Pershing. The commander in chief was no tactician. His principal procedure was to push division commanders and set rigid standards by which he could see—both visibly and on paper—that they were doing as he asked. He had reason for this. Because the AEF had come together so rapidly, he could not be sure of its quality. He believed the men were all right—they were Americans, after all—but the commanders were a mixed group, and only a few had proved themselves. To use a phrase from the horse age, he needed to keep them on a tight rein. He went too far with this, however, when he issued orders for all divisions on the line to attack on September 27 at the same time, 5:30 a.m. It was unnecessary to specify the time, and it did not suit the situation of the 35th. Traub hesitated to deviate from the commander in chief's timetable, thereby confusing the morning attack. When it failed, Pershing insisted on the 35th's making an afternoon attack, which again had an unfortunate outcome. Because of the failure of the morning attack of September 27, I Corps sent Bugge to replace Hawkins; this put Hawkins over Delaplane, and by starting Delaplane's regiment on Sunday, Hawkins destroyed the right side's ability to attack. On the left side of the division, the 137th was already coming apart, and the night attack allowed Ristine to become lost, which caused the breakup of the 139th. As a result, on Sunday morning neither Kalloch nor Mitchell could gather enough men to make a serious attack.

GHQ and I Corps bore some blame for the division's fate in the line, but the division commander, General Traub, deserved far more, and for many reasons. For one, there was his background, which did not inspire confidence in his military abilities. Like so many Regular Army officers, his principal qualification for division command was that he had graduated in the same West Point class as his commander in chief. After service in the Philippine insurrection, he taught Spanish at West Point and was the author of a book on verbs. He rose in rank and was a colonel in 1917, at which time he became a brigadier general in the automatic manner in which Regular Army colonels were promoted with the army's expansion. He served ten months as a brigade commander in the 26th Division, which placed him under General Clarence Edwards, whom Pershing and the GHQ staff considered the worst general officer in the AEF. The Germans' April 1918 trench raid was against Traub's brigade.

Personally, Traub was a braggart. In postwar hearings before the House of Representatives and the Senate concerning the 35th's high casualties, he told stories about his bravery. He related that when the 35th was falling apart, he had made a trip to the front, where the enemy had sought to relieve him. The Germans saw him walking from unit to unit, carrying a gas mask, field glasses, a mackintosh, and a swagger stick. A plane attacked, sprinkling machine gun bullets. Enemy batteries fired three hundred shells, bracketing him—shells fifteen yards to the left and fifteen yards to the right. He said to himself, "Old sport, get busy," and zigzagged to the right to escape the next shell to the left (the Germans, he said, were methodical). The shell caught him unprepared, landing two and a half feet to his left. He told the committees that the Boche was not as stupid as he thought. But of the three hundred shells wasted on him, this was the only dud—"that is the reason I am here talking to you right now."[12] He told Liggett of I Corps that in addition to machine gun bullets and shells, he almost walked into the German line, was gassed, and had a devil of a time ("You bet your life").[13] Hundreds of his officers and thousands of his men were missing, but he had survived.

Administratively, Traub was altogether without talent. Because he could not stand up to commanders above him, he often accepted advice that did not suit the division's situation. Likewise, he was incapable of reining in a subordinate if the latter was irascible and well connected within the army's command structure. This was the case with Traub's artillery commander, Brigadier General Lucien G. Berry. The artillery brigadier was the army's senior artillery officer, and he knew how to wage warfare through channels. He knew Pershing, having commanded the artillery during the expedition to Mexico. Traub thus left Berry alone, which was unfortunate, because a mistake with artillery could undermine all the work of the division.

If Traub had tried to control Berry, he would have discovered that his brigadier did not believe in airplane spotting. Berry ignored it and even told Pershing, who came through on a visit to the 35th, that airplanes were "no damn good." Traub eventually ordered Berry to use planes and said that by the end of the division's stay in the Meuse-Argonne, his brigadier could not get enough of them. In admonishing Traub for the 35th Division's debacle, First Army chief of staff, Brigadier General Hugh A. Drum, specifically mentioned the failure to use spotting.[14]

In addition, Berry did not fire his guns rapidly enough. An assistant inspector from I Corps, First Lieutenant Michel Jacobs, discovered this error on September 29 at the height of the 35th's participation in the Meuse-Argonne, as the battered regiments were attempting their last attack in line. Berry's 75-mm guns were firing at a rate of one or two shots a minute. Jacobs, of the coast artillery, told Berry that at Château-Thierry gunners in a battery rested one gun while the other three fired. But Berry kept his guns pinging away, with far too few shells in the air. Two of his three regiments were 75s, capable of thirty shots a minute.[15]

Though giving no attention to Berry's delinquencies, the division commander undertook a drastic shakeup of the infantry leadership. Traub took command on July 20, giving him plenty of time to make an impression with his standards of efficiency, which, according to him, the division never lived up to. Yet he did nothing about the division's infantry commanders until a few days before the Meuse-Argonne. Then, he relieved almost every senior line officer, for reasons that are difficult to discern. On September 21 he relieved the commander of the 69th Brigade, Nathaniel F. McClure, and replaced him with a regimental colonel, Nuttman. In his request for relief of McClure, Traub said that the general lacked punch, vim, and control and was "not my idea of a real Brigadier General, [he] must be urged, and even then does not get the results he should."[16] The commander of the 70th Brigade, Brigadier General Charles I. Martin, was relieved at the same time, and the brigade was given to Colonel Walker. Traub's reasoning here was just as murky. He cited Martin's too easy procedures and resorted to virtually the same description he offered of McClure, saying that Martin lacked push, shove, pep, energy, enthusiasm, and spirit. At the same time, he replaced his two remaining infantry regiment commanders, his chief of staff (whom the corps changed again with Colonel Bugge), and two of the three artillery colonels.

Relief of these officers just before the attack was certainly not wise, especially the relief of General Martin, who was a National Guard officer. Traub's action stirred the latent animosity between officers of the Regular Army and men and officers of the National Guard. In Kansas and Missouri, the Guard was a matter of pride. Guard units elected their officers, drilled every two weeks, and attended summer camp; they turned out in uniform on memorial occasions or for no occasion; they were proud of what they could do for their country. They believed at the outset of the war in 1917, when they were called to the colors, that they knew as much about war as the regulars, who had seen no more than skirmishes with Indians, Spanish, Filipinos, and Mexicans. As a volunteer officer, Martin had served in the Philippines under Frederick Funston, who became a major general in the Regular Army. Martin was a longtime member of the Kansas Guard and had been state adjutant general in 1917 when the Guard was inducted into federal service. He was beloved by his officers and men. Traub hardly knew him, having spoken to him, briefly, only five times.[17]

Traub's administrative incapacity also blinded him to what his incompetent signal officer, Lieutenant Colonel George A. Wieczorek, was up to, which amounted to destroying the division's ability to use signals of any sort. An officer in the coast artillery, Wieczorek had received signal corps training. His initial failure was with the division's telephone system. The French had given the division wire wound on huge spools weighing 250 pounds, which were impossible to trundle as the regiments advanced. An officer of the 137th rewound his wire on barbed-wire spindles, but his example was apparently not followed by any of the other regiments. Regimental signal officers prepared insufficient wire for the opening attack. One of them prepared only two kilometers of wire, but the first day the regiment advanced five kilometers; halfway, infantrymen saw their officer sitting on his empty spool. Moreover, the wire—a type known as "outpost, twisted pair"—was insulated by cotton, not rubber, so when it was laid on the ground, the slightest dampness, not to mention rain, broke the circuits. After withdrawal from the line, the division sent seventy miles of this wire to salvage.[18]

Almost none of the signal equipment was fit to take into battle. Thanks to Wieczorek—and the oblivious Traub—every aspect of the signal apparatus of the division was out of order. Radio might have been a possibility for holding the division together, if anyone had been successful in using it. A radio was working at division headquarters the day before the battle, but the officer in charge could not find the corps call numbers and sent a message in the clear, bringing the wrath of General Craig. As for units in the field, Hawkins could not remember whether any of them possessed radios, perhaps because he never heard from them. The radio set of one of the infantry regiments was broken, as its signalman discovered after the regiment was already on its way. The signalman of the headquarters company of the 138th Regiment had a radio working in a shell hole before Cheppy but could not reach anyone on it to relate their predicament. It did, however, obtain the time from the Eiffel Tower in Paris and pick up other traffic, which was of modest value.

Other means of communication were available. For example, flares in different colors could have been used according to a code, which had already been prepared. But when the flares were issued, it turned out that they all were "yellow smoke." Moreover, the cartridges for the flares were of a different bore from the pistols issued for them. Alternatively, panels could have been displayed to planes. Only the two attack regiments had panels, and the two support regiments leapfrogged them the first and second days. For various reasons, smaller units in the division refused to display panels, having torn them up for rags or lost them, if they ever had them to begin with. Thus, the French aero squadron attached to the 35th could obtain no panel readings from any field unit. It managed to identify the front line by observing troops there and apprised division headquarters. When headquarters received the information by code, it could not find its codebook. The 35th did not use carrier pigeons either, though they were widely used by the French; the division contained many farm youths accustomed to larger animals, and pigeons required constant attention. Later, when the 35th was in the Verdun sector, Sergeant Triplet forgot to cover a basket of the birds during a gas attack.

For liaison, the division resorted to runners, with all the confusion they produced. Runners could get lost and were slow compared to instantaneous communication by telephone or radio. Regimental commanders used their signal corps detachments as runners. One problem involving runners, for which General Traub was responsible, was his demand that officers be out in front during the attack so they could see what was going on. As a result, commanders moved their command posts frequently, and runners did not know where to go. Colonel Nuttman moved his post from one shell hole to another. His adjutant and aide told him that he had to stay in one place, but he paid no attention.[19] In the field the proper procedure was to keep command posts and other important installations on an axis, but no one did so. The problem of finding command posts arose on the first day. At 3:00 p.m. a wounded officer reached division headquarters and provided information that Varennes and Cheppy had fallen. The officer, who wished to return to his unit, asked where his regimental headquarters was. "I wish I knew," said the headquarters operations officer, Lieutenant Colonel Walter V. Gallagher, "and I wish I knew even where the brigade headquarters are."[20]

Provisions were also neglected. The men went into battle with summer clothing and encountered poor weather on the second day—incessant rain and cold. Addressing the clothing issue, Traub later explained to the House Rules Committee that he himself was wearing summer underwear. Weather in the Vosges, he said, where the 35th had taken over French positions before moving elsewhere—eventually to the Meuse-Argonne—had been wonderful, and the men did well in summer clothing. He had put in requisitions for winter clothing, but by the time it came into a railhead, the division had moved to another sector where clothing was unobtainable. He stressed this point, for he seems to have put faith in requisitions. But when the rain came, the men shivered.

Providing food for the infantry regiments on the line was another detail to which Traub gave little attention. Because of the sector's poor roads, the rolling kitchens could not get up to the front. Their fires would have been impossible anyway because of daytime smoke and visibility at night; no one thought of using charcoal. For the first two days the men ate field rations—hardtack and "bully beef." The beef was carried in two-pound cans by every fourth man, and if that individual was separated from his food-sharing friends, he ate what he could and then threw the can away; the battle area was littered with half-eaten cans of meat. Hungry soldiers rifled bodies, both American and German, looking for food; the large German cookies were a favorite. Traub's solution to the food problem was to assign it to his administrative officer, his G-1, who had other concerns. The division commander did not know what his men were eating, "but I had my G-1 and all his assistants constantly out among the troops to find out the situation, and my G-1 reported to me officially that while the men did not always have all they wanted to eat, they always had something to eat."[21]

Treatment of the wounded in the 35th's sector was another serious problem for which the division's sanitary corps made insufficient preparation. The wounded had to get along in whatever way they could. Anyone wounded away from a road was likely to lie there for hours in the rain and the cold. Litters numbered a few dozen at best, whereas casualties mounted into the thousands. The division possessed twelve mule and eleven motor ambulances. General Traub explained to members of the House Rules Committee and Senate Military Affairs Committee that every commander in the world, after ensuring the success of his operations, desired to care for his wounded. The men of the AEF who were wounded or ill had his first consideration, he stated, receiving the greatest care possible under the circumstances. He took refuge in the impossibility of prediction: "I tell you we had 7,000 wounded from our own and adjoining divisions, and how are you going to get stretchers enough for them? You cannot predict for every contingency." He hid behind descriptions of medical organization, explaining that a triage was a sorting-out place for the wounded, so that the more serious cases could be sent to hospitals.[22]

The wounded of the 35th underwent almost indescribable experiences. The division's YMCA representative, Henry J. Allen (elected governor of Kansas in November 1918), was furious over the treatment of the 10,000 Kansans in the 35th. While testifying at the hearings in Washington, he read a letter from Chicago physician Harry R. Hoffman, the division psychiatrist who had been at the front:

Imagine the plight of our wounded. There were 800 at the advanced dressing station; 1,400 more at the triage just back of the fighting lines. Some were legless; others armless; many with sides torn out by shrapnel. All, practically, were in direct pain. It was bitter cold. The mud was knee-deep. A half sleet, half rain was beating down mercilessly. And for 36 hours those 2,200 men were compelled to lie there in the mud, unsheltered. We had neither litters on which to lay them nor blankets to wrap around them.[23]

The triage was at Cheppy, but the place proved too dangerous, for the village was under shell fire. The decision was made to send the wounded to Neuvilly, below the starting line of September 26, where the fortunate ones were put, row upon row, in a half-destroyed church; the others were left lying in the rain.

The tribulations of the 35th received a surprisingly detailed investigation by the I Corps inspector, Lieutenant Colonel Robert G. Peck, and at the congressional hearings in 1919. Peck's report, highly critical, was eighty-seven pages of singlespaced typescript. Governor Allen testified at the hearings, in eloquent detail. The best the army could do was Traub's braggadocio. To little avail the War Department brought in Secretary Baker and Chief of Staff March. Baker did not know which divisions were in which corps in the Meuse-Argonne and thought that the 35th was a brigade. March spoke in general terms about the fighting and refused to go into detail.[24]

The 35th's failures might be excused by saying that the AEF had been created quickly, and time was short after the divisions were sent overseas in the spring and summer of 1918. One might say that General Pershing could not attend to all the details himself, nor could his staff subordinates or division commanders. But there was much to criticize about a commander who accepted anything his superiors asked of him and gave no attention to artillery problems, who changed subordinates at the last moment, who discriminated against National Guard officers and overlooked the failures of his signal officer, and who ignored the lack of front-line necessities such as clothing, food, and care for the wounded.

CHAPTER FIVE

Ending the Enfilade

What the First Army encountered in the Meuse-Argonne, after overcoming the initial machine gun nests, was artillery, which was a far greater killer than machine guns in World War I. The Germans had zeroed in on the American divisions from both sides of the battlefield—from the heights on the left, in the Argonne Forest, and from those on the right beyond the Meuse River. Pershing's first move after the divisional attacks petered out was to try to destroy the hostile batteries. The enfilading fire, especially from the Argonne, was too much to ignore. Every time a company emerged from a woods, the German guns began to boom.

The plight of several companies from two regiments of the 77th Division at the far left of the American line reinforced the need to get the Germans out of the Argonne. The companies were surrounded, and the men huddled in foxholes close to and even under the roots of trees on the north side of the Charlevaux valley. An inventive newspaper editor in New York, upon learning of their predicament, coined the name the Lost Battalion. It became the best-known newspaper story of the war, and everyone across the United States knew about the Lost Battalion.[1]

To silence the batteries in the Argonne and save the companies of the 77th was no easy task. The most important move was by the 1st Division, which, after replacing the 35th along its engineers' line, moved forward to a line just below Fléville. The move was costly, for the division lost nearly as many men in taking and holding the new line as had its hapless predecessor. The difference was that the 1st was battle wise, and its commander, Charles P. Summerall, kept his brigades and regiments tightly controlled. Meanwhile, the commander of I Corps, General Liggett, used part of a brigade of the 82nd Division in corps reserve in a way that Edward M. Coffman described as a stroke of imagination in an era of frontal assaults.[2] The brigade's men moved up along the east in back of the Aire, crossed the stream by fording and makeshift bridges, and attacked into the Argonne heights, supported by the tired but still fighting 28th Division. This pushed the Germans out of the forest.

Stopping the enfilade from the heights east of the Meuse was more difficult, and the attack in that direction did not get far. The hills beyond the Meuse required a large force of assaulting infantry, and after replacing divisions worn out by the initial attack all along the line, Pershing was short of infantry. After III Corps began the advance on September 26, General Bullard sent the 33rd across the Meuse because his sector had narrowed; the Meuse above Verdun turned northwest. To this force the commander in chief could add only the 29th Division. The enfilade from the heights of the Meuse continued until just after November 1, when the divisions in V and III Corps, having moved far to the north, turned right into the Meuse heights and the Woevre Plain and forced the Germans to remove their batteries.

The Lost Battalion was a story in itself, apart from the larger scene in the Meuse-Argonne. There is no question that the men were heroic in defense of their position. Their valor equaled that of General George A. Custer's men at the Little Big Horn and the earlier and similarly admirable defense of the Alamo. The newspapers were right to pick up the story of 500 men surrounded by the Germans, hanging on despite apparently hopeless circumstances and refusing to surrender.

The 77th Division became involved in the Argonne because of the failure of the First Army's initial strategy for taking the area, which was to force the Germans out of the forest by a pincer movement. In the operations plan, the intention was to take the forest by flank actions—to the left by the advance of a regiment of the 92nd Division (the African American division), along with movement north by a regiment of the French Fourth Army, the joint force moving up above Binarville. On the right of the forest, the 28th Division was supposed to advance up the Aire

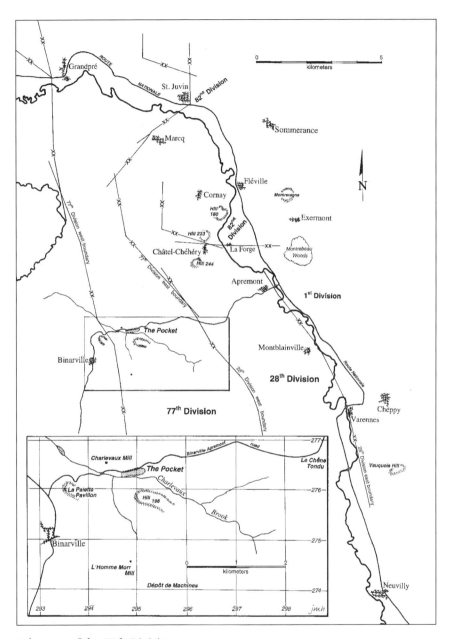

Subsector of the 77th Division

valley. Both forces would outflank the German batteries and supporting troops in the forest. In this scenario, all the 77th had to do was assist the flank forces by keeping up with them. But the flanking plan collapsed when the Franco-American force failed and the 28th did likewise, leaving the 77th to fight its way through the worst terrain of the American sector from the forest to the Meuse.

The division of Major General Robert Alexander faced the worst combination of natural and man-made obstacles of any division in the Meuse-Argonne. The forest was a large place, the size of Manhattan had the 77th jumped off from Fourteenth Street.[3] In addition, Alexander's men confronted belts of barbed wire a hundred meters wide, often between tree trunks and invisible until encountered. In back of that were machine guns, fired until the last moment, when the gunners disappeared into the forest. Guns then opened from the rear—they were echeloned. The defenders had spent a long time in the forest, since 1914. They had put in concrete pillboxes vulnerable only to mortars or 35-mm guns. They had arranged trenches in crucial places and wired between them.[4]

The 77th was too small and weak to handle such an expanse of obstacles. Alexander said, rightly, that the division lost ten men for every German casualty. Its ranks had been depleted by action on the Aisne-Marne, the follow-up to the Soissons attack. Weak in infantry, it received 4,000 replacements just before the attack on September 26. The men were untrained, many never having fired a rifle. According to one story, an officer found one man in the rear during an action, smoking a cigarette, claiming that he did not know which end of the rifle to put the cartridge into. The men had never seen a grenade. They did not know extended order drill, which meant that in combat, they would bunch. One of Alexander's brigadiers advised his officers to use these soldiers as carrying parties, but when everything was over, many of them had gone into the line, where their ignorance led to casualties.[5]

The Lost Battalion—six companies of the 308th Infantry and one of the 307th, together with elements of a machine gun battalion—went forward into what became known as "the pocket" on October 2, 1918. There were two battalion commanders: Major Charles W. Whittlesey of the First Battalion of the 308th, and Captain George C. McMurtry of the Second. The command was under the senior man, Whittlesey. The 308th was the division's left regiment, and the Whittlesey force went up a large ravine for a kilometer to the Charlevaux valley, reaching it at 5:00 p.m. and passing trenches on both sides. The relation of the valley to the ravine was as if the former constituted the transverse of a *T*, the latter the stem. They dug in on the north side, just below the Binarville-Apremont road, a reverse slope impervious to artillery fire from the north. Terrain above the road was without cover, and a clifflike rise made any descent from the crest doubly difficult. The position was an oblong, six hundred yards wide and sixty yards deep. At the bottom of the valley lay Charlevaux Brook, only a few feet wide, and the area thereabouts was marshy and open. The places to watch were the flanks, east and west, and Major Whittlesey posted them with heavy machine guns.

The German defenders then boxed the Americans in. Landwehr, or garrison, troops and men of the 76th Reserve Division—not many of them—went around Whittlesey's left flank and into the trenches to the south of the ravine, which had been empty when the Americans had passed between them earlier. During the night of October 2–3 the Germans wired the space between the trenches, creating a line. They set up a heavy mortar northwest of the American position, put machine guns on the flanks, and sent snipers into the trees on the south side of the Charlevaux valley.

The Americans' predicament is easy to imagine. Once or twice a day the enemy attacked, coming over the crest above the road and rushing down, hurling potato-masher grenades, and simultaneously attempting to come in on the flanks with machine gun and mortar support. Because of the sweeping machine guns and the snipers, the men had to remain in foxholes, and anyone moving from hole to hole during the day had to keep his head down. The wounded, placed in the middle of the pocket, received little assistance; there were only three first-aid men, no physician. Bandages ran out, and the aid men took them from the dead and then resorted to wraparound puttees. On the first full day, October 3, food ran out. Water was obtainable only at night, when carrying parties took strings of canteens down to Charlevaux Brook. The men had no protection from the weather; they had taken no blankets, pup-tent shelter halves, or raincoats, calculating that support troops would bring them up. On October 4, despite knowing the men's position (Whittlesey had sent out six carrier pigeons, and all got through), American artillery mistakenly shelled it, uprooting trees and exposing the defenders to machine gunners and snipers.[6] Burying the dead became impossible, and the smell of corpses was sickening. On October 7 the Germans sent a captured man with a message asking for surrender in the name of humanity. Upon receiving no response (newspapers reported that Whittlesey had sent back a message, "Go to hell"), the attackers made a final assault with flamethrowers.

Unbelievably, relief came on October 7. Major Whittlesey had told the men to think of the British in India during the Sepoy Rebellion, holding out for forty days in the siege of Lucknow, for such seemed the Americans' only prospect, other than surrender. But late on Monday, October 7, the defenders heard the equivalent of the bagpipes of the relieving force at Lucknow—the cough of Chauchats and the whine of Springfields. The 307th had found a gap in the wire and flanked the Germans. They gave the men what food they carried and posted the area, and the Lost Battalion slept that night without concern for what the Germans might do. The next afternoon, 194 men walked out. Ambulances took out 202, including McMurtry, who had been struck by a potato masher, the handle of which was sticking out his back.

The question remains, why was the Lost Battalion allowed to take such a difficult position so far into enemy territory (a kilometer) that the 77th could not support it? The answer is that General Pershing, in command of the First Army, and General Alexander, in command of the 77th Division, did not handle the situation well. It was a matter of command failures, not anything that Whittlesey and McMurtry, not to mention their men, had done. Such failures were common at the beginning of the Meuse-Argonne and became less frequent as the battle continued, although the AEF was such a rapid creation that it suffered from them until the end.

Like the earlier collapse of the 35th Division, the responsibility for the surrounding of the Lost Battalion lay in part with the commander of the First Army, who wanted his divisions to go forward whatever the obstacles. On September 29 the initial attack of the First Army had come to an end, and the commander in chief would renew the offensive on October 4. Meanwhile, if an opportunity for forward movement presented itself, as it did with the 77th, he welcomed it. As it turned out, the move up the ravine by the Lost Battalion was the only attack in the entire Meuse-Argonne between September 29 and October 4.

At least equal responsibility lay with Alexander, who, like Traub of the 35th, sought to do whatever Pershing desired. If the commander in chief wanted an attack regardless of flanks, Alexander would provide it.

He passed down the attack order in what critics described as his typical blustery way. Many of his colleagues in the AEF disliked him because both during and after the war—he published a well-written memoir in 1931—he had the habit of claiming to be alone in the Argonne.

Alexander's relations with his 154th Brigade commander, Brigadier General Evan M. Johnson, were poor, which did not help matters. Alexander dealt with Johnson by hectoring him. On the morning of October 2, just before the Lost Battalion went into the pocket, he called Johnson on the field telephone. When he discovered that Johnson was out, he told a member of Johnson's staff what he had intended to say personally. "You tell General Johnson," he snapped, "that the 154th Brigade is holding back the French on the left and is holding back everything on the right." The brigade "must push forward to their objective today. By 'must' I mean must, and by 'today' I mean today and not next week." When Johnson returned to his post, he did the only thing he could; he ordered Whittlesey's men forward and then sent up part of the brigade reserve, the Third Battalion of the 307th. When the reserve failed to get through (only Company K reached the pocket), he ordered the colonel of Whittlesey's regiment to attack with what was left of the 308th Regiment, together with the remaining companies of the brigade reserve. When the colonel asked for personal relief, Alexander told Johnson to go up and lead the relief of the surrounded men. Johnson's two relief attacks failed. The troops found barbed wire twenty or thirty yards deep, covered by machine guns. Johnson lost at least 100 men; the chaplain told him that he had taken out that many bodies, and there were more.[7] Alexander was ready to relieve Johnson of command, but after the 307th Regiment managed to enter Grandpré, Alexander changed his mind and recommended Johnson for promotion to major general. The recommendation was too late, however, for the division commander learned that Johnson had asked to be reassigned.[8]

Last among the command failures that were an essential part of the story of the Lost Battalion was General Alexander's giving command of the 308th Infantry to Colonel Cromwell Stacey. This was a dangerous thing to do. The Stacey case was complicated and revealed itself slowly, and Alexander might have been forgiven for not understanding it, but he had a warning of sorts. That warning came from Major General Beaumont Buck of the 3rd Division, who in the midst of the Meuse-Argonne was himself relieved for incompetence. Buck had asked the First Army to

relieve Stacey, then in command of the 30th Infantry. Given the circumstances, the First Army should have asked for a medical review board,
but perhaps because of Buck's reputation, it sent the colonel to the 77th
Division instead, where Alexander took him without question. Stacey had
a breakdown on October 4, leaving his regiment leaderless with one-third
of its companies in the pocket.[9]

Despite the popularity of the Lost Battalion among American newspaper
readers and the urgency of the situation to the men in the Charlevaux
valley, the principal problem in the Meuse-Argonne in early October was
the enfilade from German guns in the Argonne. It was necessary for
Liggett, corps commander on that side of the Meuse-Argonne, to get the
guns out of there. The German batteries in the forest, firing relentlessly
day after day, were intolerable. The ravines east of the Aire, where the
35th and then the 1st Divisions were seeking to push ahead, ran east-
west, and as long as the Germans held the Argonne heights, the enemy
batteries could enfilade the men in those ravines. The guns were less
than a mile from the Aire and could fire into V Corps as well as I Corps.

General Liggett had an idea to resolve this problem, and as it happened, Colonel Ralph T. Ward in G-3 (operations) of GHQ already had the
same idea. At First Army, General Hugh Drum talked to Pershing, and
a hurried lunch took place at I Corps on October 6 with Drum; chief of
staff at GHQ, Major General James McAndrew; and perhaps the G-3 of
GHQ, Brigadier General Fox Conner.[10] These planners agreed to an attack
on the German batteries by the reserve division of I Corps, the 82nd, in
conjunction with the forward regiments of the 28th Division in the Aire
valley, which was to take place the next morning, October 7.

It may be that the plan was drawn up too quickly. The meeting evidently was not a smooth affair. Major General George B. Duncan of the
82nd was present, along with his chief of staff, Colonel Raymond Sheldon.
Liggett's aide, Major Pierpont L. Stackpole, was also present and wrote in
his diary that Duncan was slow-witted; he "seems to be as thick as mud
and not worth a damn and neither he nor Sheldon seem to have much
conception of what they are expected to do in a tactical sense."[11] Duncan
considered the meeting close to a farce, because McAndrew seemed to
be fixated on a hill that the 28th was supposed to take, Hill 244. He complained in his memoirs, but not to the assemblage of generals, that no one

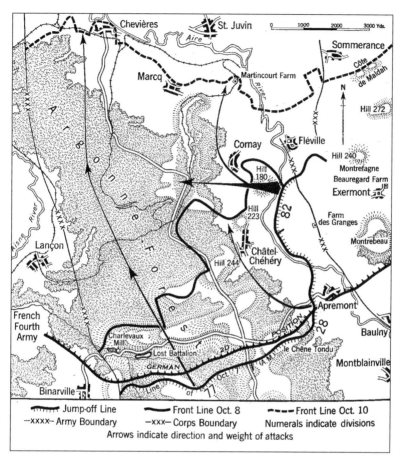

Plan of flank attack of First Army against Argonne Forest, October 7, 1918

had the slightest idea how the 82nd, then at Varennes on the east side of the Aire, would travel ten kilometers and cross the river, which was shallow (two to three feet deep) but not exactly passable, since any bridges had long since been destroyed. The area into which the division would go was a no-man's-land wedged between the 1st Division and the 28th, and German patrols penetrated it at night. As the 82nd's men turned to the left and crossed into the forest, they would have their flank in the air in case the Germans chose to descend, a maneuver that the enemy could have handled if it possessed enough troops. Once the 82nd went into the forest, there were the heights. As the 82nd's history would relate with due pride, "no more formidable natural fortifications are to be found on the entire battle front than the precipitous ridges extending from Châtel-Chéhéry and west of Cornay to the town of Marcq"—the latter on the Aire as it turned west toward Grandpré.[12]

It may have been hastily conceived, but the generals' plan was intended to resolve a virtual crisis. The initial attack of the First Army into the Meuse-Argonne had failed against the enemy's artillery. A second general attack on October 4, two days before the meeting over the Argonne guns, was failing for the same reason.

In the event, the 82nd's men did their best. The night after the meeting, the 64th Brigade under Julian R. Lindsey went up the Route Nationale in a soaking rain. The Germans across the river had the road under observation, and star shells arced, turning the night into an eerie sort of day. The road was full of trucks, wagons, and carts, and for miles the men had to walk close to and in the ditches, trying not to slip into the slime. Lindsey put across parts of two regiments. The 327th Infantry had gone up the road in battle order, the lead battalion under Major F. W. Blalock. It arrived at the ford, in the vicinity of La Forge, at 3:00 a.m., and the men went across as best they could. Engineers placed boards from rock to rock, which worked for some; the others waded. Blalock stood on the west bank and helped men up the slope. The battalion then marched north and formed on the Decauville narrow-gauge railroad east of Hill 180, the point of attack. The attack on Hill 180, on the right of the brigade sector, came at 5:00 a.m., completely surprising the defenders, who found themselves on the wrong end of a maneuver that resembled General Washington's surprise attack on the Hessians at Trenton (December 26, 1776). Companies C and D went up the hill supported by Companies A and B, the machine gun company, the 37-mm men, and the Stokes mortar platoon. All this was assisted by a heavy mist over the valley. Hill 180 was a kilometer long and ran north-south, dominating the marshland east of the river. The companies found wire on the east slope, but not enough to stop them. Captain Harrison of C Company sent the following message to battalion headquarters: "Going good. Captured 39 prisoners and 3 machine guns. No casualties yet."[13] In a short time Blalock had the hill.

Companies of the 328th Infantry on the left of the brigade sector were not so fortunate. The First Battalion (Major Boyle) assaulted Hill 223, and by noon the men were halfway up. The defenders used machine guns, the same weapons that the AEF faced so many times in the

Meuse-Argonne. Playwright Laurence Stallings, who had seen the guns at Belleau Wood and wrote an attractive if untrustworthy history of the AEF, described them as "chattering assassins," each with its "stovepipe water jacket, seven-point-six millimeter nose protruding through the flash screen and feedbelt cartridge glittering like a rattlesnake's back." No sooner was one taken when another opened, like on a checkerboard, killing the first attackers or, if only wounding them, making it impossible for them to reach their cartridge belts for first-aid packs.[14] The attack against Hill 223 and beyond to the railroad nonetheless succeeded, and General Duncan proudly related it in his memoirs. Boyle's men, like Blalock's, took the hill.

The next day the Second Battalion (Captain Tillman) jumped off to the east. The division history described that attack as "a very splendid page in the history of the division."[15] The machine gun fire was again steady and intense from the northwest and southwest as the battalion maneuvered down the western slope of Hill 223. The battalion crossed a valley of five hundred yards—no small distance—and fought through a kilometer of heavy woods. During the attack, two companies of the 327th under Captain Davis crossed the valley to reinforce the Second Battalion's right flank; they came under terrible machine gun and rifle fire, and forty men got through. As the division commander related, "Those watching this advance from the rim of the amphitheatre said the assault waves advanced across the open as if at drill and with seeming indifference to the fact that men were going down like ten pins before the ball."[16] Meanwhile, the Second Battalion of the 328th took the eastern part of the Decauville railroad. It had no liaison with Blalock's men attacking to the north, more than a kilometer away, nor for most of the day with the 28th Division to the south. The "take" of the Second was remarkable: at least 100 Germans killed, 270 prisoners, 123 machine guns, a battery of field guns, 4 antitank guns, and a quantity of small arms and ammunition.

The extraordinary feat of Corporal Alvin C. York took place on the morning of October 8, during the attack on Hill 223. The Second Battalion was held up by machine gun fire, so Sergeant Bernard Early took sixteen men to get around behind it. The group came upon an enemy battalion headquarters, and the startled Germans surrendered. It was then that trouble started. At a guttural command from somewhere nearby, the German prisoners hit the ground, and a hidden machine gun killed six of Early's men and wounded three more, including Early. York, who had dropped to the ground along with the Germans, took command. He waited for each member of the hidden gun crew to raise his head, whereupon he "jes' teched him off." Corporal York (promoted to sergeant after the action), from Pall Mall, Tennessee, had joined the army with reservations because of his religious beliefs, but a Bible-quoting battalion commander had convinced him that army service was justified. While training with the 82nd, York had been amazed by the poor marksmanship of his fellow soldiers (they "missed everything except the sky"). He had learned to shoot by hunting wild turkeys, so "it weren't no trouble nohow to hit them big army targets. They were so much bigger than turkeys' heads."

York's marksmanship and presence of mind on October 8 justified his later reputation as the most decorated soldier in the AEF. A German lieutenant, seeing that York was firing with a Lee-Enfield containing a five-round clip, decided to rush him with five other men, bayonets fixed, in the belief that one of the group would survive and kill York before he could reload. The lieutenant did not realize that York also carried a .45 Colt automatic, and he made the additional mistake of allowing his men to attack in column. York, on his feet and shooting "off-hand," dealt with them as if they were turkeys, shooting the last one first so those ahead would not take alarm and scatter. Using the unwounded men of his little group as guards, with himself at the rear, York started his prisoners back toward the American line, picking up more as he went along. He eventually brought in 132. Early later counted twenty-five dead Germans; the wounded had presumably been carried off. Taken before General Lindsey, the tall, stocky corporal made his report. "Well, York," said Lindsey, "I hear you have captured the whole damned German Army." "No sir," said York, "I only have 132."[17]

The southern part of the attack on October 7 was assigned to the 28th Division, with the 55th Brigade under temporary command of Pershing's intelligence chief, Brigadier General Dennis E. Nolan. He did his best with what he had: the 109th and 110th Regiments and the 112th from the division's 56th Brigade. Nolan had been instructed to seize Hill 244 to the south of Châtel-Chéhéry and was exhilarated by the news that his action would accompany the attack of the 82nd. In his after-action report he downplayed the capture of 244 Germans, considering it a secondary matter: "We attacked and captured Châtel-Chéhéry and the heights above it and got into the edge of the Argonne," he reported. The hill proved more troublesome than Nolan let on, however. Three hundred yards from the first machine gun position, the men encountered a second one with wire at the front and flanks. Enemy artillery fired from the Cornay ridge. Fortunately, the 28th's artillery had fired on Hill 244 in preparation for the attack, creating shell holes in which the American troops took refuge. Once they reached the top, they stalled on the crest. Nolan then received a troubling message from Major Kelly, in charge of a battalion of the 112th (56th Brigade). The message, which came in at 11:30 p.m., said that Kelly had not carried out his assignment to take the strong points along the Route Nationale. "Do you want me to proceed with the mission?" Kelly asked. "I will continue preparation awaiting your reply." Nolan told him to carry out orders, but it was too late. When Kelly attacked the next morning, he encountered heavy machine gun fire. As Nolan remarked in his report, the Germans had been retreating to the north all day and had taken up new positions. The battalions of the 55th did not secure Hill 244 until 9:30 p.m. on October 8. The general consoled himself that his brigade had advanced two kilometers. On the night of October 8 and the morning of October 9, the 82nd took over the 28th's positions.

The 82nd and 28th hence accomplished their task of pressing the German troops to withdraw, or perhaps it would be more accurate to say that the Germans decided the time had come to withdraw because of the proximity of the 1st Division below Fléville and the two divisions west of the Aire. On the morning of October 10 the 82nd brought up field guns to invest Cornay and placed heavy machine guns and 37-mm guns in the front line. It had previously taken Cornay and lost it, but this time it took the village and held it. Patrols entered Marcq on the plain beyond—their units were above the Argonne—and withdrew upon counterattack. The men could look down on the bend of the river toward Grandpré and St. Juvin, to St. Georges and Landres-et-St. Georges to the east, thence to the Côte de Chatillon and Cunel, Romagne, and Brieulles.

The thrust sideways into the Argonne, conceived by Liggett, was a success, and for that, the commander of I Corps and General Pershing could be grateful. The move on October 7–9, together with the action of the 1st Division in getting up to Fléville, pushed the German batteries out of the Argonne. The secondary achievement was freeing the Lost Battalion; there could be no doubt that pressure on enemy troops in the forest assisted the 307th Infantry in getting through and relieving Whittlesey's men. By the time the relief regiment reached Whittlesey on the evening of October 7, the Germans were in retreat. The day before, the German corps commander had given his men an extra day to eliminate the Americans. Failing to manage it with flamethrowers on October 7, they might have done it with one more attack, but their time ran out; they were in danger of being surrounded because of the threat from the 82nd and 28th.

At the time, Liggett was irritated by Lindsey's failure to get more troops into the Argonne. On the night of October 8–9, Duncan's men heard German troops and transports moving continually, passing north out of the forest and heading for the Aire bridges near Grandpré. The commander of I Corps regretted the failure to "bag" them. Moreover, if Lindsey had gotten more troops across, it might have been possible to seize Grand-pré, Landres-et-St. Georges, and the Côte de Chatillon, places that would plague the AEF in the days ahead. It could have meant occupying the Bois des Loges near Grandpré, which remained in German hands until November 2. At the time, Liggett was willing to take heads for such failures. He believed that the 77th could have relieved the Lost Battalion, that Alexander and Johnson were of little use, and that Johnson's time was about up. Duncan, according to Stackpole, was obtuse and confused. Liggett took some pleasure in Nolan's work but was unsure that he had accomplished much. In books written by Liggett in 1925 and 1928—the first assisted by Stackpole, the second by a writer for the *Saturday Evening Post*—the general softened his earlier comments, admitting that he may have asked too much.[18]

One point that no one made much of was the small number of 28th Division troops involved. In the 1930s Nolan wrote that when he took up his brigade command and counted heads in his two regiments, he discovered that he was a long way from table-of-organization complements of 4,000 men in each. He had 625 in one regiment, 525 in the other. When he asked the division adjutant why the division was reporting a much higher number, he received an awkward but honest answer. Major Rhoades replied, "They call up about 3 o'clock in the afternoon when they ought to know that nobody could know what the strength of these regiments were and I know that if I gave them some figures they would let us alone, so I gave them the first two figures that came to my mind, 1,625 and 1,575. I knew that would satisfy them as they don't know what is happening up here." Before the attack of October 7–9, Nolan left a battalion in Apremont as division reserve, comprising 100 men commanded by a sergeant. The Third Battalion of the 110th came out of the line on the night of October 8–9 commanded by its only officer, Second Lieutenant Culpepper, with a single noncommissioned officer and 55 men.[19] In sum, the numbers of troops put into the field on October 7 were not enough to accomplish much beyond their purpose, to end the enfilade and help free the Lost Battalion.

Another interesting point is that the enfilading batteries in the Argonne could have been removed with the judicious use of gas. Nolan related that on October 4 the enemy sent over a heavy artillery fire, including gas. In two battalions of the 28th's 109th Infantry, in position north of Apremont, losses from gas were severe—sixty cases, a third of them vomiting, indicating phosgene with its smell of new-mown hay. That same day, the First Army's Aisne artillery group received orders to gas the German batteries at the top of the Argonne. On the night of October 5–6, the gas—No. 9 bromacetone, a lachrymal agent—was fired above a line through the Bois de Marcq. The group received permission to put gas to the south as well, in and around Châtel, a village to the right of the Aire (not to be confused with Châtel-Chéhéry), and to gas the batteries in Cornay and near Fléville. But I Corps, which the Aisne group was attempting to help, asked for no further firing of gas. The artillery group then returned to its normal counterbattery fire.[20]

In the attack into the heights of the Meuse on October 8, the 33rd Division took the left flank, and its task seemed easy enough. On September 26 the division had had an ideal assignment as the right-hand division of III Corps. Its task had been to cross Forges Brook and hide in a forest. German artillery had sent gas shells as well as heavy explosives, firing from the heights of the Meuse and those of the whaleback, but to no avail. The first day crossing the Meuse was almost an idyllic affair, and the regiments went over in order. Walter A. McCleneghan, who later became a Methodist minister back home in Illinois, remembered that the Germans were on a high ridge on a bend of the river, a quarter mile away.[21] They looked down on the valley where the Americans were crossing the marshes, the canal parallel to the Meuse, and then the river. Unlike the Aire, the Meuse was impassable and required pontoon bridges, and the engineers prepared them. The river near Brabant-sur-Meuse was 12 feet deep and the bridge 120 feet long; near Consenvoye, the river

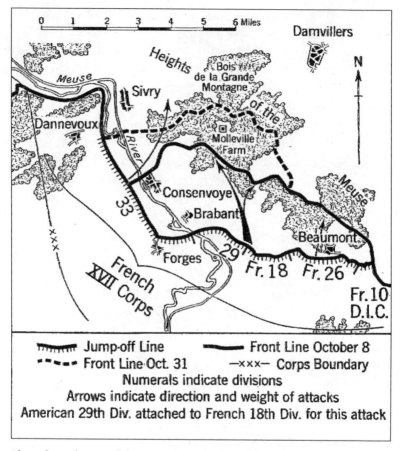

Plan of attack east of the Meuse, October 8, 1918

was 16 feet deep and the bridge 156 feet long. Engineers constructed the bridges quickly; the one at Consenvoye was ready in five and a half hours. The Germans put down gas shells, and the bridge builders wore masks. The engineers also made repairs on the Brabant-Consenvoye road on the far side of the river while working under shell fire.

The area across the Meuse reminded the men of the 33rd, which was the Illinois National Guard division, of "pasture land or former grain-fields." Lowlands sloped toward wooded heights. As troops crossed the flatlands on both sides, there was not much artillery fire. McCleneghan guessed, probably correctly, that the defenders were moving their guns back to safer places. "The occasional incoming shells did not seem to have a very good range on us and did little damage . . . somewhere off to the right a machine gun chattered in angry spells." He could see the men scattering out a half mile ahead. There were frequent orders to halt, to avoid bunching. "In the bright afternoon sunlight the whole expanse of open country and moving figures, even to my watering eyes and sometimes hazy vision, seemed like old practice maneuvers we had gone through or a motion picture filming of a battle scene 'on location.'"[22] It was a picture fixed in memory, unforgettable after fifty years.

Reality intervened as the men moved toward the sound of the guns. They had to skirt shell holes. McCleneghan noticed a soldier sitting on the edge of one, put his hand on the man's shoulder, and said, "How are you buddy, anything wrong?" He got no answer and realized that the man was dead.[23] An officer of Company I came along to check on the men and found that McCleneghan and a fellow infantryman were able to speak only in whispers. The officer may have noticed McCleneghan's bleary eyes and told the two to go to the rear: "Too much gas. Report to battalion headquarters—it's in a little clearing back there two or three hundred yards, tell them I ordered you back to the hospital."[24]

The image of pastures and grain fields disappeared after the first day, replaced by one ravine after another, all with enemy machine guns. The division history described units going forward between Consenvoye and Brabant as a humdrum affair, but the reality was a nightmare. The action "straightened out the line from Sivry to Ormes," Shipley Thomas wrote, but it was much more.[25] In two days the 33rd advanced four kilometers and took several hundred prisoners, mostly from the single Austro-Hungarian division on the western front that had replaced a first-class German division sent elsewhere. The Austrians did not want to fight and surrendered, as the Germans thought they would. For the rest of the 33rd's time east of the Meuse, it was artillery fire, machine guns, and gas. Casualties were 5,195.[26]

The right-flank division assigned to the attack, with a sector from Brabant to Samogneux, was the 29th. Its experience was not much different from that of the 33rd, except that the action concentrated on the height known as the Grande Montagne. When the 29th withdrew on October 28 it had fought north—the sectors were at a western bend of the Meuse—to the edge of the woods named after the mountain. From there, the men could gaze up to the peak. They were within a mile of the German batteries.

As McCleneghan's memoir described the 33rd's opening attack, that of Second Lieutenant Joseph Douglas Lawrence, a youthful platoon leader in the 113th Infantry, caught the 29th's. Lawrence, newly minted by the officer candidate school at Langres, was one of seven graduates who went almost immediately into the Meuse-Argonne. Only he and one other survived without bodily harm; three were killed, and two were severely wounded. The 29th's attack was nothing like that of the 33rd. The men moved forward toward the Meuse at a brisk pace; they halted at the top of a hill and shivered in the rain for half an hour before the command to fall out. There was no place to sit down except the muddy road or wet ditch banks, but many of the men lay down in the mud and went to sleep. Lawrence sat on the bank and looked at the "endless glow from the open flashes as the Franco-American and Austro-German artillery roared at each other."[27] He could not sleep because he had neither an overcoat nor a blanket and was too chilled to doze, his raincoat offering little protection. After two hours word came to fall in, and the column began moving again. He and the men passed down a steep hill to the Meuse and crossed on a pontoon bridge—not a minute too soon, for as the last man got over, a shell struck the bridge in the middle.

Thereafter it was the experience of war, including the frequent need to step aside to avoid "a bloody mess of flesh and scraps of an American uniform—evidently the unfortunate fellow had been hit by a shell." They crossed a trench with three bodies at the bottom, two American and a German, the latter on his back "with his chalky-ink swollen face hideous in death." As they went up a hill, artillery fire opened, and they jumped into shell holes or otherwise fell flat. Lawrence saw a shell hit between two men lying no more than four feet apart, covering them with dirt, but it was a dud, causing no harm. When the shelling stopped, the men went forward. Lawrence had trouble holding them in line; they bunched despite efforts by him and the sergeants.[28]

On October 10, reconnoitering a woods, the lieutenant came upon a company of Germans standing in the road. He turned and ran, and when his men saw him burst out of the woods, they did not wait for an order but turned as one and fled down the road. Lawrence overtook them a few yards in advance of the Germans. He saw a narrow-gauge railroad crossing and managed to form a line behind it, the men prone. Several were wounded before they got to the railroad. One, shot in both legs, fell on the enemy's side of the tracks and lay there with gunfire a few inches over his head. "He pleaded for us to pull him in, but we could not reach the four feet to him without exposing ourselves to certain death." The platoon fired at the Germans, who were fifty feet away; they could not see the enemy because of the underbrush but knew that they were killing them left and right, a deadly execution.[29]

Lawrence's principal engagement was manning a line with what amounted to two platoons consisting of more than 100 men he had gathered together. Small and slight, standing not over five feet five inches, he held his little force for six days on a line halfway up a hill, with no view down to the bottom where the Germans were. The men could hear the enemy attempting to go up through the brush, but by firing blindly, they managed to turn the Germans back. Lawrence had to move up and down behind the line, exposing himself to fire, to keep the men from trying to pass to the rear, especially at night. Holding the position was the worst sort of work. American and German artillery, not knowing exactly where the men on either side lay, fired uncertainly. An American shell hit a huge tree on Lawrence's line, and the upper half of the trunk fell straight down on one of the men, cutting his leg in two. Lawrence helped tie the stump. The man asked when the doctor would come, and the lieutenant assured him, "Yes, he will be here in a few minutes." The doctor did not come—none was nearby—and the man died.[30] Food came up, molasses and French bread with big holes; the molasses trickled on their hands and into their beards, where it mixed with whatever else was there. Dysentery affected everyone, and lack of sleep made them bleary-eyed.

During its time in line, the 29th engaged in a series of small actions like those described by Lawrence, and it never reached the Grande Montagne. There were a few modest successes, one of which involved a later U.S. senator, Millard E. Tydings of Maryland; he was the machine gun officer for Lawrence's regiment, the 113th. The regiment had the task of taking Etrayes Ridge, several hundred feet high, two hundred wide, and hundreds long. It was, Tydings remembered, in the shape of a ladyfinger, defended by artillery and fifty machine guns pointed down the paths the Americans would have to ascend. From all sides the Germans looked down on their foe in the ravines. The 113th's machine gun officer divided the ground to be taken into four blocks and distributed his two companies accordingly; with two platoons in a gun company, each platoon received

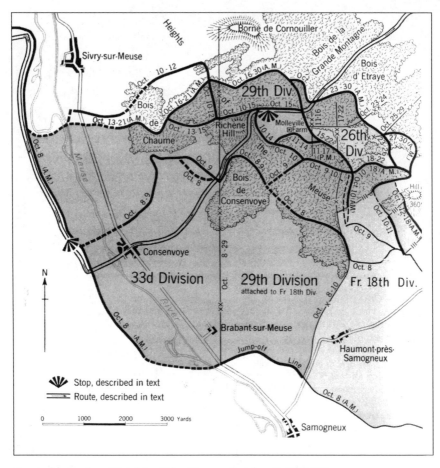

Ground gained on Heights of the Meuse, October 8–30, 1918

a block. He placed the platoons several hundred yards apart. "As the infantry started forward the first platoon commenced firing, and this fire
gradually moved, preceding the attacking troops so as to be always about
150 yards in their front." When the men advanced into a new block, the
gunners passed the work to the next platoon. This barrage moved at a
rate of one hundred meters every ten minutes, keeping the Germans
down until the infantry was upon them and took Etrayes Ridge.[31]

The 26th Division relieved the 29th on the night of the twenty-eighth.
"Douse that light, buddy," a man told one of the relief soldiers who had

lit a cigarette. The man sputtered, "You guys must think we ain't been on the front before." The 26th's men also made all kinds of noise, and Lawrence got his men out of there as fast as he could. German artillery opened on the 26th, which suffered serious losses.[32] Casualties in the 29th Division from October 8 to 28 were 5,861, not much different from those in the 33rd.[33]

Launching of the *Quistconck*. (University of Notre Dame Archives)

Production of planes was complicated. (111-Signal Corps 14509)

French 75-mm field gun. (111-Signal Corps 39958)

155-mm heavy gun. (111-Signal Corps 6367)

Renault light tank. (111-Signal Corps 29504)

Heavy Browning. (111-Signal Corps 32355)

Browning automatic rifle. (111-Signal Corps 32360)

General John J. Pershing inspects the honor guard at Chaumont. The men are wearing the campaign hats of 1898. (111-Signal Corps 26375)

Convoy at sea. (111-Signal Corps 31017)

Generals William H. Johnston and Frederick S. Foltz, September 2, 1918. (111-Signal Corps 31868)

General John L. Hines. (111-Signal Corps 30079)

Montfaucon. (111-Signal Corps 23124)

General Joseph E. Kuhn. (111-
Signal Corps 28495)

Esnes, Argonne. (111-Signal Corps 24644)

Crater on the Route Nationale. (111-Signal Corps 27411)

Exermont. (111-Signal Corps 27446)

Captain Harry S. Truman, Battery D, 129th Field Artillery Regiment, 35th Division. (Harry S. Truman Library)

Trail in the Argonne. (111-Signal Corps 30575)

Machine gunner's view. (111-Signal Corps 30576)

Pillbox. Standing next to it is Lieutenant Colonel J. Edward Cassidy. (111-Signal Corps 30577)

The pocket. The Binarville-Apremont road is two-thirds of the way up the hill. (111-Signal Corps 34664)

194 men of the Lost Battalion were able to walk out of the pocket. (111-Signal Corps 42757)

General George B. Duncan.
(111-Signal Corps 13812)

The 1st Division's guns in action. (111-Signal Corps 27421)

Going up Hill 240, the Montrefagne. (111-Signal Corps 27427)

The 1st Division's wounded in a church in Neuvilly. (111-Signal Corps 27410)

Staked barbed wire. (111-Signal Corps 12301)

Major General Charles T. Menoher opens the door for the commander in chief. (111-Signal Corps 16781)

The commander in chief decorates General Douglas MacArthur. (111-Signal Corps)

General John E. McMahon and staff. (111-Signal Corps 28294)

Church tower at
Romagne, just hit by
a shell. Towers were
favorite places for
snipers and spotters.
(111-Signal Corps
30019)

General Hunter Liggett. (111-Signal
Corps 30944)

General Robert Lee Bullard and staff, taken when he commanded the 1st Division. To the general's right is Major George C. Marshall. (111-Signal Corps 6378)

The dead at Châtel-Chéhéry. (111-Signal Corps 24931)

Ready for burial. (111-Signal Corps 24930)

Men of the 82nd Division. The placard on the left reads, "Straggler from the front lines." The right placard is not difficult to read. (111-Signal Corps 31520)

Remaining members of the 94th Aero Squadron, October 18, 1918. The others had been killed, captured, transferred, or sent back to the United States as instructors. This was the famed "hat in the ring" squadron. Third from left is Lieutenant Edward V. Rickenbacker, the air ace. (111-Signal Corps 29658)

Grandpré after capture. (111-Signal Corps 26656)

Explosion of a phosphorus grenade fired from a rifle. (111-Signal Corps 29449)

The Meuse and adjoining canal afforded opportunities for damming with tree trunks and debris. This photograph was taken near Stenay. (111-Signal Corps 34936)

Meuse-Argonne American cemetery. (The U.S. Army Military History Institute)

CHAPTER SIX

The Kriemhilde Stellung

Major General Henry T. Allen told the following story after the war: One night in the darkest hour of the Meuse-Argonne, he received an unexpected visitor, the commander in chief, who burst into his quarters, sat down at a camp table, and said to his old friend, "Things are going badly. We are not getting on as we should. But, by God! Allen, I was never so much in earnest in my life and we are going to get through."[1] The story has the ring of truth; it was no mere anecdote to celebrate the work of the man whom many Americans believed was the greatest military figure since Ulysses S. Grant. The only problem was that although Pershing may have been ready to get through, this did not give his troops the ability to do so. The First Army's green troops, as Liggett privately described them, did not yet have the experience.

After the move into the Meuse-Argonne, the divisions did not have the ability to go forward again in the way the commander in chief desired. There were two general attacks on October 4 and October 14. For October 4, Pershing took out four divisions, 125,000 men. In I Corps he replaced the 35th with the 1st; in V Corps he took out all three divisions and sent in the 32nd and, to its right, the 5th; in III Corps he kept the three divisions of September 26, and Bullard shifted the 80th to the left of the 4th and, a few days later, moved the 33rd across the Meuse. There were three successes in the October 4 attack, two by the experienced 1st and 32nd Divisions, and the other due to the competent handling of the 4th by Hines,

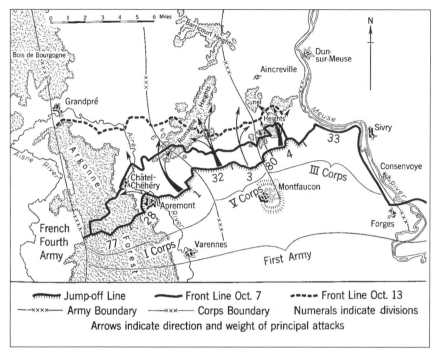

Plan of attack of First Army, October 4, 1918

who passed his men around Brieulles and went up three kilometers. The attack of the fourteenth resulted in only a single success, by the 42nd.

For the First Army's attack of October 4, Pershing did his best to recover the momentum that had slipped away on September 29. This time, the three corps were to advance independently—no holding back, as had happened when Poore's brigade reached its objective at noon on the first day and waited on that line while Booth's brigade waited behind it and the Germans reinforced Montfaucon. Once again, as in the past, Pershing believed that American determination—élan, the French called it—would show the tired Europeans what a real army could do.

He had reason to expect a positive result when the 1st Division replaced the 35th. An artillery officer was at a shell dump behind his guns when a colonel rode along the hill on horseback. "I am Colonel Ruggles of the 7th Field Artillery," he said. "I am looking for a place to put in three batteries."

"The 1st Division's coming in here?" the officer asked.

"On the way up now," the colonel said.

"It'll be a godsend to know that you're anywhere in the vicinity," said the artillery officer.[2]

The 1st Division had been at the center of AEF actions for months, and the men moved in during the night of September 30–October 1. They started out in French trucks driven by Annamese. The trucks had to come in by side roads, and the men were packed in like sardines, but it was better than walking. The latter began when troops reached the vicinity of Vauquois, the hill the 35th had so proudly taken during the first of its actions. The walk to the front remained a vivid memory for every man who did it, and Captain Shipley Thomas wrote a memorable account after the war. The men passed Vauquois and what had once been the village. Only a few stones from houses remained after the attack of September 26. After Vauquois, the scene hardly improved. There was a forest of splintered poles. A no-man's-land followed, with an outline of trenches used before the Germans learned to defend sectors by machine guns and artillery. Engineers were still working to improve the shooflies around the craters on the Route Nationale. Coming down from the front was an endless stream of trucks full of wounded. By evening, the troops reached the valley that began at Very and ran northwest to Charpentry and Baulny. Shell fire was increasing. In the darkness, the regiments—the 16th, 18th, 26th, and 28th—spread out and moved in skirmish lines. The division was now on the engineers' line that Major Stayton had established from Baulny Ridge to the northeast, the line that had saved the 35th.[3]

In the attack of October 4 the task of the 1st was to drive a stake into the German line and send the defenders back to the Kriemhilde Stellung, the strongest portion of the Hindenburg Line. The initial objective was the north edge of Montrebeau Woods, that confusion of trees and underbrush taken by the 35th on the way to Exermont and lost in the retreat. The second objective was to move up to the northwest as quickly as possible, to Fléville on the Aire, which would threaten German guns in the heights of the Argonne. The third was to encircle and take Hill 240, the Montrefagne, with the Bois de Boyon on top; the hill had been a German observation point and a place for machine guns and artillery, dominating Exermont and the area to the south.

The 1st's troops knew what to do. On the night of October 3–4 a private in a machine gun company watched carriers bring up ammunition from a dump at Charpentry (the Germans blew it up at 4:00 a.m., dropping a shell on it as soon as they realized the dump was there), and he observed the stoic behavior of the infantrymen awakened for the first-wave attack. The "boys," as the machine gunner wrote, fell in cheerfully, and as they prepared their attitude was, "Oh well, it's over the top again for us. It will be the last for many of us, but it's our job."[4]

What followed was a set-piece series of actions. It was nothing if not confidence inspiring, although for the men on the line it was anything but pleasant. Whereas the 35th knew little of liaison, the 1st knew everything. The men of the 1st opened the attack without preparation fire, although the Germans knew they were coming. The rolling barrage went three hundred feet every four minutes; infantry walked six hundred feet behind the dropping shells. The barrage was thin, through no fault of the batteries; gunners had a front of five thousand yards and only forty-eight 75s—one gun for every hundred yards. Gunners fired fast, ten shells a minute, which would have horrified General Berry of the 35th. When the guns got hot, the gunners let them cool. They waited until the infantry took the first objective, the north portion of Montrebeau Woods, then held the fire north of the woods for half an hour to protect mopping up and allow rejoining for the next move. During that time guns were moved forward, in the 1st's orderly way. The machine gunner quoted earlier looked back, and the sight of that moving line of artillery was one of his memories of the war.

From the outset, resistance was heavy, and the 1st fought its way forward. Montrebeau was alive with German machine guns and snipers, but the Americans overwhelmed them, tumbling the snipers out of the trees. Above the woods lay Exermont, the farthest point reached by the 35th, and the 1st took it back. The morning had started out foggy, which was good for the attackers, but when the fog lifted the German planes came over and radioed the location of the American line to the guns ahead, in the heights of the Argonne, and along the whaleback. The 1st's regiment on the left, the 16th Infantry, went to the left of Montrefagne, headed northwest to Fléville, and took the village, drawing back a bit to avoid enemy artillery fire that was sure to level it. On the second day the 1st took Montrefagne. Other troops had the task of turning toward the right to protect the division from enfilade fire, for the 32nd Division had not come up. In two days the 1st's line advanced seven kilometers. Subsequent days saw heavy fighting. Troops moved well above Montrefagne to even up the line with that of the 16th Infantry below Fléville, and on the right they inched forward to the Bois de Maldah.

Although the men of the 1st fought well because of their training, the division paid a high price in the attack that began October 4. Thomas's estimate of casualties was high at 9,387, the most suffered by any U.S. division in the forty-seven-day battle. The 1st's history was closer to the mark, but that was bad enough: 1,594 dead, 5,834 wounded, 39 missing, and 33 prisoners, for a total of 7,500.[5]

Individual tragedies were beyond measure. A collection of letters from Lieutenant Eldon S. Betts to his family in Illinois relates how the fighting went. The lieutenant wrote on September 28, 1918: "The end of the war is drawing near and my definition of Heaven is the U.S.A." He wrote again on October 4:

> In case I get mine tomorrow, I will write you a few lines to say good-bye and God bless you all. You have been the best of families to me and all that I have done or am, I owe to you and Mother. Don't grieve for me, as I know we shall meet on the shining sands on the other side, and, perhaps you will be proud to know that I died in a man's game, doing my bit. I am fully determined to do my best regardless of the outcome. Now goodbye, and thank you Pop, Edie and Margie, and love to all the family as well.

Betts led an attack on the morning of October 9. A friend wrote that as three platoons were advancing, with the lieutenant fifteen feet in the lead, machine guns measured his range, and he was dead before he hit the ground.[6]

One might ask whether the 1st paid too heavy a price, and whether it was attributable to the leadership of division commander Charles P. Summerall, whose reputation for bloodshed rivaled his skill with artillery. However, the casualties were not the fault of the commander, who had no choice but to order frontal assaults. The Germans had stopped the AEF, and its future in the Meuse-Argonne depended on penetrating the Giselher Stellung, which the 1st accomplished. The best day for the division was the initial one, when the 16th reached Fléville. Thereafter the men evened up the line, but it proved impossible to go farther. Summerall's aide, Lieutenant Alban B. Butler, wrote in his diary of an attempt on October 11 to get to Landres-et-St. Georges: "With less than 2,500 effectives we were unable to gain much ground. It was wicked to order our men to attack again this morning. . . . Since we entered this sector . . . we have lost between nine and ten thousand men."[7] Summerall, who was talkative, reportedly said, "Sir, when the 1st Division has only two men left they will be echeloned in depth and attacking toward Berlin!"[8] He could be overbearing, and after Soissons he dismissed his best infantry colonel, Conrad S. Babcock, for hesitating to send men into machine gun fire. With little thought he sent officers to Blois, the AEF camp for failures. He was a writer of acerbic letters and exercised that talent as army chief of staff in 1926–1930 and as president of The Citadel in South Carolina for years afterward. He lived into the post–World War II era, dying in 1964. Regardless of his faults, in 1918 Summerall was probably following Pershing's command to advance his division at all costs and to take Landres-et-St. Georges if possible.

Considering the high casualties, one wonders whether tanks might have helped. Only Renaults were available, and only a few of them. They had helped take Cheppy on September 26 and had taken Varennes but were otherwise of little value. When the 1st took Exermont it had five tanks, and a German antitank gun holed all of them. The primitive long-barreled gun of 1918 could not miss.

A tactic that was often discussed within the AEF and tried on occasion was bringing 75s up to the front line. An analysis after the war showed the idea to be unworkable; in sixty-two attempts, only three succeeded, and they occurred late in the war when German opposition was weakening. The noise of moving the guns called attention to their presence. The 1st Division made two such efforts; one required two caissons, eighteen horses, and nineteen men, and the other required twelve horses and thirteen men. In the first case, the gun had no opportunity to fire; in the second, six horses and nine men were lost. According to the division history, the use of accompanying guns "accomplished little more than to add to the heroic sacrifices of the day."[9] The trajectory of the French 75 was flat, and the gun could not fire over troops or trees. At ranges of five hundred to fifteen hundred yards, the 75s were useless; being so close to the enemy, the flashes betrayed their presence. In the 1st's attack, the 6th Field Artillery Regiment ran its guns forward as far as it could, but the tactic worked only while the fog lasted.[10] The Germans used accompanying guns, but not with troops on the move; they planted them at strong points and counted on losing them.

Another possibility the 1st might have explored was the use of gas. The Germans did not hesitate to employ it. After the 1st moved into position on the night of September 30–October 1, the men took refuge in three ravines. The Germans knew every ravine in the Meuse-Argonne and filled the three with 1,850 yellow cross (mustard) rounds, 1,135 blue cross (chlorine) rounds, and 675 green cross (phosgene) rounds. The gassing occurred at night, and high-explosive shells were mixed in to disguise the gas. The men did not realize what was happening until they smelled it. In this single attack, the 1st suffered 900 casualties. The use of gas on the battlefield was remarkably effective; it took only three gas shells to produce a casualty, compared with eight to ten high-explosive shells. On September 26 gas might have loosened the enemy's hold on Montfaucon and helped get the batteries out of the Argonne. But in September and October, AEF corps and division commanders were reluctant to call in gas, believing that it would bring retaliation. The First Army's chief of artillery, Major General McGlachlin, regretted this situation. He could do little about it. But in the attack beginning November 1, corps and army commanders felt no such hesitation.

During the attack of October 4, the other AEF divisions did what they could. For most of them, this was not much, but one of them did as well as the 1st.[11] This may have been because, in many ways, the two divisions were alike. The 1st had more training than any other division in the AEF, but the 32nd's commander was an insistent disciplinarian who believed in training and did as much of it as possible. Major General William G. Haan liked to describe his division as a fighting machine, and in a lecture presented after the war, he characterized it as such. The two divisions, the 1st and the 32nd, came into the line in the Meuse-Argonne at the same time, September 30–October 1. Their men went up to the front with the same attitude, which was a combination of competence and "getting the job done." Haan and his staff, the men following in full packs, went up through the shell-torn fields at night, ready for whatever tasks the commander in chief assigned. Just as the 1st had the task of taking back territory lost by the 35th and advancing the line as far as possible, the 32nd, replacing the 91st and 37th, had the task of taking back what the former had lost and securing more if possible.

The 32nd remained in the line longer than the 1st and, in a sort of twist, ended its stay with the equivalent of the brilliant attack that took the 16th Infantry up to Fléville: the capture of the Côte Dame Marie eight kilometers north of Montfaucon, at a cost of no casualties. The hill rose three hundred feet above its surroundings and was more than half a mile long and crescent shaped, with rises on each side. The ground in front was rolling fields with patches of scrub oak, offering little cover. The hill was a place from which German officers with field glasses could watch men struggling forward and call in artillery fire. The 32nd took it on October 14.

The division first attacked the Côte Dame Marie on October 13, and its failure that day led to its brilliant success the next. On the thirteenth Haan watched his men go forward, and when a report came in of the hill's capture, he sent it on to V Corps, from whence it was forwarded to the First Army. In his postwar lecture, the 32nd's commander related how he had mistakenly believed that his report persuaded Pershing to announce the general First Army attack of October 14, which led Haan to order his division's second attack to gain the victory he had already claimed.[12] The First Army's plan included attacks on the 32nd's left by the 42nd Division (which had replaced the 1st) and on the 32nd's right by the 5th Division. Those two divisions were to take the Côte Dame Marie by a pincer movement. The 32nd was to make a feint in front of the Côte Dame Marie.

Everything that happened on October 14 was somewhat confused, and Haan's division gained the hill by a piece of good fortune. The 32nd's regimental commanders assigned battalions to attack each tip of the hill. After attempts to get through a gap in the wire on the east side, which was defended by machine guns, the commander of the Third Battalion, 126th Infantry, called up Captain Edward B. Strom to take a few men and silence the guns. Strom and seven men climbed the face of the hillside, and for some reason, perhaps incredulity at the attempt, the defenders gave them little attention and then fired wildly, too high. Strom's group got within 150 yards and put murderous fire on the machine gun pits, using rifle grenades. The surviving Germans thought that they were surrounded and surrendered. The historian of the AEF wrote, "When Strom reported to his commander, he turned over ten machine guns, fifteen prisoners, and the key to Côte Dame Marie."[13]

On October 17 Haan wrote to Summerall, by then commander of V Corps, that the 32nd was exhausted and he did not want to hurt the division's morale by keeping it in line. It had been at the front for twenty days, and its regiments had been reduced to cadres—the 127th with 216 men in its First Battalion, 160 in the Second, and 139 in the Third. The

Third Battalion had 2 officers and 32 men in I Company, 3 officers and 21 men in K company, 3 officers and 60 men in L Company, and 2 officers and 16 men in M Company. Casualties were 5,833, with 1,179 dead. The corps commander relieved the division with gratitude.[14]

During the attack beginning October 4, III Corps' 80th Division got into the Bois des Ogons, a name that thereafter was associated with vicious fighting. It lay on the line between V Corps and III Corps, and attacks were arranged through each corps headquarters. The division pushed into the woods twice, only to be pushed back out. Its commander, Major General Adelbert Cronkhite, spoke with Bullard about a third attack and virtually asked to forgo it. "Give it up and you are a goner," was Bullard's response. "You'll lose your command in twenty-four hours. Make one more attack. This time you'll take the wood and throw the enemy out." He was right; the division took the woods.[15] On October 4 the 4th Division under Hines avoided an assault on Brieulles, skirting it with a brigade and advancing three kilometers. It was "a beautiful operation," according to Thomas, who, as a member of the 1st Division, knew about such things.[16] It penetrated the eastern end of the Kriemhilde Stellung.

Pershing was driven and determined, so when he obtained a few successes in the October 4 attack, it was only natural that he would order another general offensive as soon as possible, which turned out to be October 14. For this, he sought to bring in his remaining veteran divisions. This turned out to be only the 42nd, which replaced the 1st on the night of October 11–12. The 2nd Division was fighting under French command to the west of the Argonne in the Champagne, taking Mont Blanc with heavy casualties, and it could not arrive in time.

The plan for October 14 was as ambitious as the one ten days earlier, and again, it achieved only a small part of what Pershing hoped—this time, a single success by the 42nd Division. In the earlier attack, the commander in chief had planned on a pincer movement by the 42nd and the 5th to take the Côte Dame Marie, but the 32nd had given him Dame Marie unexpectedly. The plan for the fourteenth involved much more. This time, the 42nd and the 5th were to force the enemy out of Dame Marie by penetrating the Kriemhilde Stellung at its center. Then, the two divisions were to push north to the third portion of the Hindenburg Line on the Barricourt heights. Beyond the heights, the Meuse-Argonne was

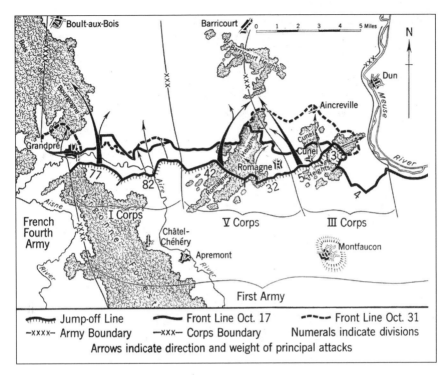

Plan of attack of First Army, October 14, 1918

open country to the river. In the event, the pincer was unnecessary, and it would not have worked anyway, because the 5th Division was unable to move forward. The 42nd stalled until the division's 84th Brigade broke through the Kriemhilde Stellung at Côte de Chatillon, after which, exhausted, it could go no farther.

The action of the 42nd is best described by brigades, for their tasks were different and their fortunes varied. On the left of the division sector was the 83rd, commanded by an attractive brigadier, Michael J. Lenihan. On the right was the 84th under Brigadier General Douglas MacArthur. The division plan was weighted against the 83rd Brigade, so much so that Lenihan should have protested. But for some reason, perhaps his innate modesty, he did not. His men had to take the two villages of St. Georges and Landres-et-St. Georges, attacking across a field a mile long. In contrast, the 84th Brigade could debouch from a woods against its objective, the Côte de Chatillon. Even worse, after Lenihan's troops got through their mile-long advance, Chatillon would be to their right rear; if the 84th had not taken it by that time (which is what happened), the Germans could enfilade the 83rd. Another difference was what the brigades would face in their sectors: when it got to the German line in front of the villages, the 83rd would encounter three lines of barbed wire; for the 84th, there would be wire, but nothing comparable. The chaplain of the 83rd's 165th Regiment, Francis P. Duffy, described it well. Duffy was no defeatist and was immensely proud of his regiment, formerly the "Fighting 69th," a New York City National Guard regiment whose history dated to the Civil War. The wire, he wrote, consisted of three thick lines, each reinforced at the rear by a machine gun trench. The first line was breast high and in places twenty feet thick, bound in small squares by iron supports. In back of it was a four-foot trench for machine guns, wide enough to allow gunners to swivel. The next two lines were at thirty-yard intervals, giving gunners fields of fire.[17] The lines started from the brigade's left; at Landres-et-St. Georges they turned southeast toward Côte de Chatillon and included two farms, La Musarde and Le Tuilerie.

The task of the 165th Regiment, once it managed to get through the mile of open field, was to pass through the wire. Ideally, artillery would have cut the wire, but here, it would be of no use. In April 1918 Colonel George E. Leach, of one of the 42nd's light artillery regiments, had tried to destroy wire by putting five hundred rounds on twenty feet of it, with no effect. As he wrote in his diary, when the war started, the standard arrangement had been to stretch wire tight, but this was abandoned in favor of staked loose sections that were impervious to artillery fire.[18] When the wire pinned the regiment, Lieutenant Colonel William J. Donovan called for mortar fire. "The mortars had pretty good effect in some areas," wrote one of the men, "but there was just too much territory to cover."[19] Tanks might have cut a path, and the 165th summoned them, but they were slow in coming. Those available were in poor mechanical condition: twenty-five started, sixteen arrived, and ten went into action and retired in disarray.

It is possible that a device invented by engineers of the 3rd Division might have helped. It caught Pershing's attention, and he invited observers from other divisions to an exhibition, which seemed to come off. The device consisted of a double roll of chicken wire with poles at both ends. Simulated attackers put down a pole on one side of a line of barbed wire, threw the roll over the wire, dropped the other pole, and rushed across.

It took just a few minutes.[20] But how the device might have functioned against the width of wire before St. Georges and Landres-et-St. Georges was a question. Observers were skeptical, and the 165th did not try it.

Like the 1st Division in the attack of October 4, the 42nd failed to gas the German positions. Most of the defenses of St. Georges and Landres-et-St. Georges—and, for that matter, of the Côte de Chatillon, including the two farms—were along the leading edges of the German line, and gas could have made those positions untenable. There was no reason to hesitate, for the Germans were using it in the 42nd's sector. In fact, much of the men's tiredness, which became more evident as the action evolved, was caused by gas inhalation.[21] But both officers and men of the division were against the use of gas.

Thus, the alternatives to a frontal attack were unworkable, unlikely to succeed, or, in the case of gas, unacceptable. As a result, the men went forward in the usual way, preceded by engineers with wire cutters, and the result was appalling. Machine gunners shot the engineers, and lines of their bodies hung over the wire.

> Groups of our lads dashed up to the wire only to be shot down to the last man. Some ran through a passage made for the roadway, the only possible method of getting through, but this of course was absolutely covered by the German guns, and every man that went through it was shot and, if not killed outright, taken prisoner. Soldiers of ours and of the Engineers with wire-cutting tools lay on their faces working madly to cut through the strands, while riflemen and grenadiers alongside of them tried to beat down the resistance. But they were in a perfect hail of bullets from front and flank, and every last man was killed or wounded.[22]

What was left of the first-wave attackers jumped into shell holes. Donovan lay in a hole attempting to direct the chaos, believing that valor would take the day. Hit in the leg, he remained for as long as he could. The impossibility of the situation became evident to everyone except for the commander of V Corps, Summerall, who remembered that his men of the 1st had fought despite losses, creating the salient that cleared the Argonne. He stalked into Lenihan's command post and relieved him, along with the 165th's colonel, Harry D. Mitchell, and Mitchell's operations officer, Captain Van Santvoord Merle-Smith.

What should we conclude about this action of the 83rd Brigade in the Meuse-Argonne? Sending a brigade across a mile of open terrain into three lines of barbed wire and machine gun trenches certainly seems to be an impossible assignment, for which blame should go first to Summerall. Like Donovan, he believed in valor, but that was no solution for what the 83rd faced. Unfortunately, Summerall had no other. He gave the brigade to Colonel Henry J. Reilly, who commanded one of the artillery regiments. Reilly's father had been Summerall's superior in the Philippines. Reilly could do nothing more with the 83rd.

The division commander, Major General Frank Menoher, was as much to blame as Summerall, for he allowed the attack. Menoher never made much of a mark with his division, despite its quality. He supported Summerall's relief of the brigade's officers, and he did nothing when Summerall also turned on the colonel of the brigade's other regiment, the 166th from Ohio. When Menoher warned Colonel Benson W. Hough, a Guard officer and a prominent lawyer in Columbus, of Summerall's displeasure with him, Hough told the division commander that he could relieve him on the spot, that his men had done all they could to support the 165th, and that although their morale was low, they were not defeated. Menoher backed off.[23]

Lenihan also deserves some blame. Although his men admired him, he was indecisive, failing to anticipate and avoid trouble. Before the attack, he called a night meeting of his colonels—a memorable affair, because they had to thread their way to his command post in Exermont (which may have been too far from the front line) while trying not to step on the bodies of men from the 35th and 1st. At the meeting, they raised two issues. One was the possibility of getting more shells for the 75s so the guns could fire more rapidly, perhaps ten shells per minute, as those of the 1st Division had done. The other, more important, was the need for the division's other infantry brigade, the 84th, to come abreast; otherwise, the Germans could enfilade the 83rd. Lenihan addressed neither issue; he just listened and said nothing.[24] The colonels went off into the night. Summerall's relief of Lenihan virtually ended his usefulness in the Meuse-Argonne. With the intervention of Liggett, who took over the First Army in mid-October, Lenihan went to the 77th, where he commanded a brigade in the last days of the war. In the post-1918 army he became a major general. After his retirement, and with the help of his wife, Mina, he wrote a charming memoir entitled "I Remember—I Remember," which included accounts of his medals. It contained a single noncommittal sentence about his being relieved of command.[25]

On the right of the 42nd's sector lay the 84th Brigade, with its goal of the Côte de Chatillon. Like the 83rd's assignment, the task of the 84th was a difficult one. Chatillon was a large hill with points to the south and northeast, each defended by an outlying farm with clustered buildings. To the southeast was Hill 288. German machine guns on the top and side of Chatillon commanded its immediate approaches. From east of the Meuse, the German batteries gave support; they were so obvious that the gunners could be seen pulling the lanyards.

As the 84th's officers analyzed its problem, there was agreement, reinforced by the example of the 83rd, that a frontal attack would not be wise. It was at this juncture that General MacArthur issued an order that, if carried out, would have brought the brigade's ruination and perhaps sent its author to Blois. His proposal—a bayonet charge at night—was so silly as to be embarrassing to even relate. The men never could have gotten close enough; the enemy would have heard them stumbling through the brush, loosening stones underfoot, and machine gunners would have cut them down. Major Ravee Norris of the brigade's Alabama regiment, the 167th, told his regiment's commander, Lieutenant Colonel Walter E. Bare, what he thought of the order, in no uncertain terms. Years later, when Colonel Reilly was putting together what he trusted would be a definitive account of the division, he included Norris's reaction: "After dark on the fourteenth, much to my surprise and consternation I got the order to assault the Côte de Chatillon with the bayonet. No firing allowed! I called up regimental post of command and protested to Bare. I said 'It is nothing short of murder to send men in on such an assault.'"[26] Bare then went to a meeting of commanders in which he argued against MacArthur, who gave up the idea.

The officers of the brigade proposed an alternative that brought success. The night before, a plane had taken a photograph of Côte de Chatillon showing a path that might be used. If the troops could approach it through a ravine while the brigade's machine guns laid down a withering and noisy barrage on the defenders, the men could move forward undetected. The plan was for the Alabamans to lead the attack. The Iowa regiment, the 168th, which had taken Hill 288 to the southeast, would also take part. Early on October 16 the regiments went forward, supported by a deafening machine gun barrage consisting of sixty guns and a million rounds and lasting forty-five minutes, which drove the defenders into bunkers. The Alabamans went up Chatillon on the left, the Iowans on the right. The latter's First Battalion, under Major Lloyd D. Ross, found a break in the wire on their side, went through, and reached the top first, where they discovered the Alabamans coming up the other side. Many heroic acts took place, for the 42nd excelled at that. Men came to places where there was no cover and ran across, appearing to the rear of German gunners. Like at St. Georges and Landres-et-St. Georges, the Germans had assumed that the Americans would try a headlong rush forward. There was one odd scene when Ross found Corporal Joseph Pruette jumping up and down on top of a dugout, shouting in apparent madness, "I've got 'em—I've got 'em." From the dugout came cries of "Kamerad." "Come out. Come out," shouted Pruette. Four officers and sixty-eight men emerged. When one of the officers saw that Pruette was only a corporal, he said in broken English that he would surrender to an officer. "To hell with that noise," Pruette shouted. "Give me those guns, or up you go in smoke."[27] At the top, the men faced two counterattacks. A timely barrage by the 5th Field Artillery Brigade held off one of them, and the Iowans and Alabamans countered the other. By nightfall, the 84th had secured the Côte de Chatillon.

After the war, Majors Norris and Ross went back to their states, and not much was heard from them. Individuals who had little to do with the capture of Côte de Chatillon offered explanations for the brigade's success. First, it was necessary to show the importance of the hill's capture, and General Reilly did that (he was promoted after he took command of the 83rd). "It was obvious," he wrote, "that the key to the situation was the Côte de Chatillon, and that only by its capture could the Germans be compelled to abandon the rest of the Kriemhilde Stellung." Four pages later, he called the hill "the pivot of the retirement of the greater part" of the German line in France.[28] The capture of the hill greatly assisted the rise of General MacArthur; he was not reluctant to describe his part in the action and gave it a philosophical twist, as was his wont. He confided to Major General Charles D. Rhodes, designated as Menoher's replacement (Menoher was going to a corps command), that many excellent fighting field officers became mere administrators when they reached the rank of general officer, and the time came in every division when commanders had to instill the fighting spirit "by personal precept and example." In the fighting on October 16, he said, he had led the brigade "through the wire."[29] MacArthur received the effusive thanks of Summer-all, and confidential reports written after the war by leading generals of the AEF concerning their subordinates, Summerall, Liggett, and Liggett's replacement at I Corps, Joseph T. Dickman, rated MacArthur "excellent." Pershing's appraisal of the commander of the 84th Brigade, offered July 1, 1922, was something less. MacArthur had retained his rank as brigadier general after the war, and Pershing may have heard the self-appraisal he offered to Rhodes. "Should serve some years in present grade before pro-motion to next higher," wrote Pershing. "Has an exalted opinion of him-self."[30] But the commanding general of the 84th Brigade was on his way up, despite the opinion of the wartime commander in chief, and Côte de Chatillon had much to do with it. MacArthur became army chief of staff in 1930 with the rank of full general—four stars—the same as Pershing during the war.

Whereas the 42nd enjoyed success in the attack of October 14, the other divisions did not do well. The worst was the 5th, afflicted with the superannuated Major General John E. McMahon. Pershing had so many tasks in the Meuse-Argonne that he had no time to measure misfits until their incompetence was upon them. Although McMahon was Pershing's age, late fifties, his chief of staff, Colonel Clement A. Trott, reported that he seemed physically incapacitated. The general had slept through the St. Mihiel attack, in which his division participated, and it took him forty-five seconds to sign his name. McMahon was also softhearted to a fault. The commander of the 9th Brigade, Joseph E. Castner, wanted to relieve Colonel Hugh D. Wise of the 61st Regiment because he was unable to get around well enough to keep track of his men; they were straggling, and the colonel was sending unreliable situation reports. McMahon refused to relieve Wise because it would ruin his career. In addition, there was the general's ignorance of how a division should advance; he had no tactical judgment. Trott said that McMahon was "not entirely up" to the demands of modern war, such as the need to support infantry with artil-lery, machine guns, and planes. During the attack, reports showed that regiments were down in strength, not even the size of battalions. The casualty lists did not explain what was happening—killed and wounded on the first day were no more than a thousand. The reason was that straggling in the 61st Regiment was spreading to other regiments. Hines, the corps commander, went up to the Bois de la Pultière and discovered another problem: McMahon had put two regiments, an entire brigade, in

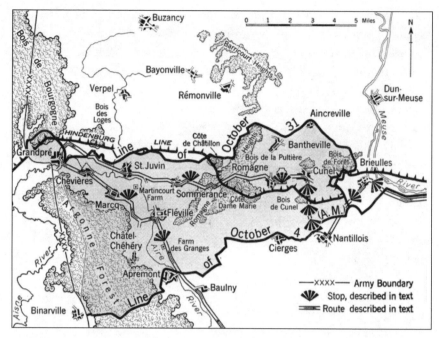

Ground gained by First Army west of Meuse River, October 4–31, 1918

a woods that required no more than two battalions—an invitation to German artillery.[31]

McMahon's case was one of the worst—perhaps the worst—in the AEF during the Meuse-Argonne. With agreement of Pershing, who happened into division headquarters on October 15, Hines sent McMahon up to the woods to thin out the troops. Rattled by the criticism, McMahon met Castner and his other brigade commander, Paul B. Malone, and kept telling them that he had "lost his job" (this was not the case, for that event happened the next day). When he insisted that Castner withdraw 200 men of the 60th and 61st Regiments, who had fought their way to the top of the nearby Bois des Rappes, Castner objected, for the men were holding. McMahon said that they were in danger of being cut off, in which case the whole brigade would collapse. He asked whether the 9th Brigade commander would obey the order, and Castner withdrew the men.[32] Hines then asked for McMahon's relief because of the bunching in the Bois de la Pultière. When he later discovered that McMahon had withdrawn men from the Bois des Rappes, he noted that doing so "cost the lives of many men and took six days to again gain the ground thus voluntarily given up." McMahon went back to the United States to command Fort Zachary Taylor in Kentucky. In February 1919 he was reduced to his Regular Army rank of colonel; he retired in October of the following year and died three months later.[33]

Poorly led divisions contained men of courage, and the 5th had many. Fighting in the Bois de la Pultière was ferocious. One of the officers reported that trails covered by enemy machine guns were worse than any Philippine jungle he had ever seen. Dozens of men were killed or wounded. The 9th Brigade lost forty-three of forty-seven new second lieutenants attempting to lead platoons through the trees and brush. In particular, two young division officers showed their leadership through acts of heroism. One was Lieutenant Samuel Woodfill from Kentucky, an individual much like Alvin York. Woodfill, an enlisted man, had been promoted to lieutenant after the war began and was given command of a company. It was during the 5th's attack on Cunel that Woodfill distinguished himself, moving ahead of his men and taking machine guns. Crawling forward, he looked for the black blankets the Germans hung above the guns to hide the flashes, aiming slightly lower to kill the gunners. In the course of taking out a group of locked-in guns, he also shot a sniper in a church tower. Near the close of his exploits he killed two Germans with a pickax he found at hand when they rose up to attack him.[34] The other officer who came to the attention of Castner was twenty-two-year-old Major Alexander N. Stark Jr. Castner said that, "without an atom of disparagement to then Lieutenant Woodfill, Major Stark was considered by my whole brigade as a far better fighting man than Woodfill, and continually showing more daring and indifference to personal danger." Nevertheless, Woodfill received the Congressional Medal, and Stark received the Distinguished Service Cross.[35]

In the final analysis, the damage done by McMahon could not be undone by relieving him of command. He destroyed the First Army attack plan of October 14. The divisions were supposed to go up to the Barricourt heights and beyond, but only the 42nd got anywhere, and in that division, only the 84th Brigade.

CHAPTER SEVEN

Reorganization

When the attacks of October 4 and 14 failed to make the gains that General Pershing had hoped for, he knew that he had to reorganize. That task consumed the last two weeks of October. There was still much to do to prepare for what proved to be the vastly successful attack of November 1, during which the divisions could finally move forward with the skill they had long lacked.

In reorganizing the line in the Meuse-Argonne, Pershing's immediate tasks were to remove inept commanders and, though he was reluctant to do so, allow the men to rest. He recognized the need to rid the AEF of commanders who could not do their jobs and bring in those who could control their divisions rather than waste them. This task he handled delicately if possible, ruthlessly if necessary. General Liggett, the new commander of the First Army, insisted that the troops be rested, and the commander in chief gave his grudging approval. Liggett saw that the troops needed to be provided with blankets and hot food and allowed to clean up. The dead had to be buried, and their replacements—men who possessed no military skills—had to be trained. Tens of thousands of stragglers (no one knew how many) were camped behind the line and had to be brought in and perhaps punished.

Roads in the Meuse-Argonne were a mess, the medical establishment was in order but needed adjustment, and the air service was unsatisfactory. The battle's infrastructure, if one could call it that, had never been secure. Operations had been organized so quickly, only two weeks after the opening of St. Mihiel, that when the men walked into the mist, fog, and smoke on the first morning of the first day, the plan had barely come together.

In preparation for the new offensive, the First Army had to tidy up the line just above the Argonne Forest, where the Germans had begun to retire but were not out yet. This meant taking the town of Grandpré at the bend of the Aire. The forthcoming offensive did not call for an initial thrust north of Grandpré toward Sedan; instead, the point of the attack would be to the right, with troops debouching out of the line before St. Georges, Landres-et-St. Georges, and Côte de Chatillon and from the Bois de Bantheville. That would be on the first day, November 1. On the second day, the divisions would move out of the area above Grandpré and head straight for the German jugular—the rail town of Sedan, whose four-track line supplied half the front from the English Channel to Switzerland.

General Pershing began the work of reorganization by ridding the AEF of incompetent major generals. A notable case was McMahon of the 5th Division, who was relieved of command on October 16 (see chapter 6). That same day, the commander in chief relieved the commander of the 3rd, General Buck, a loquacious Texan who kept informing the First Army that he had the Germans on the run, even though the enemy forces in his sector remained where they were. Pershing tried to cover up these dismissals, but the AEF inspector did not understand what Pershing was doing and began investigations. When General Drum was interviewed concerning these cases, he stated that McMahon and Buck had been transferred to the United States to train troops and that no investigations were necessary. But in dossiers on McMahon and Buck in Pershing's papers in the National Archives, it is clear that they were both relieved for cause.[1]

Major Generals Clarence Edwards of the 26th Division and Omar Bundy, once commander of the 2nd Division and then of a shadow corps in Alsace, also went back to train troops. Edwards had been a troublemaker since his arrival in France; he disliked taking advice from GHQ and was incompetent as well, a fatal combination. He possessed political influence, however, and was difficult to pry out, although all the senior generals, including Liggett (according to his aide, Stackpole), had been talking about him for months.[2] Bundy seemed old and irrelevant and was concerned mainly about his seniority; his case probably was not helped by James Harbord, Pershing's chief of staff and then head of the Services of Supply, who had served under Bundy as a brigade commander in the 2nd Division.

A special case was the relief of Major General George Cameron, who, after commanding V Corps, apparently asked to go back to his original division, the 4th. His corps had failed in the first attack in the Meuse-Argonne—notably the 79th Division under Kuhn, but the other two divisions had to be replaced as well. It was not a good score to have one's entire corps taken out. Even though, in the hectic movement of troops from St. Mihiel and elsewhere to the Meuse-Argonne for the September 26 attack, there had been no time to train the three divisions or assess the abilities of their commanders, and even though it had been Pershing, not Cameron, who had decided to send green troops to the Meuse-Argonne. Cameron had been in command of V Corps, and it had failed. His transfer to the 4th was only temporary, after which he had no place in the AEF.

It is not clear who arranged Cameron's passage back to the United States. In authority, it had to be Pershing. But behind it all might have been a telephone conversation between Cameron and Drum while the former was with V Corps. Drum had become disrespectful, in Cameron's opinion, and the corps commander said something like, "Look here, do you know that you are talking to a corps commander and a major general, and that there is only one man in this AEF who can talk to me like that and you are not that man?" While in the 4th Division, Cameron related the story to his 7th Brigade commander, Benjamin Poore. Lieutenant Charles L. Bolté (who became a general in World War II) married Poore's daughter and visited Cameron at Fort Benning in the 1920s, and Cameron also told Bolté of his run-in with Drum. Cameron believed that Drum had turned Pershing against him.[3]

At the time of these changes, Pershing gave up command of the First Army to Liggett and created the Second Army and gave it to Bullard. The new arrangement was overdue, as the commander in chief had more than he could handle. Liggett and Bullard received promotions and new authority, and there were other promotions as well: the raising of Summerall after the advance of the 1st Division was inevitable; Hines was right for III Corps, considering the way he had commanded the 4th Division; and Dickman, who took over I Corps, may have been a thick-headed German (as Stackpole wrote in his diary), but he was safe and no adventurer.[4]

While Pershing made command changes, Liggett gave his attention to the men in the divisions. They had gone into the front line with summer clothes and only raincoats—no overcoats, and no pup-tent shelter halves. After the first day, the weather had turned cold and rainy. One man, who later became a professor of English at Yale, was stationed up near the front with a medical unit and wrote on October 19 that the sun had come out for the first time in two weeks, a "glorious Indian summer day. The beeches turned russet, slopes were green or showed the brown of plowed land. The scene had a somber subdued beauty wonderfully encouraging to us who have seen so much rain and mud and drizzle and mud."[5] Then it became cold and rainy again. During the first weeks, hot food was hard to come by; rolling kitchens could not get up to the front line. Years later, veterans answering questionnaires from the Military History Institute said that they had been hungry during most of their time at the front.[6] The men were also lousy. Typical was this comment: "Couldn't sleep coo- ties were working overtime. No clothes off in weeks and we are crawl- ing with big lice."[7] The situation was no better in back of the front. The lice lived on the rats that abounded in the Meuse-Argonne. A sergeant at V Corps headquarters was in a dugout at Verrières Farm and had the chance to move from a bottom bunk, where the chicken wire sagged so close to the floor that he could feel the rats under him, to a top bunk. But he found it to be of no advantage, because "now the d— rodents prom- enade up and down the gutter, right over my nose, all night long."[8]

In two weeks, Liggett had improved the situation. Packs came up—or what was left of them after looters took their pick. Piles of blankets ar- rived. Hot food was up. The lice problem was remedied with autoclaves, showers that held a dozen men at a time. They had to undress in the cold and stand under the showerheads. At a signal, the comfortably warm wa- ter began to flow, enough to wet the shivering figures; then it turned off while they soaped. At another signal, the water came on again, perhaps for a minute, while the men rinsed off the soap—those who were slow had no second chance. When the men came out they received bundles of clothing, warm from steaming in a vat of boiling water. As the clothes cooled, they became clammy.[9]

The interlude before November 1 allowed the men to rest, although some of them had to undertake the disagreeable task of finding and bury- ing the dead. A diarist wrote that in the Argonne, bodies were "not hard to find." Chaplains, both Catholic and Protestant, helped with the work. One man noted, "I was about the only one who could stand to pull three very maggot covered bodies out of a foxhole, killed a few days before. That was the worst one I ever worked on, but once we found an American body in a cave."[10] Burying a body involved removing and keeping one of the dead man's dog tags and leaving the other on the body. The dead were buried in pits, their bodies covered with blankets and then dirt, after which a chaplain offered a prayer and a short sermon.

Two problems related to reorganizing the front were not so easily resolved: fitting replacements into units in the field and dealing with stragglers. Untrained men were useless. Liggett was under no patriotic illusion that one good American could whip any ten foreigners; he knew that "one well-trained, well-led foreigner is much more likely to whip ten good but untrained Americans." He recalled the battle of Bladensburg in 1814, when 1,500 British regulars drove 5,400 running Americans fifteen miles to the other side of Washington, which they were supposed to be defending.[11] Replacements were likely to become casualties. Every commander knew what it meant to receive men a month or two after they had been drafted into the army. A diarist complained on October 26 about what the "old men" were up against:

> This afternoon we received 27 men as replacements. Not a very good looking bunch. Some of these men never fired a rifle. They tell me they have only been in the army for a little over a month. This is awful, to think that we have to take these men up on the line. It's a crime. I feel sorry for them. Mellick and I worked with the new men all afternoon, assigned them to squads with the old men under the more experienced corporals. Actually had to show some of them how to load their rifles. Don't feel so good today.[12]

The 78th Division received 1,400 replacements on October 14 and distributed them among the regiments in proportion to losses. Most of them were of good quality—promising infantrymen, if they received training. But when the division went into the line two days later, four out of five new men became casualties.[13]

In terms of the other problem—straggling—some basic issues were in dispute. Although everyone talked about straggling and officers did their best to take measures against it, it was unclear how many stragglers there actually were and whether some men who appeared to be straggling were in fact lost or, in some cases, shell-shocked or suffering from concussions.

The provost marshal of the AEF, Brigadier General Harry H. Bandholtz, heard that the number of stragglers was between 100,000 and 150,000. This information came from a British general who had talked with Foch's chief of staff, General Maxime Weygand. Incensed, Bandholtz claimed to have evidence to the contrary and wrote to Pershing that this was just one more Allied insult to American valor.[14]

It is clear that much straggling occurred. General Haan of the 32nd said that his division had no stragglers, but this could not be believed. In one front-line division, an inspector came upon a straggler guarding a saddle with a rifle and discovered the guard's two reliefs nearby. Men who brought in the wounded returned slowly or not at all. An inspector found a wounded man on a stretcher beside a road with four bearers sitting alongside. They claimed that they could not get through Malancourt because of shelling. The inspector threatened to shoot one of them and accompanied them through Malancourt, which was not being shelled. One division reported that it had only 1,600 men in the line, including an engineer battalion; the latter at full strength would have amounted to 600 men. This division was taken out of the line and, on arrival at its rest area, had 8,418 men, not counting the engineers.[15]

Liggett was philosophical about the straggling problem and considered it common to all armies. Stragglers were "thirty-third-degree brothers" of the Ancient Order of AWOL (absent without leave). In the Civil War, the Union army had lost four times as many men to straggling as were killed. Stragglers were known as "coffee coolers" or "coffee boilers." They traveled in twos, because they liked company. When discovered, they jumped up from their fires and asked, "Lieutenant, can you tell me where the Umpteenth Regiment is?" The answer was, "Yes, right up there at the front, you damned rascal, as you well know!" The stragglers would make an effort to move but were soon back at the campfire.[16]

There was talk of shooting stragglers, but President Wilson would not allow such sentences. An inspector proposed a line of "battle police" a couple hundred yards behind the firing line, in addition to posts on the roads.[17] Duncan of the 82nd placed file closers behind each platoon, and his military police searched first-aid stations, kitchens, and YMCA huts and arrested every soldier without orders.[18] The more drastic the measures, the more effective they seemed. One I Corps officer recommended that first offenders be sent back to the front; second offenders would be imprisoned, court-martialed, and assigned the most disagreeable work possible.[19] Duncan's military police kept alphabetical lists of repeat offenders who, if caught, were put in cages and sent up to the line with signs on their backs inscribed in large letters, "STRAGGLER FROM THE FRONT LINES"; this subjected them to the ridicule of their comrades and "proved a very potent preventative of this offense." The signs, painted white, also made it difficult for these men to turn around. Perhaps the most effective measure against stragglers, because it was permanent, was that of Brigadier General Preston Brown of the 3rd, who told his police to throw grenades into all the dugouts behind the line.[20]

Duncan wrote that straggling in the AEF was never dealt with conclusively because of confusion in the back areas, where no one was really in charge. Another reason why measures failed was that Liggett's First Army commanders had their hands full. It was all they could do to prepare for the new offensive in the time allowed them.

The principal roads in the Meuse-Argonne, as well as the side roads, were still in bad shape in mid-October. The challenge facing the AEF's single engineer regiment dedicated to road repair was impossibly large, and the road problem had to be solved by makeshift means. The 23rd Engineer Regiment, organized along with other special engineer regiments by War Department Order 108 in 1917, had been recruited from all parts of the country. Its engineers came from the staffs of state highway commissions and included contractors experienced in road and bridge building and in quarry operations; many of its enlisted personnel were graduates of technical colleges. The regiment received motor trucks, repair vehicles, and special tools. It arrived in France in early 1918, when port construction and other basic engineering projects had been uppermost in the minds of AEF planners, and it was promptly broken up, its specialists and equipment dispersed throughout the Services of Supply.[21] Reassembled, it arrived at the Meuse-Argonne on the night before the battle without most of its equipment, including its trucks, which had long since been requisitioned by the SOS. Each division had an engineer regiment of 1,200 men, but they were often unavailable for roadwork; in the case of the 35th Division (and others), its engineer regiment was thrown into the line. The remaining engineer regiments did what they could about the road problem.

In I Corps, the makeshift arrangements for road repairs turned out well. At the beginning, when the roads were in terrible shape, the 317th Engineer Regiment of the 92nd Division was available. This was a fine regiment under competent command, and it gradually got everything under control. As its regimental history related, two days before the offensive, the 317th received the word to roll and barely reached its positions by the night of September 25; two of its companies went to the 77th, two to the 28th, and two to the 35th. One infantry battalion from each of the 92nd's three available regiments (the 368th was in the line) was assigned to each detachment of engineers.[22]

For the men of the 317th under Lieutenant Colonel J. Edward Cassidy, the first task was cutting wire, but they had no cutters. Luckily, Cassidy spied a narrow-gauge railroad track, followed the track to a dump, and came on a great pile of heavy-duty wire cutters. The next task was the roads. The Germans' first line of defense, a tangle of wire and anti-tank trenches, crossed the Route Nationale; Cassidy's men, together with their infantry labor force, got those obstacles out of there. Simultaneously, they attended to the craters between Boureuilles and Varennes. Then came maintenance. The roads were made of sandstone, which rain and traffic turned to mud. The high crowns allowed trucks and wagons to slide, and the mud ensured ditching. Cassidy put in timber sidings, stabilized by German iron of varied sorts found on the battlefield; then he cut the crowns and used them as fill. The sandstone was so soft that he had to resurface the roads every forty-eight hours. Crews slipped between traffic and did hasty tamping. For repair of the Route Nationale, it was impossible to bring in Telford stone from Neuvilly, six kilometers back, because of traffic and the lack of trucks; the 92nd's regiment had only a few Macks. So Cassidy's men flung everything they could into the ruts, including stone from buildings, and added to the fill by breaking up German pillboxes.

The 317th also sought to use the German rail system, with some success, but this was just beginning by early November. Cassidy and the regiment's commander, Colonel Earl I. Brown, divided the transportation work: Cassidy took the roads, and Brown took the rail lines. The Germans had relied on the latter, especially the narrow-gauge network, to bring in artillery ammunition. Brown thought that the German engineers had been careless about grading and their choice of routes, but the system of narrow-gauge lines worked. Brown also dealt with the much less extensive standard-gauge lines and had a line from St. Juvin to Buzancy well along by the time of the armistice.

In its work in I Corps, the 317th Engineers had to make do without equipment—the lack of wire cutters was just the beginning. After it opened a road between St. Juvin and Landres-et-St. Georges, a divisional truck train collided with a mule train and ditched trucks right and left. Cassidy had no Caterpillars and that night "borrowed" two from a nearby artillery regiment. When the narrow-gauge rail lines in the Argonne were ready, the 317th could obtain only three gas engines and one steam engine. First Army headquarters had plenty of steam engines but refused to part with them.

The AEF's organization of the sanitary corps in the Meuse-Argonne—the physicians, the tens of thousands of sanitary train men, and the array of hospitals—was by and large handled satisfactorily, and there was no need for stopgap measures. When the United States entered the war, the head of army medicine, Major General William Gorgas (conqueror of yellow fever in Cuba and Panama), knew that he could not rely on Regular Army medical officers to treat what would be a deluge of cases, many of them difficult. A group of civilian physicians, called in to investigate the surgical resources of the army, opened several old rosewood chests to find many "queer instruments of which we did not even know the use." One set was wrapped in a newspaper bearing the date July 11, 1898, and the headline, "Battle of Santiago."[23] Gorgas thus commissioned the best civilian physicians, such as the Mayo brothers of Minnesota, who became brigadier generals, and Cleveland surgeon George W. Crile, who became a colonel. Field hospitals were staffed with personnel recruited from civilian hospitals, and the civilians raised standards to a high level.

The future professor of English cited earlier wrote of his experience as a hospital corpsman and noted that everything came down to organization.[24] At Evacuation 8, six surgical teams managed eighteen operating tables. Each team covered three tables: one for a soldier waiting, the second for a soldier being prepared and anesthetized, and the third for a soldier undergoing surgery. Surgeons stripped off their bloody gowns and gloves, put on clean sets, and started at the next table. Each surgeon specialized in certain types of operations: wounds of the knee joint, fractures of the jaw and teeth, gunshots in eye, brain wounds, sucking wounds of the chest. On a single day, September 30, 1918, the six teams of Evac 8 operated on 206 wounded men with an average of 2.5 wounds per man. Thus, each team handled thirty-four cases in eleven hours, or more than three per hour. The death rate in the war was remarkably low. The death rate from disease and wounds in the Mexican War of 1846–1848 was 110 per year for each 1,000 men in the army; in the Civil War, it was 65; in the Spanish-American War, 26; and in World War I, 19.

One innovation that the civilian medical specialists inaugurated at the Meuse-Argonne was something they had learned during the great German offensive early in the year, when casualties from the British Fifth Army had poured into Allied hospitals, including those of the U.S. Army. British practice had been to operate on all surgical cases as they arrived, making no effort to sort them. As a result, surgeons close to the front lines often dealt with cases that were not urgent. In the Meuse-Argonne, the Americans sent two-thirds of the wounded back to base hospitals, notably those with lung perforations or through-and-through wounds that actually improved during travel time—it was a matter of letting nature take its course.

During the two weeks of reorganization, the medical teams worked on imperfections in the system, with incomplete success. One aspect of the medical scene that they could not remedy was that too many wounded men died in the field because they could not be brought down in time. On the first day, an officer of the 91st came upon train after train of stalled ambulances (or ammunition trucks substituting for ambulances), the drivers improving their time by sorting out the corpses. The road was marked by little groups of dead men, as regular as mileposts.[25]

Once the wounded arrived at field hospitals, there were medical lapses. Crile moved up and down the Meuse-Argonne checking on the situation. The hospitals, he found, were working fairly well, but on October 17 he reported that at Evacuation 114, which had no medical officer, "Everything is overflowing with patients," and "the divisions were being shot up and wards full of machine gun wounds." He also saw the results of cold and rain: pneumonia and influenza. "Every sort of infectious case was there, packed in as close as sardines with no protection. An ophthalmologist was in charge of these hundreds of cases of desperate pneumonias that are dying by the score." He blamed the army for what he saw: inexcusable disorganization, inexperienced surgeons treating serious wounds, skilled surgeons caring for the slightly wounded. He wrote, perhaps too critically, that "nothing seems to have been learned from the long years of experience of our Allies, the British and the French." He was tired, for he had been operating on twelve-hour shifts. There were 120 patients awaiting operations by surgical teams that morning, and in one night, 60 deaths.[26]

Last, in surveying the AEF's abilities and inabilities in the area of medicine, there must be mention of the influenza epidemic, which was at its worldwide height at the time of the Meuse-Argonne. The difficulty of determining its importance to the conduct of the battle is caused by a lack of statistics. The AEF counted medical cases only if patients were hospitalized. Then there was the problem of distinguishing influenza from the sector's many cases of pneumonia. There is no doubt about the effect of influenza on men in training camps in the United States, and on the men who boarded ships bound for France when the epidemic was at its height. Branch Rickey (later a well-known name in baseball) was aboard a transport during the war's last weeks and witnessed the loading of empty coffins; this bothered him, but he knew that it was sensible, considering the thousands of men on board. And before the voyage was over, he knew that the coffins had been used. The German army, it seems clear, encountered influenza well before the Americans in the AEF, who were infected when transports brought it in at the ports. One historian of the epidemic quotes Colonel Jefferson Kean, deputy chief surgeon of the AEF:

> 28 September: Influenza increasing and spreading rapidly; 1700 cases reported at Brest. Total in AEF Sept. 1–25, 11,910 cases.
> 6 October: Influenza and pneumonia have increased by thousands of cases. Case mortality of pneumonia, 32 percent. The situation is very serious.
> 11 October: Pneumonia mortality this week 45.3 percent.
> 19 October: No improvement in influenza situation in AEF.
> 26 October: Influenza and pneumonia decreasing. New cases fallen off 75 percent.[27]

In reorganizing the First Army for its new attack and, of much less importance (because of its smaller size), preparing the Second Army, one problem of infrastructure was never solved: the inadequacy of the air service. Troops in the Meuse-Argonne saw German planes dominate the air, and testimony regarding the air service's shortcomings was unending. The historian of the 33rd Division remarked rather blandly that the air service was "not as aggressive as would be desired." The commander of the 89th, General William Wright, wrote more acidulous comments in his diary. When the 79th was in trouble, it received almost no advantage from its attached aero squadron—the 214th French, which was under the American air service. The division received no reports on the position of the front line, and there was no telephone communication with the landing field at Foucaucourt. Two messages dropped at the division's command post called for "more barrage," but they had been written two hours prior to their receipt and did not give the position where the barrage was needed. The squadron's planes mistakenly dropped messages at the 4th Division's headquarters, even though the officers of the 79th had carefully pointed out its own headquarters. The 2nd Field Artillery Brigade of the 2nd Division heard nothing from the air service between November 1 and 11, compelling the guns to fire blindly; in contrast, German planes were out all the time. When the 317th Engineers worked on the roads at St. Juvin, enemy planes came over every night.[28]

How could this happen? Part of the trouble was training, or rather the lack of it. Squadrons had little or no opportunity to work with divisions, so assigning a squadron to each division was of little avail. In addition, there were not enough planes available to the AEF. Almost no American-built planes were in the air; the French furnished most of the planes the aero squadrons had—two thousand machines by the end of the war. The American air service had 45 squadrons, the British 97, and the French 260. It was true that the air service greatly increased in personnel, from 723 officers and 14,559 men in January 1918 to 7,692 officers and 74,272 men by the end of the war. But lack of planes prevented most of them from taking part in the battle.

Other difficulties limited the service. The fliers were too nonchalant, according to one critic; their routine of going up for action in the morning, returning for lunch at midday, and resuming action in the late afternoon was too civilized when the German pilots were up during much of the day.[29] Bureaucracy may have played a role as well, as the Allies liked to point out. On one occasion, the chief of staff of the 82nd Division reported to the First Army's pursuit squadron that eight German planes had been flying over the front line for the last four hours. He was told that the pursuit squadron objected to receiving information directly from divisions and that proper channels should be used.[30]

Then there was the feud between the two principal air service officers in France, Brigadier Generals Benjamin D. Foulois and William Mitchell.[31]

Both had served in the Regular Army since the Spanish-American War. Foulois had commanded the first balloon purchased by the signal corps; later, both balloons and planes were incorporated in the air service, which was under the signal corps until 1917. Foulois was an early flier and had gone up with Orville Wright. Mitchell began taking flying lessons in 1916 and was not much of a flier, which may have heightened the rivalry. Mitchell's critics cited his inability to land a plane easily, calling him the master of the "controlled crash."

In the air service, which was a young service, the rivalry had its effect, for neither man excelled at administration. Pershing had to put an engineer, Major General Mason Patrick, in charge of the service at Chaumont, while the rivals vied for command in the field. Mitchell came out on top on October 15, when he became chief of the air service of Pershing's Army Group comprising the First and Second Armies.[32]

After less than a month in command in the Meuse-Argonne, there was a question about Mitchell's attention to reconnaissance and the protection of troops from enemy spotting planes and balloons. The First Army G-2, Colonel Willey Howell, complained to General Nolan at GHQ that Mitchell was uncooperative on reconnaissance; Nolan went to Drum, who summoned Mitchell. The air service commander agreed to fly more missions but, to Nolan's disgust, "laughed off" the admonition and did not take it seriously. Mitchell maintained that weather in the Meuse-Argonne was so poor—in forty-seven days, only seven had allowed the taking of photographs—that he could do little about reconnaissance. Nolan wrote in 1935 that "there were enough interferences . . . by the weather and rain without having the opposition on good days of the aviation commander."[33] Meanwhile, German spotting planes were everywhere, and enemy balloons were up. When the planes or balloons came over, it did not take long for the shells to arrive. Challenging this spotting was dangerous, for spotting planes often had protection in the clouds above. Attacking balloons was equally dangerous. The Germans rigged them with wire cables that tore planes apart, or they sent up dummy balloons loaded with explosives. The air service reported that it shot down a hundred enemy planes and twenty-one balloons in the Meuse-Argonne, but according to the men on the ground, this had little effect.[34]

In the years after the war, when Mitchell became an advocate of bombing and strategic airpower, it seemed evident that his overactive mind had done more than its share to make the air service ineffective.

In preparation for St. Mihiel, desiring to command, he offered a policy statement that must have charmed his superiors at GHQ: "The Air Service of an army is one of its offensive arms. Alone it cannot bring about a decision. It therefore helps the other arms in their appointed mission." At St. Mihiel the air service had dominated the German air force, which did not commit its planes, probably because its troops were withdrawing from the salient. Thereafter, Mitchell began to assert his enthusiasm for bombing, which his friend General Henry H. Arnold, commander of the U.S. Army Air Forces in World War II, referred to as a desire to "blow up Germany."[35] Mitchell was so proud of a bombing attack on October 9 that involved two hundred American and French bombers that he asked Drum and Nolan to go outside their headquarters and watch the bombers go by. That particular mission dropped 39 tons on its targets. Tellingly, American bombers dropped a total of 139 tons in 1918.

Stackpole noted in his diary that the reorganization allowed only local actions during the last two weeks of October, such as tidying up the line and seizing whatever advantages were possible:

> Pershing turned up again, with his entourage and steam train. Drum and the General (as he told me) prevailed upon him to think that any aggressive attack except in a limited way in local operations should be deferred for a few days until it could be made on a wide front and until we have allowed say six divisions to get freshened up, available for such an operation. Constant general attacks with a pretty well used up force accomplish little now except an increase of already heavy daily losses.[36]

On the eastern side of the Meuse-Argonne, this meant pressure on the German batteries across the river, which continued to harass Bullard's Second Army until the capture of their sites in November. On the western side, tidying up involved the capture of Grandpré, beyond which lay farms and woods that ranged north to Sedan and the double-track railroad. After the Germans retreated from the Argonne and the lower Aire valley, they sought to hold the bend of the river dominated by the little town at the center where, moving to the west, the Aire joined the Aisne.

The hard-driving and not altogether agreeable General Robert Alexander of the 77th wanted to take Grandpré before his division was relieved and pushed his left brigade commander, Evan Johnson, to do so. He implied that if Johnson succeeded in taking the town it would repair the damage done to his reputation by his slowness in relieving the Lost Battalion. On October 14 the division began its attack by seizing the village to the east, St. Juvin, accomplished in large part by Captain Julius O. Adler commanding Company H, 306th Infantry. The captain was ordered to advance on St. Juvin from the right, with Grandpré farther down the road. After crossing the Aire, this scion of the *New York Times* (his middle initial representing the name of founder Adolph Ochs) took his company left and, by his own description, advanced in "gang formation," which apparently meant with no tactics at all. Along the way, Adler met an officer from the 82nd Division with a detachment of machine guns who approached to question the wisdom of entering St. Juvin with only a handful of soldiers. Company H numbered a mere fifty men, less than a platoon; it had a machine gun crew of four from Company B of the 305th Machine Gun Battalion under Lieutenant André. Adler replied that his orders were to take St. Juvin and Hill 182, a troublesome place (because of German machine guns) north of St. Juvin. The 82nd's officer said the northern part of the village contained "beaucoup Boches," but Adler's answer was more bravado. He claimed that he would take the village within twenty or thirty minutes. Company H entered St. Juvin at 3:45 p.m., and the action started when Adler, André, and another man turned north to reconnoiter. A German crossed their path, and Adler fired and missed; when the German turned to run, the group chased him up the hill. Nearing the top, they saw the crest lined with 125 to 150 Germans. The threesome opened fire with two pistols and a rifle, together with a Chauchat team from Company H that had come up. Fifty Germans surrendered, and the others ran.[37]

On October 15 came the attack on Grandpré, which was considerably more complicated and dangerous than the St. Juvin operation. It was only partly successful. The town's defenders fought, but the 77th managed to force them back, to General Alexander's satisfaction. The plan contemplated an attack by the First Battalion of the 307th Infantry, crossing the river; Colonel Sheldon of the 307th moved his Second Battalion to the east, hoping that it could come in from St. Juvin; and the Third Battalion was farther away, connecting with the 308th Infantry. The initial concern was getting the First Battalion across the river, which was unfordable because of rains. The men faced rifle and machine gun fire, as well as artillery from the Bois de Bourgogne above the town. The colonel relieved the battalion's commander for lack of aggressiveness and brought up a captain to replace him. The battalion's new commander sent patrols to the west, and the men found a ford that was passable. With the assistance of double-planked footbridges, the entire battalion got over. They occupied the town's east-west street, advanced into the two north-south streets, and organized for defense.[38]

In the early morning of October 16, the 78th Division came up behind the 77th and relieved it. The taking of the rest of Grandpré then became a major enterprise. Enemy troops defended the place to the end. They held a tongue of rock jutting into the town that ended in a thirty-foot drop. Artillery in the Bois de Bourgogne controlled an area to the east, Belle-joyeuse Farm, and the Bois des Loges; to the northwest, the enemy held the village of Talma, from which machine guns fired on a farm below and the road from Grandpré to Echaude.

The 78th confronted a town and environs that had not been taken, and it had its hands full. When the 312th Regiment waded across the Aire, the river was still swollen, and the men soaked their gas masks. Artillery in the Bois de Bourgogne fired gas, and a noxious cloud moved toward the regiment. As if by a miracle, the wind shifted and blew the gas up the valley. The first patrol entering the town received fire from rooftops and houses that killed or wounded every member. When troops sought to move north to flank the town from Bellejoyeuse Farm, the Germans shelled the farm with unbelievable intensity. Years later, an inhabitant of the farm who had been fifteen years old in 1918, André Godart, pointed out to writer Thomas Fleming—whose father had been a sergeant in the 78th—that the average number of shell holes per acre was 150; Godart had counted them.[39]

Everything was under shell fire or machine gun fire. Fleming's father was in a platoon of Company C of the 312th stationed just below the road out of Grandpré to the west, and machine guns in Talma had it zeroed in. One evening, Sergeant Fleming saw a major from division headquarters strolling along the road. "Get off that road, you goddamn idiot!" he shouted. But the major did not hear him. The sergeant jumped up and tackled the officer, and the two somersaulted into a shell hole half full of water. According to the younger Fleming, who heard the story more than once, the major came up out of the mud shouting about courts-martial and executions and then suddenly stopped, realizing what had happened.

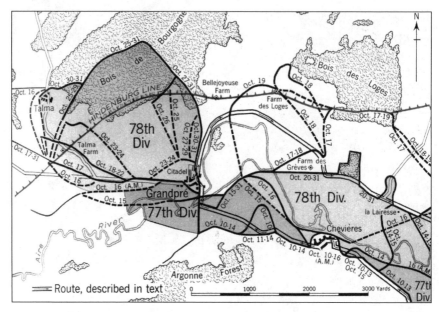

Ground gained near Grandpré by 77th and 78th Divisions, October 10–31, 1918

He then extended a gooey hand and said, "Sergeant, thanks for saving my life."[40] East of Bellejoyeuse Farm was the Bois des Loges, one kilometer square and full of east-west ravines that were like a piece of corrugated cardboard—perfect gas traps. When the 78th tried to hold the woods, its men went into the ravines to escape machine gun fire from the north and found themselves trapped in the gas; they had to stay there day and night with masks on.

The entire situation proved so difficult that on October 19, four days after the 77th had entered the town, it became doubtful that the 78th could remain. The division commander, Major General James H. McRae, and his right brigade commander, Brigadier General Mark L. Hersey, went to see General Craig at I Corps. Hersey's brigade had been shot to pieces and was down to 700 men. At midnight Craig called Drum at First Army, who talked to Liggett. Stackpole watched as Liggett, busy beyond belief with the effort to bring the battlefield into fighting trim, told Drum to tell Craig, McRae, and Hersey to hold whatever part of the Bois des Loges they could and for the rest of the division to establish a line on the

Grandpré–St. Juvin road to give the men shelter from shell and machine gun fire. They should join with the 82nd to the right and with whatever French forces remained on the left, west of Grandpré, and withdraw at once, before daybreak, without disturbing the Germans.[41] The 78th withdrew from the Bois des Loges but hung on to Grandpré. The division needed until October 27 to get the Germans out of Grandpré. The flank defenses took two more days.

During the remainder of the war, and after the armistice, a debate arose over what division, the 77th or 78th, took Grandpré. General Alexander of the 77th raised the issue, and his supporters included General Johnson, whose men had entered Grandpré. In one of the meetings of general officers that Liggett held to review the First Army's actions in the Meuse-Argonne, Alexander read a statement of a battalion commander (Major Fred A. Tillman) making the 77th's case. Liggett interrupted the division commander: "If the report of the battalion commander, which General Alexander has just read, is true, I cannot understand how bitter fighting took place for four or five days after. There is a mistake in that statement beyond any doubt. Is he an experienced man?"

"Well, he is an average major," said Alexander. He was being unfair to Tillman, whom he had promoted from lieutenant to captain for being the first officer to reach the Lost Battalion, and then to major for taking the lower street of Grandpré.

"If the town of Grandpré had been taken by the time stated by this battalion commander," continued Liggett, "then there would not have been such a fight as the 78th Division had to get it. The First Army cleared the Argonne," he concluded, "and the 77th and 78th divisions took Grandpré."[42]

CHAPTER EIGHT

Breakout

When the First Army, which constituted the bulk of the AEF, resumed its offensive against the Germans in the Meuse-Argonne on November 1, 1918, it was a far different force from the nine divisions that had jumped off on September 26. Everything was not perfect. If General Liggett had been permitted a few more weeks to reorganize the army, with more changes of command, more rest for the men, and more time to train the replacements that streamed into the divisions, its skills might have been better. Still, the army was a far more impressive force than it had been at the beginning, when men of the raw divisions had scrambled over precipices and down into the fog and smoke, trying to keep together. Pershing had opened the initial part of the battle with the tactic he knew best, which was to push commanders and men to get them moving. That tactic did not work; once the divisions came up against the German main line, they were stopped. In such fiascoes as the advance of the 35th under General Traub, they were defeated. When the commander in chief tried again on October 4 and again on October 14, these second and third attacks produced only a muddle, with the exception of the 1st, 32nd, 4th, and 42nd. Fortunately, Liggett stepped in, stopped the hammering, and gave the tired divisions a chance to rest. By November 1 the shrewd, unruffled lieutenant general was ready to show what the Americans could do.

A sign of the change—and there were many—was the use of artillery. After the war the army's artillery commander, Major General Edward F.

McGlachlin, described how he had handled his force. He had plenty of guns and an organization to back them. On a twenty-five-kilometer front he placed 1,538 pieces, not counting 38 heavy railway guns. Calibers ranged from the small guns, the 75s, up to the naval guns served by the men in the flat hats. Supporting them were ammunition trains, tractor organizations, artillery parks, repair shops, range-finding units, a meteorological station, airplane and balloon aviation squadrons, antiaircraft guns, and searchlight units. The way McGlachlin used these guns was far different from the firing by the map that had marked the preparatory fire and the crudely handled barrage of September 26, which, for all practical purposes, had been ineffective. The preparatory fire had shot up a vast expanse of real estate, making passage of the troops all the more difficult, after which the barrage got ahead of the troops and protected no one. McGlachlin ascribed to the principle that infantrymen needed protection, with no guesswork. Artillery brigade commanders brought guns up to the front line so as not to be out of range after the men went forward. The preparation was short, two hours, beginning at 3:30 a.m., and the barrage used the 155s as well as the light 75s. Gunners fired as rapidly as possible, ten to twelve shells a minute for the 75s—there was none of General Berry's pinging. The barrage was based on terrain: one hundred meters every four minutes on open ground, six minutes up slopes, eight through woods. On the 2nd Division's four-kilometer attack line was army and corps heavy artillery, three field artillery brigades, 255 heavy machine guns, 80 projectors with smoke shells, and 12 Stokes mortars. One-third of the fire from the 75s in the barrage, one battery in each three-battery battalion, was shrapnel fired just ahead of the high-explosive shells. The 75s had D shells, first produced in 1917, with a range of 11,246 meters; this gave the batteries more time after the attack before having to move up. Observers were everywhere to call in fire. Summerall, who remembered his own nineteenth-century tactics in breaching the walls of the Forbidden City, encountered McGlachlin on the field. "Oh, my God, Mac," he exclaimed, "your wonderful artillery!"[1]

The point divisions for the First Army were the two of V Corps, the 2nd and 89th; both were highly competent, ready for the fighting that lay ahead. The 2nd was a hybrid, a brigade of U.S. Army troops and one of marines. Suitably, Pershing had installed as its commander a gaunt, hard-jawed marine, Major General John A. Lejeune, filled with élan and willing to push his men, but independent minded, intelligent, tireless, and fit to command the 2nd Division in what proved to be the war's last attack. The 89th had been trained in Kansas by Major General Leonard Wood, who may have been the best trainer of troops the army had. He was also a political general, in the sense that he knew many people and did not hesitate to offer his opinions on politics and politicians, including the president of the United States, whom he cordially hated. Secretary Baker, Pershing, and President Wilson may have kept Wood from command of the division in France, but his skill remained, and the 89th was better for it. The 89th did not have the experience of the 2nd, but with Wood's training, it was just as good, as was the general commanding it. Major General William Wright was a tall man with a protruding nose and friendly, sad eyes. He kept a diary that documented what his division faced on November 1, including how he went out each day to the infantry brigadiers and colonels to measure their preparation or lack thereof.

The 2nd moved forward behind the barrage, and by the end of the first day it had gone nine kilometers. It took St. Georges and Landres-et-St. Georges with no problem at all. It is unclear why the villages fell so quickly, but it probably had to do with artillery fire. The history of one of the 2nd's infantry brigades relates that when the preparation fire opened, the sky was "alight from then until daybreak with the constant flashes seeming to come from every ravine for miles to the rear. The ground shook to the explosions. It was the supreme power of the Artillery, absolute devastation."[2] A secondary factor was the use of gas. With Summerall as corps commander and Liggett as army commander, there was no hesitation. The area in front of the 2nd was covered with phosgene. Evidence of the result was found in a German report discovered after the war; it stated that on November 1, two field hospitals admitted three hundred gas cases brought up from St. Georges, of which twenty died that day.[3]

By evening, the attack of the 2nd had been so successful that the German line was wide open, a sixteen-kilometer slot, with only a handful of troops between Buzancy and Nouart. The German 52nd Division had all but disappeared, with 1,000 men captured in Landres-et-St. Georges; only 28 noncommissioned officers and 178 men were left. Rearguard forces barely managed to get out the division artillery, eighty guns.[4]

By the morning of November 2, the gap in the enemy line was filled by the German 41st Division, coming down fast. Enemy forces began to

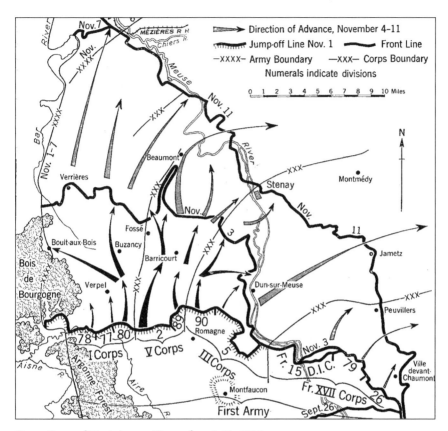

Operations of First Army, November 1–11, 1918

assert themselves with the usual machine gun nests and artillery; some pieces were brought down to the infantry line. It was then that American ingenuity stepped in, leading to one of the most spectacular tactics of the war (though it would have been disastrous earlier on any part of the western front). A conference of four colonels in the army brigade of the 2nd, led by acting brigade commander James C. Rhea, decided to try infiltration. That night the two regiments of the brigade—the 9th Infantry on the right and the 23rd on the left—took two roads through the Bois de Folie. The brigade started at 8:00 p.m., and procedure was simple: two columns. Men moved forward two by two. At the front were German-speaking scouts in patrols thrown out on either side, instructed to seize sentries as quietly as possible. If the enemy fired machine guns, the patrols threw themselves to the ground while squads in the columns

came up and enveloped the gunners. Enemy troops were altogether unprepared. Their sentries had slipped back into foxholes or huts and gone
to sleep, and so had the machine gunners. By the morning of November
3, when the forward movement came to an end, the 2nd had gone another six kilometers through terrain that would have meant heavy casualties in daytime.

On November 3 a mix-up in division attack orders made a daylight
advance impossible—runners could not get up in time to alert the regiments, which missed the barrage—so it was decided to try the infiltration tactic again, with the 9th and 23rd taking the same positions on the
right and left, respectively. Gradually the road the 23rd was on petered
out, and the regiment moved over and followed the 9th. Their route was
through a woods, the Bois de Belval, that stretched across the division
front for a depth of three kilometers. The columns started at 4:30 p.m.
in a pouring rain that helped disguise their approach, and again the defenders were caught sleeping. At one point the men came on a brilliantly
lighted farmhouse. In front of another house they found the automobile
of a German general, they believed. The troops saw batteries firing to the
south and let them continue, knowing that the fire was useless; before
long, the guns and gunners would have nowhere to go, since the Americans were on the only road. The night march of November 3–4 took the
2nd another four kilometers.

By the following night, November 4–5, the Germans had caught on
and were waiting on the road to Beaumont. That night the 2nd attacked
in broad battle formation.

The idea of night attacks looked to both the past and the future. At St.
Mihiel the 1st and 26th Divisions had advanced on the night of September
12–13. Summerall recalled those actions in commenting on the attacks of
early November.[5] At the beginning of the Meuse-Argonne, when the enemy was scrambling to fill gaps in the line, there had been opportunities
for night attacks, but the Americans had been too inexperienced to exploit
them. On the first day they attacked too slowly. Colonel Leslie J. McNair,
inclined to be critical, saw the men of the 77th Division sauntering, as he
put it, into the Argonne in broad daylight. The 28th, on the right, did the
same going up the Aire valley. Had both raced forward and continued
the attack that night, they could have made large gains; machine gunners were the Germans' only defense, and they would have been blind at
night or, if they fired, would have given away their positions. The attack

of the 35th Division on the afternoon of September 27, ordered by Pershing, lasted into the night, and companies advanced far ahead. Years later, in World War II, Sergeant Triplet of the 35th Division was a colonel with Combat Command A of the 7th Armored—4,000 men with tanks, artillery, and infantry. When the 7th got into Germany, he moved at night, taking town after town. This was in the spring of 1945, and although the German army was disintegrating, as it was in late 1918, it still had some fight left. In the second war against Iraq, in 2003, American armored divisions raced across the desert at night, tank gunners and infantrymen equipped with night-vision goggles.

In November 1918 the second of the point divisions, the 89th, made gains just as spectacular as those of the 2nd. The 89th went seven kilometers the first day, two less than the 2nd because Wright's men were in a salient, the Bantheville Woods.[6] It had come into the woods on the night of October 19–20, replacing the 32nd. The 89th's plan for November 1 was to keep the 177th Brigade in the line rather than bringing up the 178th, which was rested and in support. That way, the Germans would not expect an attack, although reconnaissance planes must have seen the buildup of artillery behind the division, so the defenders could not have been surprised. When the attack was imminent, Colonel Conrad S. Babcock of the 354th brought his men up to the edge of the woods an hour before the preparation fire. There they endured the sound of the shells going over, like so many railroad trains, and the machine gun fire that accompanied it. It seemed to be just above the heads of the men, an endless line of bullets like a gigantic shears cutting a mile-wide piece of tin.[7]

For the 89th, the first-day goal was the top of Barricourt Woods; the heights lay just beyond, the crest of the whaleback. From the heights the Germans had spotted the American artillery. In a lecture after the war, Colonel Ward of GHQ described the elevations of commanding points in the army's sector:

Montfaucon	340 meters
Argonne Forest	263 meters
Côtes de Meuse	400 meters
Romagne heights	300 meters
Cunel heights	300 meters
Bois de Bourgogne	210 meters
Barricourt heights	340 meters[8]

Babcock's 354th reached the top of the Barricourt Woods on the afternoon of the first day, and the division took the heights on the second. The men could look ahead toward the distant Meuse with its great bend west and then north toward Mouzon and Sedan. From the heights the terrain sloped down, with beautiful rolling hills and villages in between, each with a church tower. This country had eluded the AEF during its torturous weeks in the line. It was like gazing on the promised land.

The 89th, like the 2nd, had trouble on the second day, but it was short-lived, and soon the troops were going forward. The division's thousands of rifles swept back the defenders like a huge broom. According to Dale Van Every, "the operation was no longer a battle. It was a pursuit and the rapidity of the American advance depended only on the speed with which bodies of troops could be pushed forward."[9] The Germans' movement was to the Meuse, behind which they formed a line. But from the outset, that line was in doubt, for how could they protect themselves against hundreds of thousands of Americans? American casualties were acceptable, considering the gain. From November 1 to November 11, the 89th had 479 men killed, 4,662 wounded, and 168 gassed.

The advance by I Corps was not as spectacular, yet gratifyingly successful. With the assistance of the 78th, 77th, and 80th Divisions, and the 42nd (replacing the 77th) after the movement began, enemy forces were soon on their way to the Meuse. It was here that the famous (or infamous, depending on one's point of view) race for Sedan occurred. The race was the private notion of General Pershing, although he later denied any participation and sought to cover the whole business with the fact of victory.[10]

The first day did not go well for I Corps. The plan of attack was for a move forward not on November 1 but on November 2. The breakout of the 2nd and 89th in the middle of the line would flank enemy forces on both sides and compel them to retreat. But something happened, and I Corps jumped the gun. The new corps commander, Joseph Dickman, did not grasp the plan, and he allowed the 78th to attack into the Bois des Loges. Machine gun and artillery fire stopped the Americans, and by nightfall the woods were still in German hands. Prisoners said that enemy losses were slight, and the 78th suffered 519 casualties.[11] I Corps was so eager to get into the fray on November 1 that, as Liggett discovered,

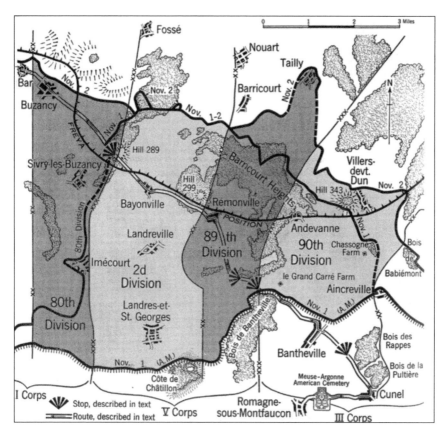

Ground gained near Barricourt Heights, November 1–2, 1918

it attacked Champigneulle above St. Juvin. Terrain around the village was open—no place for a frontal assault—and machine guns repulsed the Americans.

Dickman and the 78th did not understand Liggett's strategy of waiting until V Corps outflanked the Germans, and neither did General Pershing. The army group commander was watching everything from his steam train close to Liggett's headquarters, and that night he telephoned the First Army commander to congratulate him on V Corps' success and ask about the failure of the 78th in I Corps. Liggett told the querulous commander in chief to wait until the next morning and see what happened.

Liggett's offensive by I Corps could hardly fail. In addition to the outflanking of enemy troops above I Corps, V Corps' advance to the heights of Barricourt, the general took a special measure against the German defenders in the Bois de Bourgogne, the woods across from the Bois des Loges. First Army artillery drenched the woods with 41.4 tons of yperite, mustard gas. Gas expert Rexmond Cochrane, in his analysis of what happened in the Bois de Bourgogne, explained that army artillery always favored the use of gas, but in earlier phases of the Meuse-Argonne, the roads had been so clogged that the artillery could not get forward and was unable to reach the scene until just before the attack of November 1.[12] Few German infantrymen were in the Bois de Bourgogne, but it contained nine batteries of artillery of the German 76th Reserve Division, together with machine gunners. The action of V Corps in reaching the top of Barricourt and the gassing of the Bois de Bourgogne gave Liggett what he needed and what he had told Pershing to look for. After midnight, in the early morning of November 2, the Germans pulled out of the Bois des Loges, and later the right brigade of the 78th advanced without opposition. The left brigade moved up between the two woods, which would have been impossible before the gassing. There was silence in Bourgogne, where the yperite had destroyed seven of the nine batteries and expelled the machine gunners. The Americans saw bodies everywhere. Several days later, inhabitants of a village to the north told a unit of the 78th that many of the retreating Germans had eyes swollen almost shut and were forced to stagger rather than march.[13] The left brigade, passing between the two woods, reached the top of the Bois de Bourgogne on the evening of November 2 and made dispositions to outflank the remaining Germans in the Bois des Loges the next day, only to discover the task unnecessary.

On the second day, the three divisions of I Corps took up the pursuit, or, as Frederick Palmer described it, made up for lost time.[14] That day they went six to eight kilometers, and a similar distance on the third and following days. An engineer in the 77th wrote, "The advance of the Division from the early morning of the 2nd of November to the evening of the 6th was the most rapid in its history."[15] The advance was almost uncontested. The 42nd relieved the 77th at noon on November 5, in an unprecedented daytime relief.

The exhilaration of the advance was a result of its rapidity, but also because the ground was no longer pockmarked with shell holes, the woods were no longer splintered poles. The historian of the Iowa regiment of the 42nd was moved to near poetry in describing the scene, which was entirely different, he wrote, from "the hideous, shell-torn waste that lay behind." There were fields, timbered hills, ravines with rushing streams, groups of farm buildings "nestled" in clearings. The men "romped forward, unopposed, up hill and down, across . . . fields and orchards, splashing through tumbling brooks, pushing through the brush" as if explorers rather than infantrymen. Every now and then a village appeared, this time not a pile of rubble but houses with roofs. As soon as the Germans left, the inhabitants hung bedsheets from windows or tied undershirts to poles to show that the Germans had gone and to save themselves from artillery fire.[16] The attractiveness of the advance was marred only by the weather; the skies were leaden and overcast, and frequent rain muddied both men and horses. Adding to this cheerless part of the scene were flocks of crows scavenging on dead horses lying along the roads.[17]

The 80th Division on the right, to the right of the 77th and replacing the 82nd, did as well as I Corps' other divisions, although an investigator from G-5 (training), GHQ, who surveyed the 80th's progress wrote that it was not as skilled as its sister divisions. Still, he believed that there had been improvement over its work in the attack beginning September 26, when it had been in III Corps to the right of the 4th Division. He thought that its regiments were ignoring their Stokes mortars and that the use of 37-mm guns was inconsistent, depending on the officer in charge. The inspecting officer also took note of the division's use of white phosphorus smoke grenades, a remarkable new weapon that the 80th employed well. The phosphorus grenade was an easy way to take out machine guns. In a lecture after the war, the I Corps gas officer, Colonel John W. Schulz, noted that the 80th's units had trained with the grenades, assembling and firing them. At the beginning of the November attack, German machine gunners had crept forward before the barrage, and the grenades had driven them away. The advance was so rapid that not many opportunities arose to use the grenades. However, after other means failed to silence a nest of machine guns in a ravine north of Imecourt, the grenades forced the surrender of eight or ten guns and 200 prisoners. On the night of November 5, a machine gun held up a battalion of the 318th Infantry between St. Pierremont and Sommauthe, not far from the heights dominating Sedan. It was impossible to find the offending gun to put artillery on it, but three grenades in the general direction sent the gunners running.[18]

In the advance of I Corps, the race for Sedan was an episode of little importance, but it was memorable to the men of the 1st Division who did the racing. It began on the afternoon of November 6 and ended three days later. The idea of the race originated in a November 3 conversation between General Pershing and the commander of the French Fourth Army. Pershing, with a chip on his shoulder, told the French general that the latter had had no right to suggest in a directive that the American First Army was under French command. After receiving an apology, the American commander in chief raised the possibility that, in the general advance toward Sedan, the Americans might come closer to the city, and the French commander, in a contrite mood, agreed that in such a case the Americans could take it. Apparently, Pershing told the operations officer of GHQ, Brigadier General Conner, to involve V Corps and I Corps in a race to take Sedan. There is no evidence of the conversation, but that when Colonel Foreman asked Conner about it, the general told the colonel that the less said about the race for Sedan the better.[19] Conner told the First Army G-3, Colonel Marshall, to draw up an order for the two corps, but Marshall demurred, because neither Liggett nor Drum was in First Army headquarters. The officers decided that if Liggett had not returned by 6:00 p.m. that day, November 5, Marshall would send the order—a strange yet gentlemanly procedure. Drum came in at the last moment and added a sentence to the order stating that the boundary of the First Army with the French Fourth Army to the left would not be binding. The order went out in Liggett's name.

The trouble occurred when Summerall, the commanding general of V Corps, issued an order for the 1st Division (the reserve division of his corps) to pay no attention to the boundary with I Corps and cross it to get to the heights south of Sedan ahead of the 42nd Division. Meanwhile, Dickman, the commander of I Corps, needed no invitation to a race, since the approaches to Sedan were his territory, and his divisions, including the 42nd, were moving toward them as quickly as they could. There may have been some personal animosity between Dickman and Summerall as well. The 1st Division eventually ran into the 42nd, into the latter's field of fire. The acting commander of the 1st Division, Brigadier General Frank Parker, made several statements to lower-ranking commanders in the 42nd that he was going to carry out his orders, regardless of the 42nd or the French. The French, after a slow start, were also hastening toward Sedan and were anxious to take it. It was there that Napoleon III and his army had surrendered to the Germans in 1870, a defeat that all Frenchmen were determined to avenge. The prior arrangement between the AEF and the French had stipulated that the French would have the honor of taking Sedan. But Pershing later claimed that he had modified the arrangement to depend on which force, French or American, got there first.

The race infuriated Liggett. Pershing had gone over Liggett's head, and two of his subordinates, Marshall and Drum, had gone along with Conner in Liggett's absence. Liggett did what he could to minimize the damage and went to both corps headquarters. At I Corps he held Dickman's hand and spoke of a military atrocity. At V Corps, Summerall was out, but Liggett told the chief of staff, Brigadier General Burtt, that Burtt should have known better. As Liggett said at the time and later, if the Germans had known of the confusion and been able to counterattack, there might have been serious consequences.

Everything was back in order by November 9, but the personal irritabilities were long lasting. Liggett carefully backed away from the issue, saying nothing publicly. He later told his aide, Stackpole, that Parker was incapable of anything beyond a regimental command. Stackpole watched with care when, after the armistice, Summerall and Burtt came to lunch at First Army headquarters. They called, he wrote in his diary, to make sure that they were not under a cloud. "Nothing was said about it, but Summerall laid on the oily talk pretty thick, though he refrained from kissing the General [Liggett]." Dickman's memoirs, published in 1927, bristled with indignation at Summerall. Dickman delayed Parker's promotion to major general after the war.[20] When Pershing's memoirs appeared in 1931, the former commander in chief blamed Summerall and Parker and remarked, unctuously, that he would have disciplined them if not for everyone's contributions to the victory represented by the armistice a few days later. Summerall prepared a diatribe accusing Pershing of disloyalty and was prepared to release it to the North American Newspaper Alliance, but friends talked him out of it.[21]

An intriguing but perhaps spurious footnote to the race concerned General Douglas MacArthur of the 42nd. His principal biographer, D. Clayton James, raised the issue but admitted that it was far-fetched.[22] When 1st Division troops entered the 42nd's sector during the race for Sedan, a corporal arrested MacArthur—wearing a mashed-down regulation cap and a scarf and carrying a swagger stick—as a German spy. Released, he brushed it off as of no importance. A few days later, November 11, he took command of the 42nd Division upon the promotion of his superior,

Menoher, to corps command. However, Major General Charles Rhodes, former artillery brigadier of the 82nd, had taken command of the division just that morning, his orders dated November 9. This was interesting. MacArthur possessed more influence than a brigadier general ordinarily had. His father had been a prominent general in the Philippines, and when MacArthur was a colonel, his mother had written to General Scott, then chief of staff, that she thought "Douglas" should receive a star and be a general. She also wrote to Secretary of War Baker, with whom her son had worked in the War Department. Brigadier General LeRoy Eltinge of GHQ, deputy chief of staff, told Rhodes that the change of orders was a result of intervention from Washington, presumably Baker. But that made little sense, because Baker could not have sent such an order without consulting General Peyton March; the latter, though not averse to quarreling with Pershing, would have hesitated to make such an important assignment without consulting the AEF commander in chief.[23] MacArthur's biographer suspected that Pershing did not want Baker to find out about the race for Sedan and did what was necessary to ensure MacArthur's silence.

It is a singular tribute to the judgment of General Liggett that he did not allow the race to push him into more than momentary anger, that he restrained his impulse to speak to Pershing and continued his strategy for defeating the Germans. During the race and for days before it, the entire western front had been in motion, the line carried forward toward Germany, with northern France being freed of German occupation. Great events were taking place, diplomatically as well as militarily. President Wilson had been in touch with the German government, which, under its new chancellor, Prince Max of Baden ("Max equals Pax" was the slogan in Berlin), was asserting itself over Field Marshal Hindenburg and General Ludendorff. Prince Max was asking for peace on the basis of the Fourteen Points announced by the American president in his address to Congress on January 8, 1918. On October 25, at the behest of Ludendorff, Hindenburg asked German troops to hold the line against the Allies, to assist Germany in obtaining what he described as an honorable peace. The Berlin government at once forced the issue with the duumvirate at German army headquarters in Spa, which resulted in Ludendorff's resignation the next day. Meanwhile, the Allies under Marshal Foch had been advancing

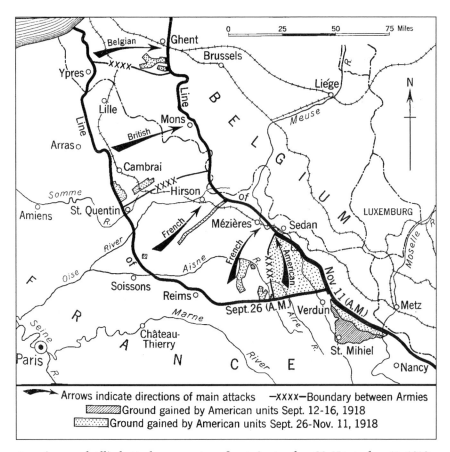

American and Allied attacks on western front, September 26–November 11, 1918

ever since the "black day" of the British breakthrough on August 8. The British and French armies opened what they hoped would be a final offensive on November 1. The British army moved toward Avesnes and the fortress of Maubeuge, which it took on November 8–9. The French took Hirson. This meant the capture of key points on the German four-track rail line, while the U.S. First Army moved toward Sedan. On November 2, American heavy guns were in range of the line, and on November 5, the light guns of I Corps arrived. The German army was in an impossible position, requiring an armistice.

Knowing what was transpiring outside the First Army's sector, but diverted momentarily by the Sedan fiasco, Liggett was turning his army

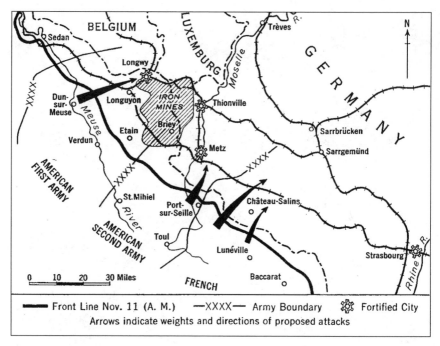

Plan of proposed American-French attack, November 14, 1918

from its previous east-west attack line to one that was north-south, putting the weight of his divisions against enemy artillery in the heights of the Meuse. This task, to which he devoted the last few days of the war, anticipated an attack on Metz by Bullard's Second Army, scheduled for November 14.

In the weeks prior to November 1–2, the batteries on the Côtes de Meuse had harassed the First Army, and attempts to get them out were unsuccessful. The heights were the best artillery position in the Meuse-Argonne; at four hundred meters, they exceeded the heights of Barricourt by sixty meters. The Verdun grouping of First Army artillery sent shells into the Côtes de Meuse almost without effect; only direct hits could take out the guns. From October 14 to November 1, the First Army sent over 48,725 yperite shells, but the success of this gassing depended on the wind and required the batteries to stay in place. A French battalion of 75s fired fifteen thousand yperite shells each day for five days and calculated that it covered five batteries the first day, four the second, three the third, one the fourth, and none the last.[24] The numbers declined too evenly, suggesting few results on any day.

Several attempts to cross the river above where the 33rd and 29th had gone over and where the 26th had replaced the 29th came to nothing. During its incursion into I Corps, the 1st Division entered the portion of Mouzon on the west bank. As patrols approached the bridge, the Germans blew it; mines exploded, buildings burst into flame, and machine guns and artillery opened fire. The 77th Division met resistance when D Company, under Captain Barber, tried to cross between Villers-devant-Mouzon and Autrecourt.[25] The company's engineers built a footbridge, but as soon as a few infantrymen had crossed, marking "the most advanced point reached by our division or any other American division during the war," artillery demolished it. In this part of the Meuse, the river was three hundred feet wide, the water icy cold. On the night of November 8, determined to save the detachment that had gotten across, the captain and part of his company went to where the footbridge had been and constructed a raft. Barber personally crossed in the face of machine gun and artillery fire and found five survivors, one wounded. He took the wounded man back first, but the raft overturned and the man was lost. Barber swam the river, stretched a rope across, and brought back the rest, one by one. A battalion of the 356th Infantry, the 89th Division under Captain Arthur Y. Wear, also tried to get across. There was no lack of volunteers to swim the river, most of whom drowned or were shot by machine gunners. Wear, who had just returned from the hospital, walked a short distance into the woods and shot himself.

The first division to get over in force was the 5th under General Ely. On October 10 it took Brieulles, which had held out for more than a month. It attempted to cross on the night of November 1, having to pass over a plain, the canal that paralleled the river, the river itself, and then another plain, while taking machine gun and artillery fire from the bluffs and hills. Three days later it gained a lodgment and took the high ground the next morning. By the evening of November 6, it had advanced two kilometers along a six-kilometer front between Brieulles and Dun-sur-Meuse. It widened this front to ten kilometers, three times the normal frontage of a division, and by the armistice, it was into the swamps and woods of the Woevre Plain. Ely's aide proudly described "a greater area than any other American division, an achievement that seemed typical of General Ely's commands."[26]

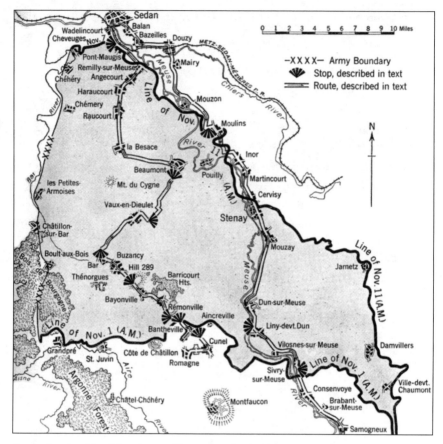

Ground gained by First Army, November 1–11, 1918

By the time the 5th was across the river and moving out, the 90th, above the 5th, was on the other side, as was the 89th above the 90th. On the night of November 10–11, the 89th's artillery shelled Pouilly for the third night to keep the defenders on edge, and this time, seven battalions crossed on pontoons turned into catamaran rafts. A regiment crossed at Stenay on the remains of the Laneuville bridge.[27]

The operations report of the 2nd Division, above the 89th, also celebrated a successful crossing. On November 10 the division sought to cross at two places—Mouzon and Letanne, to the south. Near Mouzon, the engineers had the task of swinging bridges from one side to the other. Artillery preparation began at 3:30 in the afternoon with a light harassing fire and continued until 8:30, when it turned heavy. After an hour, the artillery lifted in advance of the infantry. The enemy became aware of the bridging effort, and the crossing failed. It did, however, have the advantage of turning attention from Letanne. There, engineers got a bridge over, and marines had started to file across when, according to the operations report, "a lashing snapped and for a moment it looked as though all was lost," but a man snatched a rope and tied the break. The noise caused the Germans to open with machine guns and artillery. The first marines across silenced the machine guns, and two battalions of the 5th Marines got across, along with a battalion of the 9th Infantry. By the armistice, the 2nd's bridgehead was four kilometers wide and five deep.[28]

After the war, criticism descended on the army for allowing these attacks, with their casualties, so close to the armistice. Word had gone down to the divisions on November 8 that an armistice would be signed, but the date and hour of its going into effect were not known. Pershing learned that it would be 11:00 on November 11 at 6:00 that morning. Fighting thus continued until 11:00, which seemed useless, typical of the army. Congressional hearings took place, and Babcock of the 354th Infantry, who had seen men killed in the war's last hours, was in Washington and attended.

> It was sickening and depressing to hear officers like Brigadier General Fox Conner (West Point, 1898), my classmate, tell of the importance of our gaining a certain ridge or section of ground before the Armistice went into effect. What did these useless killings and injuries mean to officers who had never commanded men in battle, whose entire war experience was a war on paper, where the expenditure of human life was necessary but with which they had no experience, no responsibility, and apparently little sympathy.[29]

On the evening of November 11, 1918, men in the line lit bonfires and sat around them and sang, whistled, and laughed, celebrating the end of the battle of the Meuse-Argonne.

CHAPTER NINE

Victory

The cost of victory was huge: 26,277 Americans killed in the Meuse-Argonne. The question is, what went wrong? Why were the casualties so high? It is true that the Allies and Germany suffered far greater losses. Total American deaths in battle in World War I—about twice the number in the Meuse-Argonne—were minuscule compared with those of the other major participants. The army's statistician, Colonel Leonard P. Ayres, wrote that American losses were third lowest among the nations involved, including minor participants. German losses were thirty-two times as great, French twenty-eight, British eighteen.[1] But for the United States, the Meuse-Argonne was costly. The battle was not merely the largest in American history but also the deadliest. Twice as many died in the Meuse-Argonne as in the next most costly battle, Okinawa in 1945. There, deaths totaled 12,900; of those, 4,900 were navy deaths caused by kamikaze attacks.

The primary reason for the losses in the Meuse-Argonne was the failure of the Wilson administration to mobilize the economy for war. The failure of ship production had widespread effects. It meant that the bulk of the American divisions could not be brought overseas until Britain and France asked for them in January 1918. Even then, the divisions could only be transported gradually; Pershing did not have most of his divisions until the summer of 1918. After packing the men into holds, there was little room for anything else. The army stopped motor truck and animal transport in January, which meant that the American divisions in France did not have sufficient transport. Nor was there room for the supplies needed for port construction and to reinforce France's rail system. Added to this was the administration's failure to provide weapons of almost any sort. The huge economy of the United States could not turn out planes, artillery, tanks, or ammunition. Browning machine guns became available only in the last weeks of the war.

The failure of war production was accompanied by the War Department's incapacity in training. The department took its time constructing the cantonments, and when the men entered them, it allowed Regular Army officers to conduct training in trench warfare, just as the German army was transitioning to the quite different requirements of open warfare. To this error, the trainers added their belief, echoing Pershing, that the rifle was the most important weapon of modern war. They also provided bayonet training, which had no importance in the fighting of 1918. The men could not train with heavy weapons until the divisions arrived in France, although this was not the fault of the army. Unable to train men with weapons they did not have, the Regulars resorted to time-wasting activities, at which they were expert. Every morning they gave the men calisthenics, sent them off to dig trenches, taught them how to salute, and had them practice close-order drill. Training in France was no better. Pershing did not get far with his training program because, after the Germans' spring offensive, the AEF doctrine did not change, and there was not enough time for training of any sort.

The AEF found itself in the Meuse-Argonne almost before it knew what was happening, and it reacted clumsily to what it was up against, which added to casualties. In the great battle there were failures in tactics, the first and most important being in the use of artillery. The big guns were the principal killers in the war, causing 65 to 70 percent of all casualties. The AEF mastered this weapon when General McGlachlin reorganized the artillery for the attack of November 1, but only after earlier failures in the field. An error in organization assigned an artillery brigade, integral or attached, to each division in the line, whether the division needed it or not. The 77th Division retained its artillery brigade, even though artillery was of limited value in the Argonne Forest. An infantry officer later admitted that artillery fire was used largely for its morale effect; the men felt better knowing that friendly fire was ahead of them, even if it demolished trees, turned bushes into powder, and dug holes. Artillery officers followed rules for the use of guns that were theoretical rather than practical. Most of the preparatory fire for the attack of September 26 was wasted; enemy outposting in the Giselher Stellung was thin, targets few and far between and poorly identified. Similarly, the barrage did not work because, as McGlachlin's successor, Major General W. S. McNair, admitted, it was "universally" too fast and got away from the infantry; units often called back and asked for fire on places the guns had already passed.[2]

Once the battle was joined, procedures of the artillery brigades displayed egregious errors. Handling of artillery in the 35th Division was a fiasco because the guns could not get up to the front; 75s were forced into secondary roads or forest trails because of craters in the Route Nationale. The rate of fire was too slow—only one or two shots a minute, when 75s could fire as many as thirty. At a crucial time, September 29, when the right side of the 35th's attack line needed support, the division operations officer, perhaps because he was ill with pneumonia, miscalculated and started the barrage too far forward, allowing enemy machine gunners to remain until the infantry line met them. In the 77th Division, with its forested terrain, where artillery was virtually useless, Brigadier General McCloskey fired on the Lost Battalion when someone in one of his light regiments misread Major Whittlesey's location, which was exactly known. That shelling lasted an hour and thirty-five minutes.

For weeks, artillery commanders could do as they saw fit. Finally, in the attack of November 1, the First Army took control of artillery. McGlachlin and corps artillery commanders moved division artillery brigades to where they were needed. The 2nd Division received three brigades and the 89th received two, together with French regiments and dedicated army and corps guns. Direction was so specific that each artillery unit knew not only where it was to fire but also where its next position would be. Brigades opened fire close to the front line and moved forward successively; there was never an entire brigade on the road. For the attack of November 1, Mark Grotelueschen stressed the change in tactics for the heavy artillery regiments, the 155s. Those regiments constituted one-third of the First Army artillery assigned to divisions. In earlier attacks the heavy guns had fired on their own targets and resorted to targets of opportunity. On November 1 they supported the infantry: "the assault battalions must be covered by artillery in all stages of the advance."[3]

In a report after the war, General Summerall remarked on what he considered the best combination of fire, which appears to have been what McGlachlin used or close to it, with the purpose of saving American lives and destroying the enemy. What he advised was a fire of 75-mm high-explosive shells immediately in front of the infantry, a line of shrapnel one hundred meters in front of that, concentrations and lines of 155-mm shells three hundred meters in front of the shrapnel, and concentrations of eight-inch howitzers and guns firing three hundred to five hundred meters in front of that. Guns would neutralize enemy batteries by assignments of two to one. Extra guns substituted for those moving forward.[4] In an article in the *Infantry Journal,* McGlachlin reported the results of his November 1 barrage.[5] Prisoners stated that concentrations confined them to shelters and isolated them in small groups. Artillery prisoners said that they could not leave shelters to serve their guns. The Americans captured complete batteries, muzzle and breech covers in place, ammunition stacked close by.

Distinctly secondary to the importance of erroneous artillery tactics in causing casualties in the Meuse-Argonne was the lack of skill in dealing with enemy machine guns. The toll in casualties was 10 to 15 percent. In the Meuse-Argonne, machine guns served to hold back American troops. There was a basic conflict between commanders and men over machine guns; the commanders desired tactical gains, but the men, facing what Laurence Stallings described as the chattering assassins, were reluctant to place tactical success above their own lives. Pershing admonished his generals not to be stopped by, as he put it, a few machine guns. For him, the primary example was the 79th Division's delay before Montfaucon on the first day owing to a surprisingly small number of machine guns. Some days later, facing the failure of his second attack that opened October 4, Pershing sent out another admonition, well expressed by General Bjornstad in a message to commanders in III Corps:

> At 2:40 p.m. today the Army Commander expressed to the Corps Commander his great dissatisfaction with the progress of the attacking divisions, taking into consideration the fact that the enemy is not now holding his front with sufficient strength to counterattack and is, therefore, very evidently holding it merely with successive machine gun positions. He directs, through the Corps Commander, that

division commanders require brigade and regimental commanders to get in personal touch with front line conditions and see to it that energetic measures are adopted at once to reduce these machine gun nests. The Army Commander is convinced that the enemy holds principally with machine gun groups, with little support in the rear, and that these groups can be reduced by aggressive attack on the part of officers.[6]

It seems that the commander in chief gave little thought to protecting the troops, beyond his desire for energetic measures. On October 16, General Drum, probably directed by Pershing, sent out a memorandum to corps and division commanders on "Reduction of Hostile Machine Gun Nests," but it was no more specific than the solution offered by the army commander. The First Army chief of staff stated the tactical problem ably. It was necessary, he said, to occupy machine gun positions, not bypass them. As for how to do it, he advised using "all means available" and developing them "to the fullest extent." The means: rolling barrages, smoke shells, accompanying 75s, 37-mm guns, Stokes mortars, tanks, gas, machine guns and automatic rifles, rifles, hand grenades, and bayonets. "The ultimate reduction of the machine gun nest demands that the defenders be driven therefrom or captured or destroyed by the use of the bayonet or the threat of the bayonet."[7]

The answer to the human problem in attacking machine guns was more complicated. Barrages worked if artillery could be gotten into position, which was far from easy. How could one supply a rolling barrage or smoke shells if the guns were not up? Similar problems hindered the use of 37s and Stokes mortars.[8] Only two divisions had tanks on September 26, and they were nearly gone after the first days. Troop commanders did not want to employ gas. Use of machine guns and small arms against enemy machine guns required tactical suggestions, and Drum offered none. The less said about the bayonet the better.

Drum did not mention night attacks, used by the 35th at the beginning of the Meuse-Argonne and later by the 2nd. Nor did he mention (perhaps because it had just taken place) the tactic used against machine guns by the 29th on the Côtes de Meuse, where German machine guns numbered in the dozens. The 1st Landwehr Division in the Bois d'Ormont had a field strength of 148 officers and 1,879 men—not much more than two battalions—but it used 112 heavy machine guns and 216 automatic rifles. Going up Etrayes Ridge, Major Tydings sited his own machine guns by calculating squares of fire, behind which infantrymen moved up.

In the 89th Division, Colonel Babcock trained two regiments in what he described as "diamond tactics."[9] He drew them up after his bitter experience commanding a regiment of the 1st at Soissons, where, after suffering 60 percent casualties, he refused to throw more men in front of the machine guns. Summerall relieved him of command, accusing him of a lack of vigor. Before Babcock left the division, he talked to the officers and men in his regiment and elaborated the diamond idea, which, according to the 89th's division history, provided the ability to "overcome the resistance of machine guns with surprisingly small casualties." Infantry manuals prescribed flanking, but the usefulness of Babcock's tactics lay in the details, learned by training. When an enemy machine gun fired, the men lay down or got behind cover. After discovering the approximate position of the strong point, officers sent men into the attack position. At the front was a four-man group under a noncommissioned officer with an automatic rifleman, an ammunition carrier, and a rifle grenadier equipped with a tromblon for grenades, a cup-shaped mechanism that fit on the end of a Springfield. Behind the diamond, on each side, were flankers— soldiers with rifles or automatic rifles. The diamond group fired furiously so as to engage the machine gunners, while the flankers worked forward. Behind the diamond and the flankers were platoons, spread out so that they fired between the center group and its flankers. Companies came up behind in allotted order, with front-line men giving direction so that an echeloned battalion would not dissolve into small groups. Everyone fired while the flankers closed in.

It is possible that the First Army could have done much better with machine guns if the white phosphorus grenade, used by the 80th Division in I Corps' attack toward Sedan, had been available. The technology, however, was not developed until the war's last days.

It seems clear that if the AEF had devoted more attention to cleaning out machine gun nests, it could have saved many lives. In the years after the Russo-Japanese War, which had seen the use of artillery and machine guns, the Regular Army paid little attention. Training at Leavenworth, ·which was supposed to bring the Regular Army up to date, took its lessons from the Civil War and the Franco-Prussian War. After the Spanish-

American War the army basked in its experiences in the Philippines and the Caribbean. When a second real war began in Europe in the twentieth century, it sent observers but filed their dispatches in the War Department.[10]

Last among the tactics that assured casualties in the Meuse-Argonne was the AEF's reluctance, until the war's last days, to use poison gas. That reluctance was understandable. When the Germans employed it at Ypres, its use was attributed to "the Hun." There was also a vague fear that gas would bring retaliation or that troops handling the artillery, cylinders, or projectors (four-inch Stokes mortars) would allow the poison clouds to get out of hand.[11] The 26th Division had an experience that, though not publicized, became well known. Near Lahayville on May 31, 1918, part of a battalion went forward in a trench raid, and the division artillery commander (probably without consulting the division gas officer) put phosgene on the village. It happened to be on a rise of ground, and because the wind was wrong, the cloud went back on the men, who thought that they were smelling high explosives. Their major wrote that they were bothered "by the fumes from our shells, many men being rendered very sick, vomiting and gasping." Every man in the unit, 234, became a gas casualty.[12]

What commanders did not understand was that by 1918, gas was a staple of war.[13] More gas was used that year by both sides than in the previous three years combined. From the beginning of the Meuse-Argonne, the Germans used gas in ingenious ways. When the 1st Division took over the 35th's sector and the men stationed themselves in ravines, the Germans turned the ravines into gas traps. They often fired gas in quantities sufficient to cause troops to wear masks, which tired the men. They fired just enough gas shells to debilitate the troops without masks—this was a common procedure in the 42nd's sector before St. Georges and Landres-et-St. Georges and the Côte de Chatillon. The neighboring 32nd Division received the same treatment. Gradually, gas discipline deteriorated.

For days at a time a few gas shells were fired along with high explosives and shrapnel, resulting in a more or less continuous use of the respirator by our troops. Some casualties were inflicted by this means, but more especially gas discipline was put under a severe strain, as frequently, particularly in the newer divisions, the wearing of masks extended to many more troops than was necessary to actually protect against the small number of gas shells fired. The procedure was apparently a definitely planned attempt to force large numbers of our troops to repeatedly put on their masks, and in many cases needlessly, thus tending to destroy the respect of our troops for the effectiveness of gas warfare and consequently to seriously undermine their gas discipline. Following such a wearing-out shelling, the copious use of gas shells in normal concentrations was successful in inflicting fairly heavy casualties on some of our troops.[14]

In the above appraisal, Colonel Schulz mentioned the new mustard high-explosive shell. Men encountering it did not realize they were receiving gas. Failure to appreciate the importance of gas cost the First Army 18,670 casualties, or 20 percent of the wounded in the Meuse-Argonne. This was a heavy cost for failing, until the war's last days, to analyze a problem and take measures against it.

It is impossible to know how casualties might have been affected if commanders had resorted to gas from the beginning, but something needed to be done. In the middle of the First Army line on November 1, St. Georges and Landres-et-St. Georges received a drenching, together with heavy artillery fire, and gave way immediately. On the I Corps side, a brigade of the 78th Division passed up the Bois de Bourgogne and flanked the Bois des Loges, thanks to gassing of the former.[15] If the First Army had given the enemy a sure understanding that any use of gas, even small quantities, would bring massive retaliation, that might have stopped the gas casualties on both sides.

It is another story how the costly victory in the Meuse-Argonne—and the even more costly victories in other battles by the British and French—came to naught in subsequent years because of the inattention and wrongheaded policies of the nations opposing Germany in 1914–1918. For a while, the French army dominated Europe, but when its competence was waning in the 1930s, it trusted in the Maginot Line. The British government trusted in the Royal Navy, having reverted to its pre-1914 outlook that fighting on the Continent was not in its national interest. During these years, any sort of cooperation against a German military resurgence would have succeeded. But the two democratic nations did not attempt it because their peoples and governments did not wish to.

In the interwar years, the people of the United States could have ensured peace in Europe but gave it little attention, absorbed in their own, largely internal, affairs. The Paris Peace Conference failed in large part because President Wilson dominated the American delegation and refused to give attention to his Republican opponents, especially in the Senate. The presidents after him offered little leadership until events spiraled out of control. Warren G. Harding had visited Europe before his presidency but saw no European dangers, and in fact, there were none. Calvin Coolidge never left the country, except for a wedding trip to Canada and a short visit to Cuba in 1928. He once told the British ambassador's wife that he saw no reason to visit Europe, that he could learn nothing there. Herbert Hoover was the most traveled president in American history, having been a mining engineer, but he was absorbed with the Great Depression in 1930–1933. Like Hoover, Franklin D. Roosevelt had to focus on the country's economic troubles. He possessed some knowledge of Europe, sensed trouble, but did little about it, content with reciprocal trade agreements and the neutrality pronouncements of Congress. During the interwar years, the U.S. Army returned to its pre-1917 cocoon, and the U.S. Navy constructed battleships and heavy cruisers that had little to do with the possibility of another German submarine threat.

All this and more lay ahead after victory in 1918.

NOTES

Abbreviations

AEF   American Expeditionary Forces
c.-in-c.   commander in chief
GHQ   general headquarters
RG   Record Group (National Archives, College Park, Md.)

Preface

1. Paul F. Braim, *The Test of Battle: The American Expeditionary Forces in the Meuse-Argonne Campaign* (Newark: University of Delaware Press, 1987), is a general history of the AEF with only a cursory account of the battle.

Chapter 1. Preparation

1. Frederick Palmer, *Our Gallant Madness* (Garden City, N.Y.: Doubleday, Doran, 1937), 29.
2. Arthur S. Link, *Wilson the Diplomatist: A Look at His Major Foreign Policies* (Baltimore: Johns Hopkins University Press, 1957), 27; Arthur P. Dudden, ed., *Woodrow Wilson and the World of Today* (Philadelphia: University of Pennsylvania Press, 1957), 10; Arthur S. Link, *Woodrow Wilson: A Brief Biography* (Cleveland, Ohio: World, 1963), 69.
3. William J. Williams, *The Wilson Administration and the Shipbuilding Crisis of 1917: Steel Ships and Wooden Steamers* (Lewiston, N.Y.: Mellen, 1992); Jeffrey J. Safford, *Wilsonian Maritime Diplomacy: 1913–1921* (New Brunswick, N.J.: Rutgers University Press, 1978); Robert Hessen, *Steel Titan: The Life of Charles M. Schwab* (New York: Oxford University Press, 1975).
4. Daniel R. Beaver, *Newton D. Baker and the American War Effort: 1917–1919* (Lincoln: University of Nebraska Press, 1966); I. B. Holley Jr., *Ideas and Weapons: Exploitation of the Aerial Weapon by the United States during World War I: A Study in the Relationship of Technological Advance, Military Doctrine, and the Development of Weapons* (New Haven, Conn.: Yale University Press, 1953).
5. William J. Snow, *Signposts of Experience: World War Memoirs* (Washington, D.C.: U.S. Field Artillery Association, 1941).
6. S. L. A. Marshall, "On Heavy Artillery: American Experience in Four Wars," *Parameters* 8 (1978): 3–4.
7. Mark E. Grotelueschen, *Doctrine under Fire: American Artillery Employment in World War I* (Westport, Conn.: Greenwood, 2001), 132, relates that of Americans killed and wounded in the war, 56 percent were from shells and shrapnel, 32 percent from gas, and 9 percent from rifle and machine gun fire. Rexmond C. Cochrane, *The 78th Division at the Kriemhilde Stellung: October 1918* (Washington, D.C.: U.S. Army Chemical Corps, 1957), 76, calculated 20 percent gas casualties;

of the 92,022 cases admitted to hospitals from September 27 to November 16, 18,670 were gas casualties.

8. Dale E. Wilson, *Treat 'Em Rough: The Birth of American Armor, 1917–20* (Novato, Calif.: Presidio, 1989), 16.

9. Alfred D. Chandler Jr. and Stephen Salsbury, *Pierre S. Du Pont and the Making of the Modern Corporation* (New York: Harper & Row, 1971), 359–430.

10. John J. Pershing, *My Experiences in the World War,* 2 vols. (New York: Stokes, 1931), 1:221–222.

11. Robert L. Bullard, *Personalities and Reminiscences of the War* (Garden City, N.Y.: Doubleday, Page, 1925), 22.

12. Scott served from April 1917 until he left for Russia on a fact-finding mission in May. Bliss became acting chief of staff until Scott returned in August. Scott retired as chief of staff the next month, and Bliss served until he went to Europe in the autumn, when Biddle became acting chief. Bliss returned in December but was soon back in Europe, and Biddle again became acting chief until the appointment of Bliss's successor.

13. Edward M. Coffman, *The Hilt of the Sword: The Career of Peyton C. March* (Madison: University of Wisconsin Press, 1966). March's memoirs, *The Nation at War* (Garden City, N.Y.: Doubleday, Doran, 1934), were an obvious effort to counter Pershing's triumphalism in *My Experiences in the World War.* March had done well in the War Department, more than almost any other officer would have accomplished, and a good editor could have excised his splenetic comments about Pershing and perhaps his clear-eyed remarks about Secretary Baker. His account of Baker was close to humorous:

> At an early date in handling my duties, I had taken personal control of the War Department business, with the result that a custom, which had grown up under my predecessors, of chiefs of bureaus dropping in on the Secretary to discuss matters pertaining to their bureau, and to obtain personal action by the Secretary, entirely disappeared. The great mass of all military business from whatever source it emanated was handled by me, leaving the Secretary completely free to consider the higher matters of his office. . . . It gave him time, too, to write the remarkable letters which he sent to our representatives in every quarter of the globe. . . . At first he frankly did not like the situation, and spoke to me about the disappearance of the bureau chiefs from his list of callers. But he quickly saw it doubled his efficiency. (March, *Nation at War,* 371–372)

Thereupon he awarded Baker an extravagant encomium: "It is my considered opinion that Newton D. Baker is the greatest War Secretary this Nation has ever produced" (ibid., 373).

14. James W. Rainey, "Ambivalent Warfare: The Tactical Doctrine of the AEF in World War I," *Parameters* 13 (1983): 34–45; James W. Rainey, "The Questionable Training of the AEF in World War I," *Parameters* 22 (1992–1993): 89–103; Timothy K. Nenninger, "Tactical Dysfunction in the AEF: 1917–1918," *Military Affairs* 51 (1987): 177–181; Timothy K. Nenninger, "Unsystematic as a Mode of Command: Commanders and the Process of Command in the American Expeditionary Forces, 1917–1918," *Journal of Military History* 64 (2000): 739–768; Timothy K. Nenninger, "American Military Effectiveness in the First World War," in *Military*

Effectiveness: The First World War, ed. Allan R. Millett and Williamson Murray (Boston: Allen & Unwin, 1988), 116–156; Douglas V. Johnson II, "A Few 'Squads Left' and Off to France: Training the American Army in the United States in World War I" (dissertation, Temple University, 1993); Kenneth E. Hamburger, *Learning Lessons in the American Expeditionary Forces* (Washington, D.C.: U.S. Army Center of Military History, n.d.).

15. Rainey, "Questionable Training," 93.

16. "Then, by way of offering us something new to occupy our attention, a complete schedule appeared, announcing a succession of close-order drills." William L. Langer, *Gas and Flame in World War I* (New York: Knopf, 1965), 18.

17. Pershing, *My Experiences in the World War,* 1:380.

18. Robert H. Ferrell, *Collapse at Meuse-Argonne: The Failure of the Missouri-Kansas Division* (Columbia: University of Missouri Press, 2004), 10.

19. Rainey, "Ambivalent Warfare," 41.

Chapter 2. The American Expeditionary Forces

1. After the war, a controversy raged over Haig's undertaking of this disastrous offensive, especially continuing it into November 1917. Here, B. H. Liddell Hart ("How Myths Grow—Passchendaele," *Military Affairs* 28 [1964–1965]: 185) may have had the last word: "Haig had great qualities as a leader of the British Army in war—above all, the strength of his faith, confidence, and determination. These qualities were invaluable in the earlier and later stages of the war, but worked out less happily in the middle period of entrenched deadlock." Leaders of the British government proved incapable of preventing or stopping the offensive; see Brian Bond, "Soldiers and Statesmen: British Civil-Military Relations in 1917," *Military Affairs* 32 (1969): 62–75.

2. Tim Travers, "Reply to John Hussey: The Movement of German Divisions to the Western Front, Winter 1917–1918," *War in History* 5 (1998): 367–370; I am indebted to Edward M. Coffman for calling my attention to this article. In preparation for the offensive, the German high command brought in as many troops as it believed it could, given the occupation of Russia. It left forty divisions, including three of cavalry. The Italian defeat at Caporetto in October 1917 does not seem to have had any effect on the western front, even though the Austrians and Germans took 275,000 prisoners and advanced sixty miles.

3. There was more to Gough's delinquencies than failure to prepare rear trenches. "Officers who served under him formed the opinion that lives were lost in the battles he organized because he failed to coordinate artillery support with infantry assaults, failed to limit his objectives to attainable ends, failed to curtail operations that had patently failed and failed to meet the standards of administrative efficiency which the commander of the neighboring Second Army, General [Sir John] Plumer, so estimably did." John Keegan, *The First World War* (New York: Knopf, 1999), 395.

4. For the German army's preparation and conduct of the offensive, see Holger H. Herwig, *The First World War: Germany and Austria-Hungary, 1914–1918* (London: Arnold, 1997), 294–296, 351–432. Herwig's book is a revision of the British-centered school of Liddell Hart and makes full use of German and Austro-

Hungarian archives. For the causes of the near collapse of the Allied line, see Tim Travers, *How the War Was Won: Command and Technology in the British Army on the Western Front: 1917–1918* (London: Routledge, 1992), 50–91. Travers contends that Gough was partly responsible, along with the commander of the British Third Army, Sir Julian Byng, whose army retreated even more rapidly than did Gough's. Primarily, however, he blames Field Marshal Haig, who did not understand his own tactic against a German attack, which was a defense in depth. Haig made little or no effort to see what his army, corps, and division commanders were doing in preparation. Moreover, the command structure of the British Expeditionary Force was vertical, rather than horizontal, meaning that there was little liaison. In the crisis, the command structure disintegrated.

5. The Germans manufactured seven of these guns and used several, because the limit of each was fifty rounds, after which it had to be rebored. The guns were 120 feet long.

6. Allied cooperation has a large literature; see David F. Trask, *The AEF and Coalition Warmaking: 1917–1918* (Lawrence: University Press of Kansas, 1993), and Robert B. Bruce, *A Fraternity of Arms: America and France in the Great War* (Lawrence: University Press of Kansas, 2003).

7. Donald Smythe, *Pershing: General of the Armies* (Bloomington: Indiana University Press, 1988), 101.

8. Ibid., 145. The biographer wrote that Pershing "was much more fluid on the amalgamation question than people have given him credit for. All along—and Pershing was consistent on this—he maintained that should the emergency require it, he would do whatever was necessary, even to the extent of putting doughboys into Allied ranks by companies."

9. Hermann von Giehrl, "The American Expeditionary Forces in Europe, 1917–1918," *Infantry Journal* 20 (1922): 296.

10. William L. Langer, *Gas and Flame in World War I* (New York: Knopf, 1965), 9.

11. Forrest C. Pogue, *George C. Marshall: Education of a General, 1880–1930* (New York: Viking, 1963), 155, 160; George B. Duncan, "Reminiscences of the World War," 11:72–73, courtesy of Edward M. Coffman.

12. Smythe, *Pershing: General of the Armies*, 107.

13. For General Traub, see chapter 4. Smythe wrote that the French corps commander made such a liberal distribution of Croix de Guerres that it was impossible to discipline commanders in the 26th. In addition, disciplinary action would have been difficult, because trench raids almost always succeeded. Pershing thereafter forbade the acceptance of foreign medals except with the approval of GHQ.

14. For Cantigny, see Allan R. Millett, *The General: Robert L. Bullard and Officership in the United States Army: 1881–1925* (Westport, Conn.: Greenwood, 1975), 359–365.

15. Barrie Pitt, *1918: The Last Act* (London: Cassell, 1962), 156.

16. Douglas V. Johnson II and Rolfe E. Hillman Jr., *Soissons: 1918* (College Station: Texas A&M University Press, 1999), 46ff.; Mark E. Grotelueschen, *Doctrine under Trial: American Artillery Employment in World War I* (Westport, Conn.: Greenwood, 2001), 61, 68, 71. Casualties are in *Report of the Secretary of War to the President: 1926* (Washington, D.C.: Government Printing Office, 1926), 226.

17. For casualties at St. Mihiel, see *Report of the Secretary of War,* 235.

18. Grotelueschen, *Doctrine under Trial,* 76n.

19. Clark to Pershing, Sept. 15, 1918, box 2, entry 22, RG 200, Pershing papers.

20. Martin Blumenson, *The Patton Papers,* 2 vols. (Boston: Houghton Mifflin, 1974), 1:591–592.

21. Allan R. Millett, "Over Where? The AEF and the American Strategy for Victory, 1917–1918," in *Against All Enemies: Interpretations of American Military History from Colonial Times to the Present,* ed. Kenneth J. Hagan and William R. Roberts (Westport, Conn.: Greenwood, 1986), 235–256.

22. George C. Marshall, *Memoirs of My Service in the World War: 1917–1918,* ed. James L. Collins Jr. (Boston: Houghton Mifflin, 1976), 146; D. Clayton James, *The Years of MacArthur: 1880–1941* (Boston: Houghton Mifflin, 1970), 206–210; Smythe, *Pershing: General of the Armies,* 188.

23. Hunter Liggett, *A.E.F.: Ten Years Ago in France* (New York: Dodd, Mead, 1928), 159.

24. Max von Gallwitz to Thomas M. Johnson, Mar. 20, 1928, "German Fifth Army Report," box 17, Hugh A. Drum papers. General Drum, to whom Johnson sent the letter, was chief of staff of the First Army. "The subject was cause for controversy for many years after the war. In the early postwar years Drum vigorously defended, both publicly and privately, Pershing's decision. He said 'that wasn't our purpose. The real objective was the Meuse-Argonne campaign.'" In a lecture at the Army War College in 1934, he changed his mind. Elliott L. Johnson, "The Military Experiences of General Hugh A. Drum from 1898–1918" (dissertation, University of Wisconsin, 1975), 315–316.

25. Notes on conversation between Pershing and Foch, folder 986-A, box 3143, GHQ G-3, entry 267, RG 120; "Notes on Conference between General Pershing, Marshal Foch, and General Pétain at Bombon," Sept. 2, 1918, *United States Army in the World War,* 17 vols. (Washington, D.C.: Government Printing Office, 1948), 2:589–592.

26. Clark to Pershing, Sept. 1, 1918, box 2, entry 22, RG 200, Pershing papers.

27. Roy V. Myers memoir, 39, Myers papers.

28. Drum learned of the Meuse-Argonne the evening of Foch's visit to Pershing. "The Military Experiences of General Hugh A. Drum," 304, citing the final report of G-3, First Army, and an entry in Pershing's diary. "I did not learn of the change in the plans until the concentration movements for St. Mihiel had gone so far that no change of the first line divisions could be made with any prospect of carrying out the two operations during the time specified." Drum to George C. Marshall Jr., Dec. 9, 1920, "Correspondence with Col. G. C. Marshall, Jr.," box 14, Drum papers.

29. Walton Clark Jr., "Three Brothers in World War I," 197, 108th Field Artillery Regiment, 28th Division survey. Division and other surveys are in the U.S. Army Military History Institute, Army War College, Carlisle Barracks, Carlisle, Pa.

30. Col. G. M. Russell, "Intelligence Section, 5th Army Corps, Argonne-Meuse Operations," lecture, Jan. 27, 1919, folder 299, box 30, GHQ c.-in-c. reports, entry 22, RG 120.

31. Crile papers.

32. Dale Van Every, *The A.E.F. in Battle* (New York: Appleton, 1928), 317–318.

Chapter 3. First Days

1. Foch's directive of September 6 said that the objective of the First Army was "the capture of the Hindenburg position along the front Brieulles-sur-Meuse, Romagne-sous-Montfaucon, and Grandpré, developing later in the direction of Buzancy-Stonne with the view of overflowing the enemy line . . . towards the East."
2. Gallwitz in George S. Viereck, ed., *As They Saw Us: Foch, Ludendorff and Other Leaders Write Our War History* (Garden City, N.Y.: Doubleday, Doran, 1929), 239.
3. Roy V. Myers memoir, 42, Myers papers.
4. Ray Neil Johnson, *Heaven, Hell, or Hoboken* (Cleveland, Ohio: Hubbell, 1919), 105–106.
5. Walton Clark Jr., "Three Brothers in World War I," 201, 108th Field Artillery Regiment, 28th Division survey.
6. *The Cannoneers Have Hairy Ears: A Diary of the Front Lines* (New York: Sears, 1927), 179.
7. Vernon R. Nichols, "Our Battle of the Argonne," *Infantry Journal* 16 (1919): 188.
8. The heroic pilot, W. Clarkson Potter, died October 10 in a crash behind the enemy line. C. G. Barth, *History of the Twentieth Aero Squadron: First Day Bombardment Group, First Pursuit Wing, Air Service, First Army, American Expeditionary Forces* (Winona, Minn.: Winona Labor News, n.d.), 37.
9. *Cannoneers Have Hairy Ears,* 181–182; Eileen F. Lebow, *A Grandstand Seat: The American Balloon Service in World War I* (Westport, Conn.: Praeger, 1998), 135–136.
10. W. Kerr Rainsford, *From Upton to the Meuse: With the Three Hundred and Seventh Infantry* (New York: Appleton, 1920), 158–159.
11. *History of the 306th Field Artillery* (New York: Knickerbocker, 1920), 37.
12. Jonas E. Warrell memoir, Warrell papers.
13. The memoir is pasted in a copy of *The Cannoneers Have Hairy Ears: A Diary of the Front Line,* Granger papers.
14. "Brief History in the Case of Brigadier General Frederick S. Foltz," box 8, entry 22, RG 200, Pershing papers. On September 9 General Johnston had recommended General Foltz for promotion to major general.
15. Johnson, *Heaven, Hell, or Hoboken,* 96.
16. Charles S. Farnsworth, "Report of Meuse-Argonne Offensive, Sept. 26–Oct. 2, 1918," Oct. 18, 1918, 33.6, box 5, 37th Division historical, entry 1241, RG 120. An observer for G-5, GHQ, Major Lloyd R. Fredendall, blamed the engineer regiment for failing to make a reconnaissance of no-man's-land ahead of the jump-off point and for failing to bring up road material. "Recent Operations," Oct. 4, 1918, 16931-24, box 1397, adjutant general, entry 6, RG 120. He noted that two or three times the engineers left the roads to serve as division reserves.
17. The parts of the Hindenburg Line were named after Wagnerian witches: Giselher, Kriemhilde, and Freya. The first centered on Montfaucon and the second, the strongest, on the Romagne heights. The Freya, in the Buzancy heights, was not fully prepared.
18. Nolan comments on General Pershing's memoirs, 497–498, Nolan papers.
19. Lebow, *A Grandstand Seat,* 137.
20. Christian A. Bach and Henry H. Hall, *The Fourth Division: Its Services and Achievements in the World War* (Garden City, N.Y.: Fourth Division, 1920), 166.

21. Harvey Cushing, *From a Surgeon's Journal: 1915–1918* (Boston: Little, Brown, 1936), 462.
22. Edward A. Davies diary, 26–27. For the 79th's action, see Elbridge Colby, "The Taking of Montfaucon," *Infantry Journal* 47 (1940): 139–140. Casualties were high: 597 killed, 2,375 wounded, and 473 gassed, for a total of 3,445.
23. "The Seventy-ninth Division: 1917–1918" (War College, 1925), copy in U.S. Army Military History Institute library.
24. The War College officers remarked that the other divisions in V Corps, the 91st and 37th, had fifty-nine and twenty-six days of training in France, respectively. They drew no conclusion as to the wisdom of putting three poorly trained divisions in a single corps.
25. All this came out after Noble protested his relief, which forced a review by Brewster of GHQ. As might be expected, the inspector backed Kuhn. "Finding and Recommendation in case of Brig. Gen. R. H. Noble," box 3411, inspector general reports, GHQ, entry 1241, RG 120. Noble was sent to Blois and reduced to colonel one day after the armistice; he retired in 1922. Before assignment to the 79th, he had been attached to the 77th, then under Major General George B. Duncan. Duncan reported that Noble lacked "background of military knowledge and ability in directing the work of others," that he was "undeveloped in capacity for command," and noted, "I would not be satisfied with General Noble in command of a brigade in this division." Timothy E. Nenninger, "John J. Pershing and Relief for Cause in the American Expeditionary Forces, 1917–1918," *Army History* (2005): 27.
26. Col. Alfred W. Bjornstad, hearings before the Committee on Military Affairs, U.S. Senate, 68th Congress, 2nd session, pt. 1, Jan. 9, 12–14 (Washington, D.C.: Government Printing Office, 1925). Bjornstad's action in Bullard's absence raised an issue that confused command in the Meuse-Argonne at the beginning of the battle: the latitude enjoyed by chiefs of staff when their superiors were in the field. The German army had a tradition of allowing staff officers to supervise battles, as in the case of Hentsch, and the AEF was developing one. Pershing often left his headquarters at Chaumont, and the chief of staff (Harbord and later Major General James McAndrew) sent messages on his behalf, as did the assistant chiefs of the G branches for administration (G-1), intelligence (G-2), operations (G-3), supply (G-4), and training (G-5). Similarly, Drum ran First Army headquarters at Souilly. Interestingly, when Hines became commander of III Corps in mid-October, after Bullard took command of the Second Army, Bjornstad sent just one order in Hines's name without telling him; Hines went to First Army headquarters and forced the transfer of his chief of staff to the 7th Division. In 1925 Bjornstad could not mention this fact until it arose in his promotion hearings. Hines, then chief of staff of the army in Washington, brought it up.
27. Booth wrote triumphantly at the bottom of a copy of the Pershing letter: "Thus there is ended a research of thousands of pages of records, and interviews, both verbal and written, with hundreds of officers, covering a period of approximately twenty years." "Booth, E. F., Major General," box 9, Drum papers; B. A. Poore, "My Experiences in the American Expeditionary Forces, 1918–1919," Poore papers.
28. Coleman diary, Sept. 26, 1918.

29. A member of Pétain's staff told Major Clark that "I personally saw two U.S. artillery regiments bivouac on roads." Col. Nodé Langlois, in Clark to Pershing, Oct. 11, 1918, box 2, entry 22, RG 200, Pershing papers.

30. Roy V. Myers memoir, 49, Myers papers.

31. Gallwitz to T. M. Johnson, Mar. 20, 1928, "German Fifth Army Report," box 17, Drum papers; Erich Ludendorff, *Ludendorff's Own Story: August 1914–November 1918*, 2 vols. (New York: Harper, 1919), 2:373; Frederick Palmer, *Our Greatest Battle (the Meuse-Argonne)* (New York: Dodd, Mead, 1919), 142.

Chapter 4. The 35th Division

1. *American Troops at the Argonne*, hearings before the Committee on Military Affairs, U.S. Senate, 65th Congress, 3rd session, Feb. 18, 1919, 50 (Washington, D.C.: Government Printing Office, 1919).

2. The basic source for any analysis of the 35th Division in the initial phase of the Meuse-Argonne is the report of the I Corps inspector, Lieutenant Colonel Robert G. Peck, "St. M. & M.A., 35th Division (No. 1)," box 16, Drum papers (hereafter cited as Peck report). There is a copy in 333.9 Robert G. Peck, box 969, entry 26, RG 159. For details of what follows, see Robert H. Ferrell, *Collapse at Meuse-Argonne: The Failure of the Missouri-Kansas Division* (Columbia: University of Missouri Press, 2004). Two excellent contemporary accounts, both by newspapermen, are Clair Kenamore, *From Vauquois Hill to Exermont: A History of the Thirty-fifth Division of the United States Army* (St. Louis: Guard, 1919), and Charles B. Hoyt, *Heroes of the Argonne: An Authentic History of the Thirty-fifth Division* (Kansas City, Mo.: Franklin Hudson, 1919). For the regiments, see Kenamore's *The Story of the 139th Infantry* (St. Louis: Guard, 1920); James E. Rieger, "139th Infantry A.E.F.—Fourth Missouri Infantry," in *History of the Missouri National Guard* (n.p.: Missouri National Guard, 1934); Evan A. Edwards, *From Doniphan to Verdun: The Official History of the 140th Infantry* (Lawrence, Kans.: World, 1920); and William S. Triplet, *A Youth in the Meuse-Argonne: A Memoir, 1917–1918*, ed. Robert H. Ferrell (Columbia: University of Missouri Press, 2000). For the 129th Field Artillery, see Jay M. Lee, *The Artilleryman: The Experiences and Impressions of an American Artillery Regiment in the World War, 129th F.A. 1917–1919* (Kansas City, Mo.: Spencer, 1920).

3. Norman S. Hall and Sigrid Schultz, "Five Red Days: The True Story of the 35th Division in the Meuse-Argonne Battle," *Liberty* 4 (May 14, 1927): 9–14, contains the Huellesheim diary.

4. Triplet, *A Youth in the Meuse-Argonne*, 168.

5. Interviewed by the corps inspector, Delaplane was unsure who started the battalion. A War College study said that it was Hawkins, which seems reasonable. "The Thirty-fifth Division: 1917–1919" (War College, 1921–1922), copy in U.S. Army Military History Institute library.

6. Triplet, *A Youth in the Meuse-Argonne*, 222–224.

7. The best description of what happened on the right of the division line is in the report of the I Corps inspector.

8. Parker C. Kalloch Jr. to adjutant general, Washington, D.C., June 9, 1919, "35th Division," box 16, Drum papers.

9. Edward P. Rankin Jr., *The Santa Fe Trail Leads to France: A Narrative of Battle Service of the 110th Engineers (35 Division) in the Meuse-Argonne Offensive* (Kansas City, Mo.: Richardson, 1933). Rankin was a company commander.

10. After the war Ralph Truman remained in the Guard, and when the 35th Division again entered federal service in 1940, he was its commanding general. The War Department relieved him the next year, along with virtually all other Guard generals who were commanding divisions.

11. *Report of the Secretary of War to the President: 1926* (Washington, D.C.: Government Printing Office, 1926), 230.

12. *Losses of 35th Division during the Argonne Battle,* hearings before the Committee on Rules, U.S. House of Representatives, Feb. 20, 1919, 89 (Washington, D.C.: Government Printing Office, 1919).

13. Ibid., 69; Stackpole diary, Oct. 2, 1918.

14. Testimony of Colonel Bugge, Peck report; the report is not paginated. Lieutenant Colonel Peck's recommendations appear verbatim in Drum to Traub, Oct. 26, 1918. The last point, number seventeen, pertained to Berry: "That the Artillery Commander, Brig. Gen. L. G. Berry, failed to cooperate with and make full use of the Air Service until ordered to do so." Berry was irritated at being singled out in Drum's criticism of the division, which became known to the officers and men and threatened to blight his army career. In addition, he suffered the indignity of being interrogated by Colonel Upton Birnie Jr. on April 6, 1919, just before the 35th sailed for the United States. Evidently, Brigadier General Fox Conner, GHQ, thought the 35th needed another look. Birnie found Berry evasive, unwilling to answer questions directly. Months later, Berry wrote to General Liggett objecting to the criticism. Liggett wrote to Drum, who replied that he had sent Liggett everything he could pertaining to the issue. Berry then wrote to the adjutant general, who said that no action had been taken on the issue of the air service and, after consulting General Pershing, closed the case. "1919," box 1, Berry papers.

15. For Jacobs's criticism, see "Report Concerning 35th Division in Action," Oct. 1, 1918, box 3410, inspector general, GHQ, RG 120.

16. "Relief History in Case of Brig. Gen. N. F. McClure, 69th Infantry Brigade," box 8, entry 22, RG 200, Pershing papers. Traub described McClure's leadership as poor. "He is not a decided character" and should be "demoted and assigned to some other duty than the active command of troops in the field and . . . replaced by a real live Brigadier General." McClure did not protest his relief until after leaving the division, because he believed that it would be unfair to Traub, who had many things to do just before the division attacked. Later he made a full protest, which received cursory attention. He was demoted to his Regular Army rank of colonel.

17. "Brief Statement of Facts in the Case of Brigadier General Charles I. Martin, formerly commanding the 70th Infantry Brigade," box 10, entry 22, RG 200, Pershing papers. For the meetings with Traub, see Martin's testimony before the Senate Armed Services Committee in *Army Appropriation Bill, 1920,* hearings before the Committee on Military Affairs, U.S. Senate, 65th Congress, 3rd session (Washington, D.C.: Government Printing Office, 1919), 6 n.

18. This wire, incidentally, was the same kind sent to the 79th Division, which, like the 35th, had problems with telephone communications and resorted to runners. A curious fact in the history of the 35th is that the division's artillery brigade had

good wire and enjoyed easy communication throughout the four days of action. General Berry must have known, or should have known, that the infantry regiments were using outpost, twisted pair wire. His relations with General Traub were formal; the two had their command posts within fifty feet of each other yet communicated by typewritten letter. Berry was wary of Traub, unsure of how he might be treated, and it is entirely possible that he let Traub get into trouble.

19. The adjutant of the 69th Brigade was Major Dwight F. Davis, who became secretary of war in the Coolidge administration (1924–1929).

20. Peck report.

21. *Losses of Thirty-fifth Division during the Argonne Battle,* Feb. 20, 1919, 90.

22. Ibid., 70, 88.

23. Ibid., Feb. 17, 35–36.

24. For the Peck report, see note 2; for the congressional hearings, see *Losses of Thirty-fifth Division during the Argonne Battle* (House) and *American Troops at the Argonne* (Senate); for General Martin's relief, see *Army Appropriation Bill, 1920.* Testimony of Secretary Baker and General March during the hearing of January 24, 1919, is in *Losses of Thirty-fifth Division,* 4–20.

Chapter 5. Ending the Enfilade

1. The reporter was Fred S. Ferguson; the editor was from the United Press.

2. Edward M. Coffman, *The War to End All Wars: The American Military Experience in World War I* (New York: Oxford University Press, 1968), 323.

3. Meiron Harries and Susie Harries, *The Last Days of Innocence: America at War, 1917–1918* (New York: Random House, 1997), 370. For the Lost Battalion, see Robert H. Ferrell, *Five Days in October: The Lost Battalion of World War I* (Columbia: University of Missouri Press, 2005), and Alan D. Gaff, *Blood in the Argonne: The "Lost Battalion" of World War I* (Norman: University of Oklahoma Press, 2005), which correct and amplify Thomas M. Johnson and Fletcher Pratt, *The Lost Battalion* (Indianapolis: Bobbs-Merrill, 1938).

4. Robert Alexander, *Memories of the World War: 1917–1918* (New York: Macmillan, 1931), 190.

5. On October 11, Colonel A. C. Read of the advance office of the inspector general informed GHQ about the 850 replacements sent to the 307th Regiment and the 1,250 sent to the 308th on September 23. "These men were almost entirely uninstructed in everything that a soldier should know, and were very poorly disciplined. G-1 at advanced army headquarters does not know from what replacement division these replacements came." On the memorandum is a handwritten note by the acting inspector general, Colonel Jospeh I. Baer: "Many of these men did not know how to load a rifle. The sending of such men to an organization in the advance is little short of murder. How we have escaped a catastrophe is a clear demonstration of the German demoralization. The matter must be looked into thoroughly and responsibility must be fixed." File 1008, box 125, general correspondence 1917–1918, GHQ inspector general, entry 584, RG 120. Baer sent a memorandum to Brigadier General Spinks of the inspector's office recommending an investigation and referred to "the other replacement question," which

may have been the advisability of establishing a replacement organization rather than breaking up divisions.

6. The commander of the 52nd Field Artillery Brigade was Brigadier General Manus McCloskey. There was no investigation.

7. Report to First Army inspector by Capt. Albert T. Rich, assistant inspector, Oct. 11, 1918, First Army reports, box 3410, GHQ, entry 24, RG 120.

8. Johnson was as prickly as Alexander, but in terms of ability in the field, he was probably a good deal better. He also wrote well, and the report on his brigade in the 77th Division historical file—a copy is in the Drum papers—constitutes the best day-by-day account of the moves to relieve the Lost Battalion. For the chaplain's report of the bodies, see note 7, Captain Rich to First Army inspector. From the 77th Division, Johnson moved to the 79th, then the 7th. After the war he was military attaché in Rome, and in 1921 he wrote to Pershing asking for both the Distinguished Service Medal, often awarded to commanders, and the Distinguished Service Cross, a battlefield award; he desired the latter for leading attacks to save the Lost Battalion. Pershing, then chief of staff, pigeonholed the request, sending it without recommendation to the committee on decorations. Folder 12, box 7, entry 22, RG 200, Pershing papers. Johnson should not have written to Pershing, but he may have thought he needed to because Alexander was blocking the awards.

9. Major John C. H. Lee, a colonel and chief of staff in the 89th Division in the Meuse-Argonne, and a lieutenant general in World War II, wrote to Pershing about Stacey in 1920. The former commander in chief, on the advice of his aide, Major (formerly colonel) John C. Quekemeyer, sent the letter to a board. Folder 14, box 21, entry 22, RG 200, Pershing papers. Stacey did get back his rank as colonel in 1920, and he retired in 1930. Timothy K. Nenninger, "John J. Pershing and Relief for Cause in the American Expeditionary Forces, 1917–1918," *Army History* (2005): 26. This article corrects my *Five Days in October,* 46–47, where I erred in relating Stacey's Regular Army rank as lieutenant colonel instead of major.

10. Drum to Liggett, July 28, 1917, "Liggett, Hunter," box 20, Drum papers. In a response dated August 1, Liggett wrote that Conner was present; Drum was uncertain about this.

11. Stackpole diary, Oct. 6–7, 1918. Duncan wrote that Lieutenant Colonel Gordon Johnston, then assigned to I Corps headquarters, undertook a reconnaissance between the 1st Division and the 28th and saw General Summerall, commander of the 1st Division, and Brigadier General Frank Parker, commander of the 1st Brigade. Neither knew anything about the forthcoming attack by the 82nd and 28th. They said that such a maneuver would have been impossible even for their own experienced troops and that they never would have attempted it without staff work. Headquarters generals, Duncan concluded, found theory easier than practice. "The culmination of effort by Corps Headquarters seemed to be in preparation of an order which could be handed down as a literary and military masterpiece which took hours to perfect after oral direction had been given as to what to expect. It was a much simpler matter to work out a troop movement on the map than it was to execute it on the ground. Orders for attack seemed to be studied as map problems only, much as is done at the service schools." Later, General Drum gave a talk to 82nd Division officers and said that the division had

not attacked properly and had engaged in "milling around." Johnston, who was present, remarked on the lack of planning that surrounded the I Corps decision to use the 82nd. George B. Duncan, "Reminiscences of the World War," 2:146–149.

12. *Official History of the 82nd Division, American Expeditionary Forces* (Indianapolis: Bobbs-Merrill, 1919), 39–40.

13. Ibid., 50–51.

14. Laurence Stallings, *The Doughboys: The Story of the AEF, 1917–1918* (New York: Harper & Row, 1963), 271.

15. *Official History of the 82nd Division,* 58–59.

16. George B. Duncan, "General Missions of the 82nd Division in the Argonne-Meuse Offensive," 3, army course lectures, Feb. 3, 1919, folder 4, box 31, entry 22, RG 200, Pershing papers.

17. Dwight D. Lee, *Sergeant York: An American Hero* (Lexington: University Press of Kentucky, 1985), 27–84. The basic facts of York's heroism seem beyond question, but the particulars are in dispute. Other members of Early's squad claimed to have had a greater role. Tom Skeyhill, ed., *Sergeant York: His Own Life Story and War Diary* (Garden City, N.Y.: Doubleday, Doran, 1928), in which York collaborated, is uncertain in provenance, especially the diary with its colloquialisms. The very place where the action occurred is uncertain. *New York Times,* June 20, 2006.

18. Stackpole diary, Oct. 7–10, 1918; Hunter Liggett, *Commanding an American Army: Recollections of the World War* (Boston: Houghton Mifflin, 1925), 188–189; Coffman, *War to End All Wars,* 325.

19. Nolan comments on General Pershing's memoirs, 506–507, Nolan papers; after-action report, Sept. 28–Oct. 9, 1918, undated, ibid.

20. Rexmond C. Cohrane, *The Use of Gas in the Meuse-Argonne Campaign: September–November 1918* (Washington, D.C.: U.S. Army Chemical Corps, 1958), 34–35.

21. McCleneghan memoir. This is a remarkable account, composed after the war; the first part is handwritten on Knights of Columbus stationery. It appeared in serial form in the *Rockport (Ill.) Star.* Years later, in 1973–1974, the author added several chapters.

22. McCleneghan memoir, 66–67.

23. Ibid.

24. Ibid., 69.

25. Shipley Thomas, *The History of the A.E.F.* (New York: Doran, 1920), 294.

26. Frederic Louis Huidekoper, *History of the 33rd Division, A.E.F.* (Springfield: Illinois State Historical Library, 1921), 1:166–167. The author added casualties of attached units. When the army published its casualties for the war in 1926, its total for the 33rd Division was 4,574, of which 429 men were killed, 191 died of wounds, and the rest were wounded. *Report of the Secretary of War to the President: 1926* (Washington, D.C.: Government Printing Office, 1926), 230. As was true of Huidekoper's total, this included casualties for the division's initial attack west of the Meuse.

27. Joseph Douglas Lawrence, *Fighting Soldier: The AEF in 1918,* ed. Robert H. Ferrell (Boulder: Colorado Associated University Press, 1985), 75.

28. Ibid., 81, 86.

29. Ibid., 94.

30. Ibid., 112–113.

31. L. S. Upton and Millard E. Tydings, "Capture of Etrayes Ridge: A Machine Gun Study," *Infantry Journal* 31 (1927): 133–136; Millard E. Tydings, *The Machine Gunners of the Blue and Gray Division (Twenty-ninth)* (n.p.: n.d.).
32. Lawrence, *Fighting Soldier,* 133.
33. Rexmond C. Cochrane, *The 29th Division in the Côtes de Meuse: October 1918* (Washington, D.C.: U.S. Army Chemical Corps, 1959), 61. Cochrane included cases of psychoneurosis and illness, as well as the missing. The 29th was a fresh division when crossing the Meuse, so the army's statistical calculations of 1926 were close to the mark: 732 men killed, 227 died of wounds, and 4,048 wounded, for a total of 5,007. *Report of the Secretary of War,* 228.

Chapter 6. The Kriemhilde Stellung

1. Frank H. Simonds, *They Won the War* (New York: Harper, 1931), 18–19.
2. *The Cannoneers Have Hairy Ears: A Diary of the Front Lines* (New York: Sears, 1927), 210.
3. Shipley Thomas, *The History of the A.E.F.* (New York: Doran, 1920), 259–260.
4. Herbert L. McHenry, *As a Private Saw It: My Memories of the First Division, World War I* (Indiana, Pa.: Halldin, 1988), 48.
5. Thomas, *History of the A.E.F.,* 317; *History of the First Division during the World War: 1917–1919* (Philadelphia: Winston, 1922), 213. Rexmond C. Cochrane, *The 1st Division in the Meuse-Argonne: 1–12 October 1918* (Washington, D.C.: U.S. Army Chemical Corps, 1957), 127, put casualties, killed, wounded, and gassed (the last at 1,400), as 6,628. The army's statistics published in 1926, which included casualties for November 1918, were 1,437 killed, 514 died of wounds, and 7,258 wounded, for a total of 9,209. *Report of the Secretary of War,* 226.
6. Betts papers; McHenry, *As a Private Saw It,* 64.
7. Quoted in Cochrane, *The 1st Division in the Meuse-Argonne.*
8. Douglas V. Johnson II and Rolfe E. Hillman Jr., *Soissons: 1918* (College Station: Texas A&M University Press, 1999), 41.
9. A. J. Dougherty, "Accompanying Guns," *Infantry Journal* 17 (1920): 487–490; Cochrane, *The 1st Division in the Meuse-Argonne,* 22; *History of the First Division during the World War,* 186.
10. *A History of the Sixth Regiment Field Artillery First Division United States Army* (Ransbach, Germany, 1919), 68–70.
11. Paul J. Jacobsmeyer, "Intelligence in the American Expeditionary Forces: The Experience of the Thirty-second Division, September 1917–November 1918" (master's thesis, University of Wisconsin, 1986).
12. "You can imagine, therefore, the state of my mind when I learned the cold facts that we had not captured the key position. . . . For just about five minutes, when the real facts became positively known to me . . . I suffered the greatest depression of my life." William G. Haan,"The Division as a Fighting Machine," *Wisconsin Magazine of History* 4 (1920): 14–15.
13. Edward M. Coffman, *The War to End All Wars: The American Military Experience in World War I* (New York: Oxford University Press, 1968), 327–329. That afternoon and evening, the rest of the Third Battalion, together with the Second, followed

Strom's men to the top. The 127th Regiment moved up the west side of the hill from the rear, only to find the German defenders gone.

14. W. G. Haan to Summerall, Oct. 17, 1918, Haan papers, State Historical Society of Wisconsin, courtesy of Paul J. Jacobsmeyer; the original is in the Summerall papers. Casualties of the 32nd Division in the Meuse-Argonne, which included action just before the armistice, were 1,145 killed, 415 died of wounds, and 4,992 wounded, for a total of 6,552. *Report of the Secretary of War,* 229.

15. Robert Lee Bullard, *Personalities and Reminiscences of the War* (Garden City, N.Y.: Doubleday, Page, 1925), 176.

16. Thomas, *History of the A.E.F.,* 295.

17. Francis P. Duffy, *Father Duffy's Story: A Tale of Honor and Heroism, of Life and Death with the Fighting Sixty-ninth* (Garden City, N.Y.: Garden City, 1919), 265–267.

18. George E. Leach, *War Diary* (Roanoke, Va.: Rainbow Division Veterans, 1962), 56–57.

19. Albert M. Ettinger and A. Churchill Ettinger, *A Doughboy with the Fighting Sixty-ninth: A Remembrance of World War I* (Shippensburg, Pa.: White Mane, 1992), 161.

20. Beaumont B. Buck, *Memories of Peace and War* (San Antonio, Tex.: Naylor, 1935), 218–225.

21. Rexmond C. Cochrane, *The 42nd Division before Landres-et-St. Georges: October 1918* (Washington, D.C.: U.S. Army Chemical Corps, 1960), 87–88.

22. Duffy, *Father Duffy's Story,* 272.

23. R. M. Cheseldine, *Ohio in the Rainbow: Official Story of the 166th Infantry, 42nd Division, in the World War* (Columbus, Ohio: Heer, 1924), 256.

24. Henry J. Reilly, *Americans All: The Rainbow at War* (Columbus, Ohio: Heer, 1936), 649.

25. The memoir is in the Lenihan papers. The inspector of V Corps, Colonel S. Field Dallam, investigated the general's relief but apparently it did not go beyond V Corps; see "reports of investigation," corps inspector, entry 1138, RG 120. His report contains statements by Summerall, Lenihan, Mitchell, Chaplain Duffy, Merle-Smith, and First Lieutenant Harold J. Betty. The most interesting is Merle-Smith's, which amounts to a brief in support of Lenihan. A holder of the Distinguished Service Cross for heroism in the Aisne-Marne, a Princeton graduate, and a New York lawyer who later became assistant secretary of state, Merle-Smith said that Summerall had asked too much of the brigade. See Richard M. Huber, *Big All the Way Through: The Life of Van Santvoord Merle-Smith* (Princeton, N.J.: Class of 1911, 1952). The corps commander afterward relented in his relief of Merle-Smith.

26. Reilly, *Americans All,* 680–685.

27. John H. Taber, *The Story of the 168th Infantry,* vol. 2 (Iowa City: State Historical Society, 1925), 191–192.

28. Reilly, *Americans All,* 657.

29. Charles D. Rhodes diary, Oct. 27–28, 1918.

30. Efficiency reports, July 1, 1922, box 23, entry 22, RG 200, Pershing papers.

31. "Brief History in the Case of Major General J. E. McMahon, N.A.," box 8, entry 22, RG 200, Pershing papers.

32. McMahon's meeting with Castner and Malone is in Castner's letter to the American Battle Monuments Commission, May 13, 1930, "Fifth Division," box 16, Drum papers.

33. "Brief History in the Case of Major General J. E. McMahon, N.A." For the general's return, see Timothy K. Nenninger, "John J. Pershing and Relief for Cause in the American Expeditionary Forces, 1917–1918," *Army History* (2005): 30.

34. *Congressional Medal of Honor, the Distinguished Service Cross, and the Distinguished Service Medal* (Washington, D.C.: Government Printing Office, 1920), 17; Lowell Thomas, *Woodfill of the Regulars: A True Story of Adventure from the Arctic to the Argonne* (Garden City, N.Y.: Doubleday, Doran, 1929), 17; *New York Times*, Aug. 14, 1951; Tony Miller, "Samuel Woodfill: The Outstanding Soldier of the A.E.F.," *Traces of Indiana* 12 (2000): 15–25.

35. Castner to Maj. Gen. Drum, May 16, 1930, enclosing letter to the American Battle Monuments Commission. Stark's Distinguished Service Cross citation was "for extraordinary heroism in action near Côte St. Germain, France, November 7, 1918. His battalion being stopped by machine-gun fire, in the attack of November 7, 1918. Maj. Stark personally led it in a renewed attack and thus succeeded in gaining the Côte St. Germain. Maj. Stark personally encouraged his men to advance against odds." *Congressional Medal of Honor, Distinguished Service Cross, and Distinguished Service Medal*, 739.

Chapter 7. Reorganization

1. "Brief History in the Case of Major General J. E. McMahon, N.A.," box 8, entry 22, RG 200, Pershing papers; "Brief History of the Case of Major General B. B. Buck, N.A," ibid. Pershing's chief of staff at GHQ, Major General McAndrew, sent a smooth letter to both generals:

> G.H.Q., October 20, 1918
> Dear . . . :
> As you probably know, General Pershing has from the beginning tried to establish in the organization of our Army the sound principle of an interchange of officers between the A.E.F. and the home units. This practice has been followed for the past six months in the case of General Staff officers and Regimental officers with excellent results.
> The need of interchange between higher officers of combat units is even greater, as we find that divisions, brigades, etc., require in their organization the training and services of officers who have had actual experience in the A.E.F. This view was presented to the Secretary of War during his recent visit here.
> Inaugurating this principle, and following the Secretary's return to Washington, authority has been cabled to return to the States several General Officers, including yourself.
> It is understood here that in compliance with General Pershing's specified request you will retain your present rank and will be assigned to duty training divisions, or in command of training camps or other duty appropriate to such rank.
> General Pershing feels that the order herewith returning you to the States should not go to you without this explanation of its meaning and intent. He wishes you a safe and pleasant return home and every good that the future can bring to you.
> It is unnecessary for me to add how heartily I join in these wishes.
> Sincerely yours,

2. Stackpole diary, passim. Craig wrote a report for Liggett dated August 6, 1918, recommending the breakup of the 26th Division for replacements. The commander of

I Corps did not support Craig's suggestion. After the war, Craig wrote to Harbord explaining that Liggett was strongly conservative concerning Edwards, except in private conversation (this last he penned in a postscript). Craig to Harbord, June 3, 1919. Brigadier General Fiske, G-5, GHQ, told Edwards's replacement, Brigadier General Frank Bamford, that the 26th was the poorest division in the AEF (box 10, entry 22, RG 200, Pershing papers). The relief dossier for Edwards (box 8, entry 22, RG 200) has no adverse reports except an unflattering appraisal when Edwards served in Hawaii in 1914 or 1915.

3. B. A. Poore, "My Experiences in the American Expeditionary Forces, 1918–1919," 23, Poore papers; General Bolté told Edward M. Coffman of his talk with Cameron (letter, Dec. 19, 1977). Stackpole wrote in his diary (Oct. 22, 1918):

> General Cameron called on General Liggett and had a rather long conference, from which I absented myself as I could not attend without a rather conspicuous intrusion. Cameron had an envelope in his hand when he came out and I daresay got General Liggett to sign some damn fool soft-hearted stuff, which may cause the ruin of both of them in these days of captious judgments. Cameron in my opinion is a treacherous eel. Later it appears that Cameron has been relieved from the 4th Division and is going home, but without reduction in rank. He wanted to learn from General Liggett why he had been relieved and the latter told him he did not know. Cameron told him many things about his talks with Pershing, including the allusion to the tired condition of the troops, and General Liggett told Cameron he thought he could find in his own utterances the reason, as even though what he said might be true, Pershing did not want to hear them. General Liggett said Cameron had a letter announcing the fact of his relief, and apart from his inquiry as to why he had been relieved gave no evidence of disappointment or disposition to complain or protest—and so far as I know General Liggett did not commit himself to pro or con in the business and did not sign anything. And the sooner Cameron and Edwards, who thank God is also relieved, get out of reach, the better pleased I shall be.

In 1939 Drum was greatly disappointed when Pershing threw his support to Brigadier General Marshall for the position of army chief of staff, and he drafted a letter to the former commander in chief in which he cryptically referred to the command troubles of 1918; his service as First Army chief of staff, he said, included "with great possible embarrassment a willing acceptance of much of the vindictiveness associated with your handling of the Edwards and Cameron cases in the A.E.F., although I personally had no direct association with either case." There is no evidence that Drum sent the letter. Elliott L. Johnson, "The Military Experiences of Hugh A. Drum from 1898–1918" (dissertation, University of Wisconsin, 1975), 289.

4. After the war, Dickman commanded the Third Army, which went into Germany. Stackpole's postwar diary entries comment on Dickman's slowness. When the general published his memoirs, there was a stodginess about them that may have influenced Liggett's aide.

5. Frederick A. Pottle, *Stretchers: The Story of a Hospital Unit on the Western Front* (New Haven, Conn.: Yale University Press, 1929), 246.

6. Paul F. Braim, *The Test of Battle: The American Expeditionary Forces in the Meuse-Argonne Campaign* (Newark: University of Delaware Press, 1987) , 155.

7. Hale Hunt diary, Oct. 19, 1918.

8. A. Draper Dewees diary, Oct. 13–20, 1918.

9. Charles Howard Donnelly, "Autobiography," 388–389, Donnelly papers. "Here also the regimental delousing machine caught up with us after the long march overland to the Argonne. Every man in the regiment was given a fine hot bath. Their clothes were baked in steam to free them of 'cooties' (lice). The entire brigade enjoyed the bath and many a thanks went out to the generous citizens of Philadelphia, who had put up the $10,000 to produce the machine and send it abroad." Walton Clark Jr., "Three Brothers in World War I," 228, Walton Clark Jr. papers.

10. Hale Hunt diary, Oct. 14, 1918.

11. Hunter Liggett, *A.E.F: Ten Years Ago in France* (New York: Dodd, Mead, 1928), 211.

12. Edward A. Davies diary.

13. Operations report, 33.6, box 7, 78th Division historical, entry 1241, RG 120.

14. Bandholtz diary, Oct. 16, 1919. This is a postwar diary, August 1919 to February 1920. Drum on October 19 estimated 119,327. Edward M. Coffman, *The War to End All Wars: The American Military Experience in World War I* (New York: Oxford University Press, 1968), 332.

15. Robert C. Humber, "Absences and Desertions during First World War," Army War College study no. 35, U.S. Army Military History Institute.

16. Liggett, *A.E.F: Ten Years Ago in France,* 209–210.

17. "Memorandum for brigade, regimental, and line commanders," Oct. 20, 1918, box 2, 32nd Division historical, entry 1241, RG 120.

18. George B. Duncan, "General Missions of the 82nd Division in the Argonne-Meuse Offensive," folder 4, box 31, entry 22, RG 200, Pershing papers.

19. Lt. Col. Troup Miller, "Plan of communication, supply and evacuation, 1st Corps, for St. Mihiel Offensive and Meuse-Argonne Offensive," folder 3, box 31, entry 22, RG 200, Pershing papers.

20. Stackpole diary, Oct. 18, 1918.

21. William B. Parsons, *The American Engineers in France* (New York: Appleton, 1920), 296–312, 358–363. Parsons was colonel of the 11th Engineers.

22. J. Edward Cassidy, "History of the 317th Engineers (Sappers)," box 14, 92nd Division historical, entry 1241, RG 120. Cassidy's history, 126 double-spaced typescript pages, is accompanied by an album of photographs.

23. George Crile, *An Autobiography,* 2 vols. (Philadelphia: Lippincott, 1947), 2:271.

24. Pottle, *Stretchers,* 226–227.

25. *The Cannoneers Have Hairy Ears: A Diary of the Front Lines* (New York: Sears, 1927), 180.

26. Crile, *Autobiography,* 2:350–351.

27. Carol R. Byerly, *Fever of War: The Influenza Epidemic in the U.S. Army during World War I* (New York: New York University Press, 2005), 98.

28. Frederic Louis Huidekoper, *History of the 33rd Division, A.E.F.* (Springfield: Illinois State Historical Library, 1921), 1:171; William M. Wright, *Meuse-Argonne Diary: A Division Commander in World War I,* ed. Robert H. Ferrell (Columbia: University of Missouri Press, 2004), 131–132 (Oct. 29–30, 1918); "The Seventy-ninth Division, 1917–1918" (War College, 1924), copy in U.S. Army Military History Institute library; Col. Dan T. Moore, operations report, 33.6, box 78, 2nd

Division historical, entry 1241, RG 120; Cassidy, "History of the 317th Engineers (Sappers)," 214–215.

29. Eileen F. Lebow, *A Grandstand Seat: The American Balloon Service in World War I* (Westport, Conn.: Praeger, 1998), 139.

30. Report of G-3, First Army, 120.03, box 3384, entry 24, RG 120.

31. Alfred F. Hurley, *Billy Mitchell: Crusader for Air Power* (Bloomington: Indiana University Press, 1975); James J. Cooke, *Billy Mitchell* (Boulder, Colo.: Lynne Rienner, 2002); Douglas Waller, *A Question of Loyalty: Gen. Billy Mitchell and the Court-martial that Gripped the Nation* (New York: HarperCollins, 2004).

32. "If more experienced aviation officers had been available, as one member of the AEF staff later noted, Pershing might well have fired both Mitchell and Foulois." Hurley, *Billy Mitchell*, 34.

33. Dictation, Jan. 31, 1936, Nolan papers: "Mitchell had one excuse after another; he didn't want them to do it; he didn't want to do the routine photographing and observation missions that are absolutely essential to the working of the Intelligence and without which Howell couldn't function as General Pershing as Army Commander thought those were being executed promptly. . . . Mitchell was straightened out on it and he laughed it off, as usual."

34. Babcock memoir, 617–618. "Our air service is useless, apparently. We get no information from it and the Boche apparently does as he pleases. Our planes seem to fly on lower levels than the Boche and most of their reconnaissance work is over our lines. The Boche have brought down an observation balloon for the last three days—today we have no balloon up." Wright, *Meuse-Argonne Diary*, 232.

35. Henry H. Arnold, *Global Mission* (New York: Harper, 1949), 52.

36. Stackpole diary, Oct. 20, 1918.

37. Adler's account is in Robert Alexander, *Memories of the World War: 1917–1918* (New York: Macmillan, 1931), 250–252.

38. A narrative of the taking of Grandpré is in the Sheldon papers.

39. Thomas J. Fleming, "Two Argonnes," *American Heritage* 29, no. 6 (1968): 91.

40. Ibid., 90.

41. Stackpole diary, Oct. 19, 1918.

42. Robert Alexander, "Operations of the Division, 26th of September to the 11th of November," First Army course lecture, Feb. 3, 1919, folder 273, box 29, GHQ c.-in-c. reports, entry 1241, RG 120. Tillman's report, "The Capture of Grand Prè," is in the Sheldon papers.

Chapter 8. Breakout

1. Edward F. McGlachlin, "Army Artillery in Meuse-Argonne," *Infantry Journal* 23 (1923): 550. "And then the lazy boom and explosion of the naval bombardment [at Guam]. I couldn't help but compare it to the preparatory bombardment the morning of November 1st, 1918—that tremendous sound." Robert Wallace Blake, *From Belleau Wood to Bougainville: The Oral History of Major General Robert Blake USMC and the Travel Journal of Rosselet Wallace Blake* (Bloomington, Ind.: Authorhouse, 2004), 82.

2. *A History of the Sixth Regiment Field Artillery First Division United States Army* (Ransbach, Germany, 1919), 82.

3. Rexmond C. Cochrane, *The Use of Gas in the Meuse-Argonne Campaign, September–November 1918* (Washington, D.C.: U.S. Army Chemical Corps, 1958), 56–57.

4. Rexmond C. Cochrane, *The 89th Division in the Bois de Bantheville: October 1918* (Washington, D.C.: U.S. Army Chemical Corps, 1960), 70.

5. "Comments by the Corps Commander upon the Operations of the Fifth Army Corps," box 16, Drum papers.

6. Because of the salient—the Bantheville Woods—the 89th had a more difficult time than the 2nd in preparing for the offensive. It had come into the woods ten days before the 2nd, which replaced the 42nd the night before the attack. The 89th had to fight to hold the woods, gaining ground during the day and losing it at night. To hold the north edge, General Wright at first put in companies, then battalions. On October 26 the Germans resorted to gas to separate Wright's front-line troops in the woods from their support. Getting food and ammunition to the battalions at the top and sides of the woods became a major enterprise. Carrying parties tried to go around the woods, and German artillery made the trips difficult. The historian of the AEF and gas warfare, Cochrane (*89th Division in the Bois de Bantheville*, 89), raised the question of whether the 89th should have remained in the Bantheville Woods and concluded that the AEF never learned that it was not necessary to keep terrain once it was taken. Filling the upper part of the woods with mustard gas would have solved the 89th's problem, for the Germans could not have held such a contaminated area. When the time came for the offensive, the 89th's troops could have gone around the side of the woods. Cochrane was probably right. The 89th remained in the woods at a considerable cost; the 353rd and 354th Regiments lost 1,200 men, 400 from the gassing.

7. Conrad S. Babcock memoir, 625.

8. Folder 307, box 30, GHQ c.-in-c. reports, entry 1241, RG 120.

9. Dale Van Every, *The A.E.F. in Battle* (New York: Appleton, 1928), 367.

10. Donald Smythe, "A.E.F. Snafu at Sedan," *Prologue* 5 (1973): 135–149.

11. Cochrane, *Use of Gas in the Meuse-Argonne Campaign*, 65–67; Rexmond C. Cochrane, *The 78th Division at the Kriemhilde Stellung: October 1918* (Washington, D.C.: U.S. Army Chemical Corps, 1957), 50–54.

12. Cochrane, *Use of Gas in the Meuse-Argonne Campaign*, 15–16.

13. Report on operations, Dec. 29, 1918, 33.6, box 7, 78th Division historical, entry 1241, RG 120.

14. Frederick Palmer, *Our Greatest Battle (the Meuse-Argonne)* (New York: Dodd, Mead, 1919), 593.

15. Gilbert W. Crawford et al., eds., *The 302nd Engineers: A History* (n.p.: n.d.), 102.

16. John H. Taber, *The Story of the 168th Infantry*, vol. 2 (Iowa City: State Historical Society, 1925), 218–219.

17. Joseph M. Glass, Henry L. Miller, and Osmund O'Brien, *The Story of Battery D 304th Field Artillery: September 1917 to May 1919* (New York: Commandy-Roth, 1919), 72.

18. Folder 300, GHQ c.-in-c. reports, box 30, entry 1241, RG 120.

19. Foreman to Drum, "Sedan Incident," box 20, Drum papers.

20. Stackpole diary, May 6, 1919, November 14, 1918; Joseph T. Dickman, *The Great Crusade: A Narrative of the World War* (New York: Appleton, 1927), 189, 193. The leading article on the episode is Donald Smythe, "A.E.F. Snafu at Sedan," *Prologue* 5 (1973): 135–149.

21. Why Pershing let this statement about the 1st Division appear in his memoirs is impossible to say. Perhaps the only conclusion one can draw is that he had so much assistance with his memoirs that he did not notice it. A better course would have been silence. In early 1919 he toured the divisions and spoke to the troops, and his custom was to send letters of commendation. His letter to the 1st Division went to its new commander, General McGlachlin, on March 20, 1919, and included praise for the race to Sedan: "In the Meuse-Argonne battle the division was twice thrown into the line—on October 1st, at which time it pushed forward in spite of heavy resistance, and on November 5th, when, after a march of 20 kilometers to reach the jumping-off line, it attacked the enemy and marched on Sedan." 11.4, box 12, First Division historical, entry 1241, RG 120.

22. D. Clayton James, *The Years of MacArthur: 1880–1941* (Boston: Houghton Mifflin, 1970), 241.

23. Rhodes diary.

24. Cochrane, *Use of Gas in the Meuse-Argonne Campaign*, 40–42.

25. Crawford et al., *The 302nd Engineers*, 109–110. "For this very brave act, each man of the Co. 'D' detachment was cited in divisional orders but it is the opinion of those who are familiar with the affair, that a far higher honor should have been awarded to Captain Barber for his great courage and perseverance."

26. Arthur P. Watson, "America's Greatest World War Battle Leader," 18, Watson papers.

27. Dewees diary, 7.

28. "2nd Division operations on third phase of the Meuse-Argonne offensive," 33.6, box 31, 2nd Division historical, entry 1241, RG 120.

29. Babcock memoir, 645–646, 648. See also Joseph C. Persico, *Eleventh Month, Eleventh Day, Eleventh Hour: Armistice Day, 1918, World War I and Its Violent Climax* (New York: Random House, 2004).

Chapter 9. Victory

1. Leonard P. Ayres, ed., *War with Germany: A Statistical Summary*, 2nd ed. (Washington, D.C.: Government Printing Office, 1919), 120.

2. McNair lecture, folder 292, GHQ c.-in-c. reports, box 30, entry 1241, RG 120.

3. Mark E. Grotelueschen, *Doctrine under Trial: American Artillery Employment in World War I* (Westport, Conn.: Greenwood, 2001), 128.

4. "Study on Organization, Armament and Employment of Artillery," Jan. 4, 1919.

5. Edward F. McGlachlin, "Army Artillery in Meuse-Argonne," *Infantry Journal* 23 (1923): 544–552.

6. Field messages, 32.16, box 24, III Corps historical, RG 120, courtesy of Mark E. Grotelueschen.

7. 191–202, box 1, organizational records, First Army, entry 765, RG 120.

8. Accompanying guns of any sort—75s, 37s, Stokes mortars—worked well if they were in position. The flat fire of 75s and 37s worked for machine guns in the open, and the curved fire of Stokes mortars was better if the guns were hidden. The problem was getting the accompanying guns up to the front. The six-horse teams required to move the 75s made that impossible. Carts for 37s and mortars required roads or open, flat ground. After the war, Brigadier General Paul B.

Malone, commandant of the 5th Division training school, sought ways of bringing up 37s and mortars. He and his staff proposed a modified Browning cart drawn by a mule or a special pack carried by a mule. Malone had served in GHQ and with the 32nd Division and wrote directly to Pershing on May 4, 1919 (folder 16929-6, G-3 GHQ, entry 1241, RG 120). There is no evidence of a reply.

9. Babcock memoir, 654–658a.

10. "The reports coming in from abroad detailing the information concerning the war which was now becoming a real war were filed in the War College files without any of it being made available to the military services at large." Ralph H. Van Deman, *The Final Memoranda: Major General Ralph H. Van Deman, USA Ret., 1865–1952, Father of U.S. Military Intelligence*, ed. Ralph E. Weber (Wilmington, Del.: Scholarly Resources, 1988), 20.

11. The projector was an eight-inch tube, closed at the bottom, from which a drum discharged thirty pounds of gas, phosphorus, or high explosive. It was fired electrically, in batteries of twenty. Any number of projectors could be discharged simultaneously. The range was eighteen hundred yards. The four-inch Stokes mortar differed only in caliber from the three-inch, and each bomb carried seven pounds. It was capable of ten to twenty shots per minute. The range for gas was 840 yards. The third means of delivery, cylinders, held sixty pounds of gas, carried by the wind to escape at or near the front. They were heavy and cumbersome and more dependent on the weather than the other methods of delivery, making them unsuitable for the Meuse-Argonne. A shell from a 75-mm artillery piece delivered one pound of gas.

12. Rexmond C. Cochrane, *The 26th Division East of the Meuse: October 1918* (Washington, D.C.: U.S. Army Chemical Corps, 1960), 19–25.

13. By the time the AEF was in France, gas warfare was revealing tactical novelties. The varieties of gas and the means of projecting them were well known, and tactics became imaginative, including "localized cloud shoots, colored gas shoots (blue and green cross mixtures), gas bursts, follow-up yellow cross contamination, and widespread harassment with HE and gas mixtures." Rexmond C. Cochrane, *The Use of Gas in the Meuse-Argonne Campaign: September–November 1918* (Washington, D.C.: U.S. Army Chemical Corps, 1958), 1–2.

14. Lecture, "Explanation and Execution of Gas Plans for St. Mihiel and Meuse-Argonne Operations," 12, Jan. 13, 1919, folder 300, GHQ c.-in-c. reports, box 30, entry 1241, RG 120.

15. The First Army fired a total of 85.8 tons of gas during the Meuse-Argonne. Gassing the Bois de Bourgogne required 41.4 tons, some of the rest was used at St. Georges and Landres-et-St. Georges, and the balance was used on German batteries east of the Meuse, where the army used gas from the beginning.

BIBLIOGRAPHY

Papers and Diaries

Unless otherwise noted, the following collections are in the U.S. Army Military History Institute, Army War College, Carlisle Barracks, Carlisle, Pennsylvania.

Henry S. Allen papers, Library of Congress
Raymond B. Austin papers
Conrad S. Babcock papers, Hoover Institution, Stanford, Calif.
Kenneth Gearhart Baker papers
Newton D. Baker papers, Library of Congress
Newton D. Baker papers, Western Reserve Historical Society, Cleveland, Ohio
Harry Hill Bandholtz papers
Lucien G. Berry papers
Elden Sprague Betts papers, Illinois State Historical Library, Springfield
Tasker H. Bliss papers, Library of Congress
Perry L. Boyer diary
Charles H. Brent diary and papers, Library of Congress
Karl B. Bretzfelder diary and papers
Beaumont B. Buck papers
Robert Lee Bullard diary and papers, Library of Congress
Mervyn F. Burke papers
Alexander H. Case papers
Harold Dean Cater papers
John Dodge Clark papers
Walton Clark Jr. papers
Frederick W. Coleman diary
Joseph L. Collins Sr. diary and papers, Center of Military History, Washington, D.C.
Harold E. Craig diary and papers
George W. Crile diary and papers, Western Reserve Historical Society, Cleveland, Ohio
Benedict Crowell papers, Western Reserve Historical Society, Cleveland, Ohio
Edward A. Davies diary, Evanston Historical Society, Evanston, Ill.
Charles G. Dawes diary and papers, Northwestern University, Evanston, Ill.
A. Draper Dewees diary
Charles Howard Donnelly papers
William J. Donovan papers
Hugh A. Drum diary and papers
Francis Joseph Duffy diary and papers, courtesy Edward G. Duffy
Harold B. Fiske papers, National Archives
Rudolph H. Forderhase papers
Gerald F. Gilbert diary and papers
Farley E. Granger papers
John L. Hackley papers, Liberty Memorial, Kansas City, Mo.
Johnson Hagood II papers
Leroy Y. Haile papers
Harry P. R. Hansen papers

James G. Harbord papers, Library of Congress
James G. Harbord papers, New-York Historical Society
Dudley J. Hard diary, Western Reserve Historical Society, Cleveland, Ohio
Nelson J. Hawley papers, Missouri Historical Society, St. Louis
Ralph Hayes papers, Library of Congress
Malcolm B. Helm papers
W. D. Heselton papers
Charles W. Hill papers
John L. Hines papers, Library of Congress
John L. Hines papers
Horace Hobbs diary and papers
Wilder C. Hopkins papers
Hale Hunt diary
Ervin M. Johannes diary, Indiana University, Bloomington, Ind.
Michael J. Lenihan papers
Peyton C. March papers, Library of Congress
Walter A. McCleneghan papers, Illinois State Historical Library, Springfield
Frank Ross McCoy papers, Library of Congress
Charles H. Merritt diary and letters
Clarence J. Minick diary, Liberty Memorial, Kansas City, Mo.
George Van Horn Moseley diary and papers, Library of Congress
T. Bentley Mott diary and papers, Virginia Historical Society, Richmond
Paul Murphy papers
Roy V. Myers papers
Dennis E. Nolan papers
John J. Pershing diary and papers, Library of Congress
Benjamin A. Poore papers
Henry J. Reilly papers
Charles D. Rhodes diary
William A. Seward papers
Raymond Sheldon papers
Elmer W. Sherwood diary and papers, Indiana University, Bloomington, Ind.
Pierpont L. Stackpole diary, George C. Marshall Library, Lexington, Va., courtesy
    Larry Bland
Charles P. Summerall papers, Library of Congress
Milton B. Sweningsen papers
Frank L. Thompson diary
Harry S. Truman papers, Harry S. Truman Library, Independence, Mo.
Ralph E. Truman papers, Harry S. Truman Library, Independence, Mo.
Jonas E. Warrell papers
Arthur P. Watson papers
Charles L. White diary, Indiana State Library, Indianapolis

Books, Articles, Dissertations, and Theses

Albertine, Connell. *The Yankee Doughboy.* Boston: Brandon, 1968.
Alexander, Robert. *Memories of the World War: 1917–1918.* New York: Macmillan, 1931.
Allen, Hervey. *Toward the Flame: A War Diary.* New York: Farrar & Rinehart, 1934.

American Armies and Battlefields in Europe. Washington, D.C.: Government Printing Office, 1938.

American Troops at the Argonne. Hearings before the Committee on Military Affairs, U.S. Senate, 65th Congress, 3rd session. Washington, D.C.: Government Printing Office, 1919.

Amis, Reese. *History of the 114th Field Artillery.* N.p.: n.d.

Andrews, J. H. M., J. S. Bradford, and Charles Elcock. *Soldiers of the Castle: A History of Company B, Engineer Battalion, National Guard of Pennsylvania.* Philadelphia: Hofflich, 1929.

Armstrong, David A. *Bullets and Bureaucrats: The Machine Gun and the United States Army, 1861–1916.* Westport, Conn.: Greenwood, 1982.

Army Appropriation Bill, 1920. Hearings before the Committee on Military Affairs, U.S. Senate, 65th Congress, 3rd session. Washington, D.C.: Government Printing Office, 1919.

Arnold, H. H. *Global Mission.* New York: Harper, 1949.

Ashworth, Tony. *Trench Warfare 1914–1918: The Live and Let Live System.* New York: Holmes & Meier, 1980.

Asprey, Robert B. *At Belleau Wood.* New York: Putnam's, 1965.

———. *The German High Command at War: Hindenburg and Ludendorff Conduct World War I.* New York: Morrow, 1991.

Ayres, Leonard P., ed. *The War with Germany: A Statistical Summary.* 2nd ed. Washington, D.C.: Government Printing Office, 1919.

Bacevich, A. J. *Diplomat in Khaki: Major General Frank Ross McCoy and American Foreign Policy, 1898–1949.* Lawrence: University Press of Kansas, 1989.

Bach, Christian A., and Henry N. Hall. *The Fourth Division: Its Services and Achievements in the World War.* Garden City, N.Y.: Fourth Division, 1920.

Baker, Horace A. *Argonne Days.* Aberdeen, Miss.: Aberdeen Weekly, 1927.

Baker, Kenneth Gearhart. "Oatmeal and Coffee." *Indiana Magazine of History* 97 (2001): 26–76.

Barth, C. V. *History of the Twentieth Aero Squadron: First Day Bombardment Group, First Pursuit Wing, Air Service, First Army, American Expeditionary Forces.* Winona, Minn.: Winona Labor News, n.d.

Bartlett, Merrill L. *Lejeune: A Marine's Life, 1867–1942.* Columbia: University of South Carolina Press, 1991.

Beaver, Daniel R. *Modernizing the American War Department: Changes and Continuity in a Turbulent Era, 1885–1920.* Kent, Ohio: Kent State University Press, 2006.

———. *Newton D. Baker and the American War Effort: 1917–1918.* Lincoln: University of Nebraska Press, 1966.

Bjornstad, Col. Alfred W. Hearings before the Committee on Military Affairs, U.S. Senate, 68th Congress, 2nd session. 2 pts. Washington, D.C.: Government Printing Office, 1925.

Blackburn, Marc K. *The United States Army and the Motor Truck: A Case Study in Standardization.* Westport, Conn.: Greenwood, 1996.

Blake, Robert Wallace. *From Belleau Wood to Bougainville: The Oral History of Major General Robert Blake USMC and the Travel Journal of Rosselet Wallace Blake.* Bloomington, Ind.: Authorhouse, 2004.

Bland, Larry, and Sharon R. Ritenour, eds. *The Papers of George Catlett Marshall: The Soldierly Spirit, December 1880–June 1939.* Baltimore: Johns Hopkins University Press, 1981.

Blumenson, Martin. *The Patton Papers.* 2 vols. Boston: Houghton Mifflin, 1974.

Bond, Brian. "Soldiers and Statesmen: British Civil-Military Relations in 1917." *Military Affairs* 32 (1969): 62–75.

———. *The Unquiet Western Front: Britain's Role in Literature and History.* Cambridge: Cambridge University Press, 2002.

Boyd, Thomas. *Through the Wheat.* Lincoln: University of Nebraska Press, 2000.

Braim, Paul F. *The Test of Battle: The American Expeditionary Forces in the Meuse-Argonne Campaign.* Newark: University of Delaware Press, 1987.

Brannen, Carl Andrew. *A Marine in the Great War.* College Station: Texas A&M University Press, 1996.

Browne, George. *An American Soldier in World War I,* edited by David L. Snead. Lincoln: University of Nebraska Press, 2006.

Bruce, Robert B. *A Fraternity of Arms: America and France in the Great War.* Lawrence: University Press of Kansas, 2003.

Buck, Beaumont B. *Memories of Peace and War.* San Antonio, Tex.: Naylor, 1935.

Bullard, Robert Lee. *Personalities and Reminiscences of the War.* Garden City, N.Y.: Doubleday, Page, 1925.

Bullard, Robert Lee, and Earl Reeves. *American Soldiers Also Fought.* New York: Longmans, Green, 1936.

Burg, Maclyn P., and Thomas J. Pressly, eds. *The Great War at Home and Abroad: The World War I Diaries and Letters of W. Stull Holt.* Manhattan, Kans.: Sunflower University Press, 1999.

Byerly, Carol R. *Fever of War: The Influenza Epidemic in the U.S. Army during World War I.* New York: New York University Press, 2005.

Cain, James M. "The Taking of Montfaucon." *American Mercury* 17 (1929): 136–143.

The Cannoneers Have Hairy Ears: A Diary of the Front Lines. New York: Sears, 1927.

Chambers, John Whiteclay. *To Raise an Army: The Draft Comes to Modern America.* New York: Free Press, 1987.

Chandler, Alfred D. Jr., and Stephen Salsbury. *Pierre S. Du Pont and the Making of the Modern Corporation.* New York: Harper & Row, 1971.

Chastaine, Ben H. *History of the 18th U.S. Infantry, First Division: 1812–1919.* New York: Hymans, n.d.

Cheseldine, R. M. *Ohio in the Rainbow: Official Story of the 166th Infantry, 42nd Division, in the World War.* Columbus, Ohio: Heer, 1924.

Chinn, George M. *The Machine Gun: History, Evolution, and Development of Manual, Automatic, and Airborne Repeating Weapons.* Washington, D.C.: Government Printing Office, 1951.

Clifford, John Garry. *The Citizen Soldiers: The Plattsburg Training Camp Movement: 1913–1920.* Lexington: University Press of Kentucky, 1972.

Cochrane, Rexmond C. *The 1st Division in the Meuse-Argonne: 1–12 October 1918.* Washington, D.C.: U.S. Army Chemical Corps, 1957.

———. *The 26th Division East of the Meuse: October 1918.* Washington, D.C.: U.S. Army Chemical Corps, 1960.

———. *The 29th Division in the Côtes de Meuse: October 1918.* Washington, D.C.: U.S. Army Chemical Corps, 1959.

———. *The 33rd Division along the Meuse: October 1918.* Washington, D.C.: U.S. Army Chemical Corps, 1958.

———. *The 42nd Division before Landres-et-St. Georges: October 1918.* Washington, D.C.: U.S. Army Chemical Corps, 1960.

———. *The 78th Division at the Kriemhilde Stellung: October 1918*. Washington, D.C.: U.S. Army Chemical Corps, 1957.

———. *The 79th Division at Montfaucon: October 1918*. Washington, D.C.: U.S. Army Chemical Corps, 1960.

———. *The 89th Division in the Bois de Bantheville: October 1918*. Washington, D.C.: U.S. Army Chemical Corps, 1960.

———. *The 92nd Division in the Marbache Sector*. Washington, D.C.: U.S. Army Chemical Corps, 1959.

———. *The Use of Gas in the Meuse-Argonne Campaign: September–November 1918*. Washington, D.C.: U.S. Army Chemical Corps, 1958.

Coffman, Edward M. "The AEF Leaders' Education for War." In *The Great War, 1914–18: Essays on the Military, Political and Social History of the First World War*, edited by R. J. Q. Adams. London: Macmillan, 1990.

———. "American Command and Commanders in World War I." In *New Dimensions in Military History: An Anthology*, edited by Russell F. Weigley. San Rafael, Calif.: Presidio, 1975.

———. "The American Military Generation Gap in World War I: The Leavenworth Clique in the AEF." In *Command and Commanders in Modern Warfare*, edited by William Geffen. Colorado Springs: U.S. Air Force Academy, 1969.

———. *The Hilt of the Sword: The Career of Peyton C. March*. Madison: University of Wisconsin Press, 1966.

———. "March and Pershing." In *The John Riggs Cincinnati Lectures in Military Leadership and Command: 1986*, edited by Henry S. Bausum. Lexington, Va.: VMI Foundation, 1986.

———. *The Old Army: A Portrait of the American Army in Peacetime, 1784–1898*. New York: Oxford University Press, 1986.

———. *The Regulars: The Army Officer, 1898–1941*. Cambridge, Mass.: Harvard University Press, 2004.

———. *The War to End All Wars: The American Military Experience in World War I*. New York: Oxford University Press, 1968.

Colby, Elbridge. "The Taking of Montfaucon." *Infantry Journal* 47 (1940): 128–140.

Congressional Medal of Honor, the Distinguished Service Cross, and the Distinguished Service Medal. Washington, D.C.: Government Printing Office, 1920.

Conner, Virginia. *What Father Forbad*. Philadelphia: Dorrance, 1951.

Cooke, James J. *The All-Americans at War: The Eighty-second Division in the Great War, 1917–1918*. Westport, Conn.: Praeger, 2002.

———. *Billy Mitchell*. Boulder, Colo.: Lynne Rienner, 2002.

———. *Pershing and His Generals: Command and Staff in the AEF*. Westport, Conn.: Praeger, 1997.

———. *The Rainbow Division in the Great War*. Westport, Conn.: Praeger, 1994.

———. *The U.S. Air Service in the Great War: 1917–1919*. Westport, Conn.: Praeger, 1996.

Craighill, Edley. *History of the 317th Infantry*. Tours, France: Deslis, n.d.

Cramer, C. H. *Newton D. Baker: A Biography*. Cleveland, Ohio: World, 1961.

Crawford, Charles. *Six Months with the 6th Brigade*. Kansas City, Mo.: Barnett, 1927.

Crawford, Gilbert H., et al., eds. *The 302nd Engineers: A History*. N.p.: n.d.

Crile, George. *An Autobiography*. 2 vols. Philadelphia: Lippincott, 1947.

Crozier, Emmet. *American Reporters on the Western Front: 1914–1918*. New York: Oxford University Press, 1959.

Cuff, Robert D. "Newton D. Baker, Frank A. Scott, and 'the American Reinforcement in the World War.'" *Military Affairs* 34 (1970): 11–13.

Cushing, Harvey. *From a Surgeon's Journal: 1915–1918.* Boston: Little, Brown, 1936.

DeWeerd, Harvey A. *President Wilson Fights His War: World War I and the American Intervention.* New York: Macmillan, 1968.

Dickman, Joseph T. *The Great Crusade: A Narrative of the World War.* New York: Appleton, 1927.

Dillon, Robert Sherwood. *An American Soldier in World War I.* Washington, D.C.: Five & Ten, 2005.

Dougherty, A. J. "Accompanying Guns." *Infantry Journal* 17 (1920): 487–490.

Doughty, Robert A. *Pyrrhic Victory: French Strategy and Operations in the Great War.* Cambridge, Mass.: Harvard University Press, 2005.

Dudden, Arthur P., ed. *Woodrow Wilson and the World of Today.* Philadelphia: University of Pennsylvania Press, 1957.

Duffy, Francis P. *Father Duffy's Story: A Tale of Humor and Heroism, of Life and Death with the Fighting Sixty-ninth.* Garden City, N.Y.: Garden City, 1919.

Edwards, Evan A. *From Doniphan to Verdun: The Official History of the 140th Infantry.* Lawrence, Kans.: World, 1920.

Eisenhower, John S. D. *Yanks: The Epic Story of the American Army in World War I.* New York: Free Press, 2001.

Ettinger, Albert M., and A. Churchill Ettinger. *A Doughboy with the Fighting Sixty-ninth: A Remembrance of World War I.* Shippensburg, Pa.: White Mane, 1992.

Ferrell, Robert H. *Collapse at Meuse-Argonne: The Failure of the Missouri-Kansas Division.* Columbia: University of Missouri Press, 2004.

———. *Five Days in October: The Lost Battalion of World War I.* Columbia: University of Missouri Press, 2005.

———. *Woodrow Wilson and World War I: 1917–1921.* New York: Harper & Row, 1985.

Final Report of John J. Pershing: Commander-in-Chief American Expeditionary Forces. Washington, D.C.: Government Printing Office, 1920.

Fleming, Thomas J. *The Illusion of Victory: America in World War I.* New York: Basic Books, 2003.

———. "Two Argonnes." *American Heritage* 29, no. 6 (1968): 44–48, 88–94.

The Forty-seventh Infantry: A History, 1917-1918-1919. Saginaw, Mich.: Seemann, 1919.

Gaff, Alan D. *Blood in the Argonne: The "Lost Battalion" of World War I.* Norman: University of Oklahoma Press, 2005.

Garlock, G. W. *Tales of the Thirty-second.* West Salem, Wis.: Badger, 1927.

Gavin, Lotti. *American Women in World War I: They Also Served.* Niwot: University Press of Colorado, 1997.

Geelhoed, E. Bruce, comp. and ed. *The Kniptash Diaries: 1917–1919.* Muncie, Ind.: Ball State University, 1999.

Geffen, William. "The Leavenworth 'Clique' in World War I: A Military View." In *Command and Commanders in Modern Warfare,* edited by William Geffen. Colorado Springs: U.S. Air Force Academy, 1969.

Giehrl, Hermann. "The American Expeditionary Forces in Europe: 1917–1918." *Infantry Journal* 19 (1921): 131–138, 264–270, 377–384, 534–540; 20 (1922): 140–149, 292–303.

Glass, Joseph M., Henry L. Miller, and Osmund O'Brien. *The Story of Battery D 304th Field Artillery: September 1917 to May 1919.* New York: Commandy-Roth, 1919.

Grotelueschen, Mark E. *Doctrine under Trial: American Artillery Employment in World War I.* Westport, Conn.: Greenwood, 2001.

Gudmundsson, Bruce I. *Stormtroop Tactics: Innovation in the German Army, 1914–1918.* Westport, Conn.: Praeger, 1989.

Haan, William G. "The Division as a Fighting Machine." *Wisconsin Magazine of History* 4 (1920): 3–26.

Haber, L. F. *The Poisonous Cloud: Chemical Warfare in the First World War.* Oxford: Clarendon, 1986.

Hagood, Johnson. *The Services of Supply: A Memoir of the Great War.* Boston: Houghton Mifflin, 1927.

Hall, Norman S., and Sigrid Schultz. "Five Red Days: The True Story of the 35th Division in the Meuse-Argonne Battle." *Liberty* 4 (May 14, 1927): 9–14.

Hamburger, Kenneth E. *Learning Lessons in the American Expeditionary Forces.* Washington, D.C.: U.S. Army Center of Military History, n.d.

Harbord, James G. *The American Army in France: 1917–1919.* Boston: Little, Brown, 1936.

———. *Leaves from a War Diary.* New York: Dodd, Mead, 1925.

Harries, Meiron, and Susie Harries. *The Last Days of Innocence: America at War, 1917–1918.* New York: Random House, 1997.

Hawley, Ellis W. *The Great War and the Search for a Modern Order: A History of the American People and Their Institutions, 1917–1933.* New York: St. Martin's, 1979.

Herwig, Holger H. *The First World War: Germany and Austria-Hungary, 1914–1918.* London: Arnold, 1997.

Hessen, Robert. *Steel Titan: The Life of Charles M. Schwab.* New York: Oxford University Press, 1975.

History of Company F, 316th Infantry 79th Division, A.E.F. in the World War 1917-18-19. Philadelphia: Company F, 1930.

History of the First Division during the World War: 1917–1919. Philadelphia: Winston, 1922.

A History of the Sixth Regiment Field Artillery First Division United States Army. Ransbach, Germany, 1919.

History of the 306th Field Artillery. New York: Knickerbocker, 1920.

Hogan, Martin J. *The Shamrock Battalion of the Rainbow: A Story of the "Fighting Sixty-ninth."* New York: Appleton, 1919.

Holley, I. B. Jr. *Ideas and Weapons: Exploitation of the Aerial Weapon by the United States during World War I: A Study in the Relationship of Technological Advance, Military Doctrine, and the Development of Weapons.* New Haven, Conn.: Yale University Press, 1953.

Hoyt, Charles B. *Heroes of the Argonne: An Authentic History of the Thirty-fifth Division.* Kansas City, Mo.: Franklin Hudson, 1919.

Huber, Richard M. *Big All the Way Through: The Life of Van Santvoord Merle-Smith.* Princeton, N.J.: Class of 1911, 1952.

Hudson, James J. *Hostile Skies: A Combat History of the American Air Service in World War I.* Syracuse, N.Y.: Syracuse University Press, 1968.

Huelfer, Evan Andrew. *The "Casualty Issue" in American Military Practices: The Impact of World War I.* Westport, Conn.: Praeger, 2003.

Huidekoper, Frederic Louis. *History of the 33rd Division, A.E.F.* Springfield: Illinois State Historical Library, 1921.

Hurley, Alfred F. *Billy Mitchell: Crusader for Air Power.* Bloomington: Indiana University Press, 1975.

Jacobsmeyer, Paul J. "Intelligence in the American Expeditionary Forces: The Experience of the Thirty-second Division, September 1917–November 1918." Master's thesis, University of Wisconsin, 1986.

James, D. Clayton. *The Years of MacArthur: 1880–1941.* Boston: Houghton Mifflin, 1970.

Johnson, Douglas V. II. "A Few 'Squads Left' and Off to France: Training the American Army in the United States in World War I." Dissertation, Temple University, 1993.

Johnson, Douglas V. II, and Rolfe E. Hillman Jr. *Soissons: 1918.* College Station: Texas A&M University Press, 1999.

Johnson, Elliott L. "The Military Experiences of Hugh A. Drum from 1898–1918." Dissertation, University of Wisconsin, 1975.

Johnson, Hubert C. *Breakthrough: Tactics, Technology, and the Search for Victory on the Western Front in World War I.* Novato, Calif.: Presidio, 1994.

Johnson, Ray Neil. *Heaven, Hell, or Hoboken.* Cleveland, Ohio: Hubbell, 1919.

Johnson, Thomas M. *Without Censor: New Light on Our Greatest World War Battles.* Indianapolis: Bobbs-Merrill, 1928.

Johnson, Thomas M., and Fletcher Pratt. *The Lost Battalion.* Indianapolis: Bobbs-Merrill, 1938.

Kaspi, André. *Le Temps des Américains: Le concours américain à la France en 1917–1918.* Paris: Université de Paris, 1976.

Keegan, John. *The First World War.* New York: Knopf, 1999.

Keene, Jennifer D. *Doughboys, the Great War, and the Remaking of America.* Baltimore: Johns Hopkins University Press, 2001.

Kenamore, Clair. *From Vauquois Hill to Exermont: A History of the Thirty-fifth Division of the United States Army.* St. Louis: Guard, 1919.

———. *The Story of the 139th Infantry.* St. Louis: Guard, 1920.

Kennett, Lee. *The First Air War: 1914–1918.* New York: Free Press, 1991.

Kindsvater, Peter S. *American Soldiers: Ground Combat in the World Wars, Korea, and Vietnam.* Lawrence: University Press of Kansas, 2003.

Kitchen, Martin. *The Silent Dictatorship: The German High Command under Hindenburg and Ludendorff, 1917–1918.* New York: Holmes & Meier, 1976.

Lane, Jack C. *Armed Progressive: General Leonard Wood.* San Rafael, Calif.: Presidio, 1978.

Langer, William L. *Gas and Flame in World War I.* New York: Knopf, 1965.

Lawrence, Joseph D. *Fighting Soldier: The AEF in 1918,* edited by Robert H. Ferrell. Boulder: Colorado Associated University Press, 1985.

Leach, George E. *War Diary.* Roanoke, Va.: Rainbow Division Veterans, 1962.

Lebow, Eileen F. *A Grandstand Seat: The American Balloon Service in World War I.* Westport, Conn.: Praeger, 1998.

Lee, Dwight D. *Sergeant York: An American Hero.* Lexington: University Press of Kentucky, 1985.

Lee, Jay M. *The Artilleryman: The Experiences and Impressions of an American Artillery Regiment in the World War, 129th F.A. 1917–1919.* Kansas City, Mo.: Spencer, 1920.

Lejeune, John A. *The Reminiscences of a Marine.* Philadelphia: Dorrance, 1930.

Liddell Hart, B. H. "How Myths Grow—Passchendaele." *Military Affairs* 28 (1964–1965): 184–186.

Liggett, Hunter. *A.E.F.: Ten Years Ago in France.* New York: Dodd, Mead, 1928.

————. *Commanding an American Army: Recollections of the World War.* Boston: Houghton Mifflin, 1925.

Link, Arthur S. *Wilson the Diplomatist: A Look at His Major Foreign Policies.* Baltimore: Johns Hopkins University Press, 1957.

————. *Woodrow Wilson: A Brief Biography.* Cleveland, Ohio: World, 1963.

Little, Arthur W. *From Harlem to the Rhine: The Story of New York's Colored Volunteers.* New York: Covici, Friede, 1936.

Livesay, William G. "A Trained Regiment in Combat." *Infantry Journal* 27 (1925): 42.

Losses of Thirty-fifth Division during the Argonne Battle. Hearings before the Committee on Rules, U.S. House of Representatives. Washington, D.C.: Government Printing Office, 1919.

Lowry, Bullitt. *Armistice 1918.* Kent, Ohio: Kent State University Press, 1996.

Ludendorff, Erich. *Ludendorff's Own Story: August 1914–November 1918.* 2 vols. New York: Harper, 1919.

Lukacs, John. "The Poverty of Anti-Communism." *National Interest* 55 (1999): 75–82.

March, Peyton C. *The Nation at War.* Garden City, N.Y.: Doubleday, Doran, 1934.

Marshall, George C. *Memoirs of My Service in the World War: 1917–1918,* edited by James L. Collins Jr. Boston: Houghton Mifflin, 1976.

Marshall, S. L. A. "On Heavy Artillery: American Experience in Four Wars." *Parameters* 8 (1978): 2–20.

McGlachlin, Edward F. "Army Artillery in Meuse-Argonne." *Infantry Journal* 23 (1923): 544–552.

McHenry, Herbert L. *As a Private Saw It: My Memories of the First Division, World War I.* Indiana, Pa.: Halldin, 1988.

Meigs, Mark. *Optimism at Armageddon: Voices of American Participants in the First World War.* New York: New York University Press, 1997.

Miles, L. Wardlaw. *History of the 308th Infantry: 1917–1919.* New York: Putnam's, 1927.

Miller, Henry W. *The Paris Gun: The Bombardment of Paris by the German Long Range Guns and the Great German Offensives of 1918.* New York: Cape & Smith, 1930.

Miller, Tony. "Samuel Woodfill: The Outstanding Soldier of the A.E.F." *Traces of Indiana* 12 (2000): 15–25.

Millett, Allan R. *The General: Robert L. Bullard and Officership in the United States Army, 1881–1925.* Westport, Conn.: Greenwood, 1975.

————. "Over Where? The AEF and the American Strategy for Victory, 1917–1918." In *Against All Enemies: Interpretations of American Military History from Colonial Times to the Present,* edited by Kenneth J. Hagan and William R. Roberts. Westport, Conn.: Greenwood, 1986.

Millett, Allan R., and Williamson Murray, eds. *Military Effectiveness: The First World War.* Boston: Allen & Unwin, 1988.

Nenninger, Timothy K. "John J. Pershing and Relief for Cause in the American Expeditionary Forces, 1917–1918." *Army History* (2005): 21–32.

————. *The Leavenworth Schools and the Old Army: Education, Professionalism, and the Officer Corps of the United States Army, 1881–1918.* Westport, Conn.: Greenwood, 1978.

————. "Tactical Dysfunction in the AEF: 1917–1918." *Military Affairs* 51 (1987): 177–181.

————. "Unsystematic as a Mode of Command: Commanders and the Process of Command in the American Expeditionary Forces, 1917–1918." *Journal of Military History* 64 (2000): 739–768.

Nichols, Vernon R. "Our Battle of the Argonne." *Infantry Journal* 16 (1919): 183–199, 267–281.

Official History of the 82nd Division, American Expeditionary Forces. Indianapolis: Bobbs-Merrill, 1919.

Order of Battle of the United States Land Forces in the World War: American Expeditionary Forces: General Headquarters, Armies, Army Corps, Services of Supply, Separate Forces. Washington, D.C.: Government Printing Office, 1937.

Palmer, Frederick. *Our Gallant Madness.* Garden City, N.Y.: Doubleday, Doran, 1937.

———. *Our Greatest Battle (the Meuse-Argonne).* New York: Dodd, Mead, 1919.

Parsons, William Barclay. *The American Engineers in France.* New York: Appleton, 1920.

Patton, Gerald W. *War and Race: The Black Officer in the American Military, 1915–1941.* Westport, Conn.: Greenwood, 1981.

Pearlman, Michael S. *Warmaking and American Democracy: The Struggle over Military Strategy, 1700 to the Present.* Lawrence: University Press of Kansas, 1999.

Pershing, John J. *My Experiences in the World War.* 2 vols. New York: Stokes, 1931.

Persico, Joseph E. *Eleventh Month, Eleventh Day, Eleventh Hour: Armistice Day, 1918, World War I and Its Violent Climax.* New York: Random House, 2004.

Pitt, Barrie. *1918: The Last Act.* London: Cassell, 1962.

Pogue, Forrest C. *George C. Marshall: Education of a General, 1880–1930.* New York: Viking, 1963.

Pottle, Frederick A. *Stretchers: The Story of a Hospital Unit on the Western Front.* New Haven, Conn.: Yale University Press, 1929.

Rainey, James W. "Ambivalent Warfare: The Tactical Doctrine of the AEF in World War I." *Parameters* 13 (1983): 34–45.

———. "The Questionable Training of the AEF in World War I." *Parameters* 22 (1992–1993): 89–103.

Rainsford, W. Kerr. *From Upton to the Meuse: With the Three Hundred and Seventh Infantry.* New York: Appleton, 1920.

Rankin, Edward P. Jr. *The Santa Fe Trail Leads to France: A Narrative of Battle Service of the 110th Engineers (35th Division) in the Meuse-Argonne Offensive.* Kansas City, Mo.: Richardson, 1933.

Reardon, Carol. *Soldiers and Scholars: The U.S. Army and the Use of Military History, 1865–1920.* Lawrence: University Press of Kansas, 1990.

Reilly, Henry J. *Americans All: The Rainbow at War.* Columbus, Ohio: Heer, 1936.

Rendinell, J. R., and George Pattullo. *One Man's War.* New York: Sears, 1928.

Report of the Secretary of War to the President: 1926. Washington, D.C.: Government Printing Office, 1926.

Rieger, James E. "139th Infantry A.E.F.—Fourth Missouri Infantry." In *History of the Missouri National Guard.* N.p.: Missouri National Guard, 1934.

Rogers, Horatio. *World War I through My Sights.* San Rafael, Calif.: Presidio, 1976.

Ross, Warner A. *My Colored Battalion.* Chicago: Ross, 1920.

Safford, Jeffrey J. *Wilsonian Maritime Diplomacy: 1913–1921.* New Brunswick, N.J.: Rutgers University Press, 1978.

Sherwood, Elmer W. *A Soldier in World War I: The Diary of Elmer W. Sherwood,* edited by Robert H. Ferrell. Indianapolis: Indiana Historical Society Press, 2004.

Simonds, Frank H. *They Won the War.* New York: Harper, 1931.

Simpson, Albert F., ed. *The World War I Diary of Col. Frank P. Lahm, Air Service, A.E.F.* Maxwell Air Force Base, Ga.: Aerospace Studies Institute, 1970.

Skeyhill, Tom, ed. *Sergeant York: His Own Life Story and War Diary.* Garden City, N.Y.: Doubleday, Doran, 1928.

Smith, Gene. *Still Quiet on the Western Front: Fifty Years Later.* New York: Morrow, 1965.

Smythe, Donald. "A.E.F. Snafu at Sedan." *Prologue* 5 (1973): 135–149.

———. *Guerrilla Warrior: The Early Life of John J. Pershing.* New York: Scribner, 1973.

———. *Pershing: General of the Armies.* Bloomington: Indiana University Press, 1988.

Snow, William J. *Signposts of Experience: World War Memoirs.* Washington, D.C.: U.S. Field Artillery Association, 1941.

Stallings, Laurence. *The Doughboys: The Story of the AEF, 1917–1918.* New York: Harper & Row, 1963.

Straub, Elmer Frank. *A Sergeant's Diary in the World War.* Indianapolis: Indiana Historical Bureau, 1923.

Summary of Operations in the World War (by divisions, separately published). Washington, D.C.: Government Printing Office, 1943–1944.

Taber, John H. *The Story of the 168th Infantry.* Vol. 2. Iowa City: State Historical Society, 1925.

Terraine, John. *To Win a War: 1918, the Year of Victory.* Garden City, N.Y.: Doubleday, 1987.

Thomas, Lowell. *Woodfill of the Regulars: A True Story of Adventure from the Arctic to the Argonne.* Garden City, N.Y.: Doubleday, Doran, 1929.

Thomas, Shipley. *The History of the A.E.F.* New York: Doran, 1920.

Thompson, Hugh S. *Trench Knives and Mustard Gas: With the 42nd Rainbow Division in France,* edited by Robert H. Ferrell. College Station: Texas A&M University Press, 2004.

Trask, David F. *The AEF and Coalition Warmaking: 1917–1918.* Lawrence: University Press of Kansas, 1993.

———.. *General Tasker Howard Bliss and the "Sessions of the World," 1919.* Philadelphia: American Philosophical Society, 1966.

———. *The United States in the Supreme War Council: American War Aims and Inter-Allied Strategy, 1917–18.* Middletown, Conn.: Wesleyan University Press, 1961.

Travers, Tim. *How the War Was Won: Command and Technology in the British Army on the Western Front, 1917–1918.* London: Routledge, 1992.

———. *The Killing Ground: The British Army, the Western Front and the Emergence of Modern Warfare, 1900–1918.* London: Allen & Unwin, 1987.

———.. "Reply to John Hussey: The Movement of German Divisions to the Western Front, Winter 1917–1918." *War in History* 5 (1998): 367–370.

Triplet, William S. *A Youth in the Meuse-Argonne: A Memoir, 1917–1918,* edited by Robert H. Ferrell. Columbia: University of Missouri Press, 2000.

Twichell, Heath Jr. *Allen: The Biography of an Army Officer, 1859–1930.* New Brunswick, N.J.: Rutgers University Press, 1974.

Tydings, Millard E. *The Machine Gunners of the Blue and Gray Division (Twenty-ninth).* N.p.: n.d.

United States Army in the World War. 17 vols. Washington, D.C.: Government Printing Office, 1948.

Upton, L. S., and Millard E. Tydings. "Capture of Etrayes Ridge: A Machine Gun Study." *Infantry Journal* 31 (1927): 133–136.

Van Deman, Ralph H. *The Final Memoranda: Major General Ralph H. Van Deman, USA Ret., 1865–1952, Father of U.S. Military Intelligence,* edited by Ralph E. Weber. Wilmington, Del.: Scholarly Resources, 1988.

Vandiver, Frank E. *Black Jack: The Life and Times of John J. Pershing.* 2 vols. Fort Worth: Texas Christian University Press, 1977.

Van Every, Dale. *The A.E.F. in Battle.* New York: Appleton, 1928.

Venzon, Anne Cipriano, ed. *The United States in the First World War: An Encyclopedia.* New York: Garland, 1995.

Viereck, George S., ed. *As They Saw Us: Foch, Ludendorff and Other Leaders Write Our War History.* Garden City, N.Y.: Doubleday, Doran, 1929.

Vilensky, Joel A. *Dew of Death: The Story of Lewisite, America's World War I Weapon of Mass Destruction.* Bloomington: Indiana University Press, 2005.

Votaw, John F. *The American Expeditionary Forces in World War I.* Oxford: Osprey, 2005.

Waller, Douglas. *A Question of Loyalty: Gen. Billy Mitchell and the Court-martial that Gripped the Nation.* New York: HarperCollins, 2004.

Ward, Larry Wayne. *The Motion Picture Goes to War: The U.S. Government Film Effort during World War I.* Ann Arbor, Mich.: University Microfilms International, 1985.

Ward, Robert D. "A Note on General Leonard Wood's Experimental Companies." *Military Affairs* 3 (1971): 92–93.

Weigley, Russell F. *The American Way of War: A History of United States Military Strategy and Policy.* New York: Macmillan, 1973.

———. *History of the United States Army.* New York: Macmillan, 1967.

Wharton, James B. "A Battalion in Action." *Infantry Journal* 16 (1919): 455–463.

Williams, Ashby. *Experiences in the Great War: Artois, St. Mihiel, Meuse-Argonne.* Roanoke, Va.: Stone, 1919.

Williams, William J. *The Wilson Administration and the Shipbuilding Crisis of 1917: Steel Ships and Wooden Steamers.* Lewiston, N.Y.: Mellen, 1992.

Wilson, Dale E. *Treat 'Em Rough: The Birth of American Armor, 1917–20.* Novato, Calif.: Presidio, 1989.

Winter, Jay, Geoffrey Parker, and Mary R. Habeck, eds. *The Great War and the Twentieth Century.* New Haven, Conn.: Yale University Press, 2000.

Wright, William M. *Meuse-Argonne Diary: A Division Commander in World War I,* edited by Robert H. Ferrell. Columbia: University of Missouri Press, 2004.

Young, Hugh. *A Surgeon's Autobiography.* New York: Harcourt, Brace, 1940.

Zabecki, David T. *Steel Wind: Colonel Georg Bruchmueller and the Birth of Modern Artillery.* Westport, Conn.: Praeger, 1994.